Cryptography for Security and Privacy in Cloud Computing

Cryptography for Security and Privacy in Cloud Computing

Stefan Rass
Daniel Slamanig

**ARTECH
HOUSE**

BOSTON | LONDON
artechhouse.com

Library of Congress Cataloging-in-Publication Data
A catalog record for this book is available from the U.S. Library of Congress.

British Library Cataloguing in Publication Data
A catalogue record for this book is available from the British Library.

ISBN-13: 978-1-60807-575-1

Cover design by Vicki Kane

© 2014 ARTECH HOUSE
685 Canton Street
Norwood, MA 02062

Contents

Chapter 1

Introduction

1.1 MODERN CRYPTOGRAPHY

Cryptography as we understand it now is a quite young discipline. While encryption has been in use for millennia, notions like public key signatures have been around for less than 50 years. As is common practice in research, many new cryptographic techniques have been developed to tackle either a theoretical question or foreseeing a soon-to-be-reality application. Cloud computing is one of these new areas, where cryptography is expected to unveil its power by bringing striking new features to the cloud.

The most popular and best standardized cryptographic primitives are key agreement and derivation mechanisms and encryption as well as digital signatures and message authentication codes, respectively. Common to all these techniques is their main focus on confidential and/or authentic exchange of data between two or more parties, leaving all matters of storage and processing with the peers. Equally well-known are many techniques to authenticate or identify an individual or entity; however, the most popular among these also refer to matters between two parties.

Distributed systems gave rise to challenges ranging much beyond problems of limiting access at the storage site (via authentication) or during transportation (via encryption). Encryption keeps the payload secure but does not hide the communication as such. Authentication normally implies the showing of an identity. More sophisticated techniques can tie an access permission to arbitrary attributes, so that neither an identity nor any other personal information must be revealed. Data residing at some remote storage system must not necessarily be trusted to be consistent or available. Cryptography offers techniques to certify such claims and to access data without even revealing the usage pattern. Moreover, if the data is stored remotely,

1

what should stop the keeper from using the data itself? Encryption is a trivial way to prevent all sorts of reading or meaningful manipulation, but today cryptography can control the usage of data at a much more fine-grained level and also allows computations on encrypted or authenticated data while preserving confidentiality and authenticity, respectively.

Today, security must be understood in a much more diverse sense rather than the humble requirements of confidentiality, integrity, availability, and authenticity (CIA+). For example, confidentiality may refer to data, but also to an identity, an algorithm, or even a behavior pattern. Identity protection can be twofold, either preventing inference of attributes from data (data anonymization) or hiding the identity of communication peers from each other (communication anonymity). Likewise, availability is not necessarily a designed feature of a system, but also a fact that needs proof and verification over the whole system life cycle.

Contemporary cryptography offers an incredibly rich set of tools and solutions to tackle all of these issues, a selection of which is compiled in this book.

1.2   CLOUD COMPUTING

Cloud computing is an evolving paradigm whose basic attempt is to shift computing and storage capabilities to external service providers. From a business perspective, it means on-demand provisioning of soft- and hardware at any (negotiable) level of granularity. In this view, we often distinguish the loan of software (*software as a service*, SaaS), platforms (*platform as a service*, PaaS) or both (*infrastructure as a service*, IaaS). Depending on where the cloud resources are located, private clouds are distinguished from public clouds, where the latter are open for any customer, which is not the case for private clouds. Hybrid clouds form a mix in between. A related yet different classification separates clouds based on their intended usage. The division in this sense is into computational clouds and cloud storage (the latter occasionally being coined *database as a service*). The treatment in this book will not rely on any such differentiations, as our main intention is to provide an easily accessible introductory compendium to some quite little known yet powerful techniques for providing security and privacy via cryptography for the cloud.

The main scenario for which we discuss cryptographic solutions is an application in which a customer hands over data to a cloud provider for storage, processing, or both. Central to our treatment is the assumption that the cloud provider acts as a distrusted black box from the client's perspective, whose duty and interest is the protection of information and privacy. The techniques presented are partially to be used at the service provider's or client's side, but in any case should protect the interests of both, to establish a successful and trustworthy service.

1.3 DIGITAL IDENTITY, AUTHENTICATION, AND ACCESS CONTROL

Technically, cloud services are offered by renting computing infrastructure (hardware and/or software) to a customer. This may happen on a pay-per-use basis, or by consuming some amount of resource that has been bought in advance. In either case, authentication and access controls are of crucial interest for both sides. Besides the obvious requirement for the cloud provider to give no more resource than what has been paid for and for the client to get no less than what has been paid for, access control and authentication must be considered at a much more fine-grained level.

Since the cloud is probably open to multiple independent customers, access control issues exist from and to the outside and between the clients, and furthermore inside the client's data. Client processes must run (physically or at least logically) separated from each other, but access to the client's data must also be controllable at a level of detail as dictated by the given application. For some applications, pure separation of processes is, however, not possible, if the cloud is supposed to compute on the data from multiple clients (e.g., for statistical calculations). Access control is thus a highly nontrivial matter of granting and revoking rights to specific users or groups, and access to the data should be controllable by the data owner at an arbitrarily fine granularity. Usually, those rights are tied to certain attributes or a digital identity. Both can be of interest when a whole group of users will be addressed (via common attributes), or access will be granted in an anonymous fashion. In either case, the access granting token is usually some piece of information that may be, but not necessarily is, a set of attributes that are unique for an individual, which would be a digital identity, or a general piece of information that is *not* linkable to an identity. The latter would be coined a credential or token.

Access control via a humble password login is probably not the way to go, since methods to either elicit the password from an unaware user or bypassing the check by outsmarting the implementation are not negligible threats. Much more elegant solutions are offered by cryptography, where the ability to access a certain piece of information rests on the knowledge of some secret information. Contrary to a simple yes/no decision made somewhere inside a code or software, the cryptographic approach avoids possible bypasses by letting the access system be open for anyone, yet it cannot be tricked into yielding the right results without the right inputs, namely the secret access credential.

Parts of the sequel are dedicated to a discussion on how digital identities, credentials, and access controls can be set up, and what different techniques are offered by cryptography. Especially in a cloud environment, where a service access is not only bound to an identity but may also be temporarily limited, tokens can be made to expire automatically after a certain period of time or a number of usages. Suitable constructions will be presented in the upcoming chapters.

1.4   PRIVACY-ENHANCING TECHNOLOGIES

Privacy is of increasing interest and importance in electronic interaction. While this aspect was more or less neglected in the early days of the Internet, in recent years it has emerged to be a hot topic in the (applied) cryptography and computer security research community. Among other reasons, this interest is occurring because the use of the Internet is becoming more and more ubiquitous and users disclose a lot of information that leaves information traces that can be assumed to last forever and can be maliciously used.

The emerging field of cloud computing especially demands adequate measures in order to preserve user privacy. In cloud computing, potentially sensitive data is stored and processed remotely in computing farms of cloud providers. Thereby, the anytime anywhere access via the Internet increases the number of potential adversaries. External attackers may penetrate the cloud provider or employees of these providers may conduct insider attacks and leak information. Furthermore, due to law enforcement, when computing farms are located in other countries, users' data may be accessed by law enforcement agencies without permission or knowledge of the users. Thereby, besides classical privacy of communicated and stored data, the protection of relationships of users with particular actions and their outcomes also becomes very important. For instance, it may not be necessary to know the exact content of a message transmitted over a network. But the sole fact that a user invokes a specific service, communicates with a specific user, or the knowledge about the frequency of service invocation or sent messages may already provide enough information to an adversary. Hence, the protection of the users' privacy requires more than just encryption of transmitted and stored data and can basically be achieved by providing privacy through anonymity.

Concerns regarding privacy and security actually seem to be the biggest hurdle for the adoption of cloud computing by security-conscious enterprises or consumers. These concerns are, however, justified and far from being purely academic, as many examples support, such as data corruption in Amazon's Simple Storage

Service (S3) and an access control bug in Google Docs that provided users access to documents for which they had never been granted access, to name only a few [1]. Related incidents and outages are currently reported frequently in the media and for instance compiled at [2].

In recent years, privacy-enhancing technologies (PETs) have gained significant attention in the research community and cover many aspects in the areas of human computer interfaces, configurable policy languages, web service federations, infrastructures, and privacy-enhancing cryptography, with the aim of protecting the privacy of users. With the introduction of paradigms such as *privacy by design*, which aims at considering privacy and data protection throughout the entire life cycle of technologies, it is now understood that privacy is an important issue that should start at the earliest design stage and proactive privacy protection should be an important design goal of technology.

1.5 OUTLINE

This book covers various cryptographic methods to improve security and privacy in cloud computing. Basically, it must be stressed that many topics in the context of this book are extremely dynamic and continuously evolving. Thus, we do not claim to cover *all* issues in this field. For instance, many cloud services require some form of payment that may also be subject to privacy issues. Work in this direction has been started recently [3–5], but this will not be covered here. Nevertheless, we hope that we have compiled an interesting and inspiring selection of different techniques in this field.

In particular, this book will provide an overview of various nonstandard techniques of security and cryptography, especially those that seem to be particularly useful in a cloud computing environment. Our presentation will be as practical and self-contained as possible, thus sparing much of the underlying mathematics for the sake of clarity and compactness. To this end, we mostly describe the general design ideas underneath a cryptographic primitive and illustrate it with simple example schemes wherever possible and appropriate.

Before we get started, however, let us briefly clarify what is *not* going to come next. We will not dig into technical details of cloud computing [6–8], such as potentials and risks of virtualization technologies (although a brief discussion of the latter will follow in Chapter 6). Furthermore, we leave legal aspects as for instance discussed in [9] out of our scope, especially since regulations are very specific and perhaps widely different among countries. Finally, platform or hardware specifics are as well not part of our treatment and can be found in various textbooks on virtualization.

As a rough roadmap to the contents, the book will be divided into chapters covering the following areas:

Fundamentals: Chapter 2 can be used to refresh the reader's knowledge about the basic mathematical tools and important cryptographic primitives along with their security requirements.

Protection of identities: Privacy is a major concern and obstacle for the adoption of cloud computing. Chapter 3 presents techniques to protect identities inferred from a protocol participation (anonymous communication, authentication, and access control), as well as information leakage from pure data (data anonymization). Furthermore, techniques to hide access patterns from cloud providers are presented.

Privacy-enhancing encryption: Processing data within a cloud presents various challenges in terms of security, and Chapter 4 is devoted to a discussion on how cryptography can realize access control quasi as a built-in feature of encryption, and how encrypted data can be processed without opening the encryption.

Remote data storage: Chapter 5 discusses how to safely store data at a potentially untrusted storage site. Here, the focus is on how to assure the consistent existence and availability of data in the cloud, deduplication of data, and how to enable search on encrypted data.

Practical issues: Chapter 6 rounds out the picture by going into a discussion about what cannot be done using cryptography alone. We also briefly discuss various nontechnical aspects like standardization in cloud computing, cloud-related offerings, and implementations of cryptographic primitives presented in the previous chapters.

References

[1] R. A. Popa, J. Lorch, D. Molnar, H. J. Wang, and L. Zhuang, "Enabling Security in Cloud Storage SLAs with CloudProof," in *USENIX Annual Technical Conference*, 2011.

[2] Cloud Outages. http://cloutage.org/, 2013.

[3] V. M. Pacheco and R. S. Puttini, "SaaS Anonymous Cloud Service Consumption Structure," in *ICDCS 2012 Workshops*, pp. 491–499, IEEE, 2012.

[4] D. Slamanig, "Efficient Schemes for Anonymous Yet Authorized and Bounded Use of Cloud Resources," in *SAC*, vol. 7118 of *LNCS*, pp. 73–91, Springer, 2012.

[5] M. Pirker, D. Slamanig, and J. Winter, "Practical Privacy Preserving Cloud Resource-Payment for Constrained Clients," in *PETS*, vol. 7384 of *LNCS*, pp. 201–220, Springer, 2012.

[6] R. Buyya, J. Broberg, and A. M. Goscinski, *Cloud Computing Principles and Paradigms*. Hoboken, NJ: Wiley Publishing, 2011.

[7] K. Hwang, J. Dongarra, and G. C. Fox, *Distributed and Cloud Computing: From Parallel Processing to the Internet of Things*. San Francisco, CA: Morgan Kaufmann Publishers Inc., 1st ed., 2011.

[8] T. Mather, S. Kumaraswamy, and S. Latif, *Cloud Security and Privacy: An Enterprise Perspective on Risks and Compliance*. Sebastopol, CA: O'Reilly Media Inc., 2009.

[9] R. D. Butters, R. Scott, and M. Stallion, *Understanding the Legal Risks of Cloud Computing: Navigating the Network Security and Data Privacy Issues Associated with Cloud Services (Special Report)*. New York: Thomson Reuters Westlaw, 2012.

Chapter 2

Fundamentals

We denote scalar values by lowercase Latin or Greek letters like a, b, α, κ, and so forth. The absolute value of a scalar a is denoted as $|a|$. Vectors are bold printed, like $\mathbf{x}, \mathbf{y}$, with the ith coordinate in $\mathbf{x}$ indicated via a subscript as x_i. Uppercase (Latin or Greek) letters like S, Σ, X denote sets or random variables. For a set S, the number of elements (cardinality) is written as $|S|$. We write $x \in S$ and $x \notin S$ to denote that x is contained in the set S or not contained in S respectively. Furthermore, we write $x \in_R S$ as shorthand notation for drawing an element x uniformly at random from the set S. The set of n-tuples with components from S is written as the n-fold cartesian product $S^n := S \times S \times \cdots \times S$. The symbol $S^{n \times m}$ is the set of all $(n \times m)$-matrices with elements from S, denoted by uppercase boldface letters like $\mathbf{M}$. The power set of S is written as 2^S. Algebraic structures are written in sans serif font, such as G, R, F. Algorithms are denoted by typewriter letters (A, Encrypt, etc.).

Whenever Σ is an alphabet (technically a set), then Σ^n is the set of all strings consisting of n characters from Σ. Likewise, Σ^* denotes the set of all strings over Σ with arbitrary length. When $x, y \in \Sigma^*$ are two strings, then $x \| y$ denotes either the plain string concatenation or any other encoding from which x and y can be recovered uniquely. The symbol $|x|$ for $x \in \Sigma^*$ denotes the length of the string (in characters).

The set $\mathcal{O}(g)$ is the set of all functions $f : \mathbb{N} \to \mathbb{N}$ for which a constant $c > 0$ and an integer n_0 exists, such that $f(n) \leq c \cdot g(n)$ whenever $n \geq n_0$. Likewise, $\Omega(g)$ denotes the set for which $f(n) \geq c \cdot g(n)$ under the same setting as before.

2.1 NUMBER THEORY

Setting up a cryptosystem usually requires the generation of large primes often having a particular form. To get a prime without further constraints, it is best to generate large random numbers and test for primality using the Miller-Rabin test (see [1]), which is implemented in many mathematical software tools or programming libraries. For instance, the Java programming language provides the class `BigInteger` and the respective method `isProbablePrime` can be used for that matter.

Given two integers x, n and $n \neq 0$, we can write $x = q \cdot n + r$, where q is called the *quotient*, and $0 \leq r \leq n - 1$ is the *remainder*. Given x, n, we shorthand the quotient q as $x \operatorname{DIV} n$ or x/n, and the remainder r as $x \operatorname{MOD} n$. The latter operation is often called a *reduction of x modulo n*. By convention, it is understood that $a \operatorname{MOD} n$ is always nonnegative, otherwise we keep adding n until the result becomes zero or positive. It is easy to see that MOD is linear; that is, $(x \circ y) \operatorname{MOD} n = [(x \operatorname{MOD} n) \circ (x \operatorname{MOD} n)] \operatorname{MOD} n$, for any operation $\circ \in \{+, -, \cdot\}$ holds. In other words, the result remains correct regardless of whether the modulo reduction happens before or after the arithmetic operation plus, minus, or multiply. It is, however, advisable to modulo-reduce a result immediately after the arithmetic operation to keep it within the range between 0 and $n - 1$ and thus keeping the costs for arithmetic operations low. Notice, however, that different moduli *cannot* be interchanged in general; that is, $(a \operatorname{MOD} n) \operatorname{MOD} m \neq (a \operatorname{MOD} m) \operatorname{MOD} n$ whenever $m \neq n$ except for trivial cases. Computing a division modulo n is more complicated and rests on the extended Euclidian algorithm, which is provided by many numeric libraries directly.

If $x \operatorname{MOD} n = 0$, then we say that n *divides* x, and write $n|x$. The largest number g that divides two given integers x, y is denoted as $\gcd(x, y)$. If $\gcd(x, y) = 1$, then we call x, y *relatively prime* or *coprime*. For any $x, y \in \mathbb{Z}$, there is a representation of their greatest common divisor as

$$\gcd(x, y) = ax + by \tag{2.1}$$

for two integers $a, b \in \mathbb{Z}$. Many mathematical and number-theoretic programming libraries provide implementations of the Euclidian and extended Euclidian algorithm to compute the greatest common divisor as well as its representation (2.1). Chapter 6 provides hints and links to respective resources, and we therefore confine ourselves to describing algorithms that usually *do not* ship with such programming libraries. We capture the required functionality as follows:

Definition 2.1. The *Euclidian algorithm* is a function, denoted as $\gcd(x, y)$, which takes two nonnegative integers x, y and returns the largest value $g \in \mathbb{N}$ dividing both x and y. The *extended Euclidian algorithm* is a procedure denoted as $\text{EEA}(x, y)$ and returns a triple $(g, a, b) \in \mathbb{Z}^3$ such that $\gcd(x, y) = g = ax + by$.

Two values x, y satisfying $x \,\text{MOD}\, n = y \,\text{MOD}\, n$ are said to be *congruent*, and we write

$$x \equiv y \quad (\text{mod } n)$$

in that case. Congruences behave in many ways like equations; that is, the congruence remains true when transformations (additions, multiplications, exponential function, etc.) are applied to both sides. However, solving a linear congruence for an unknown, say finding x in the congruence

$$ax \equiv b \quad (\text{mod } n), \tag{2.2}$$

upon given a and b, is somewhat more involved, and rests on computing greatest common divisors and properties of the modulus. Long story short, here is the solvability criterion for linear congruences:

Fact 2.1. Let a linear congruence of the form (2.2) be given.

- If $\gcd(a, n) = 1$, then there is exactly one solution $x < n$, computed as follows: compute $(g, u, v) = \text{EEA}(a, n)$ and set $x = (u \cdot b) \,\text{MOD}\, n$.

- If $\gcd(a, n) = g > 1$, then (2.2) has exactly g solutions, computed as follows: use the extended Euclidian algorithm to solve the congruence

$$(a \,\text{DIV}\, g) \cdot y \equiv (b \,\text{DIV}\, g) \quad (\text{mod } (n \,\text{DIV}\, g))$$

for y. For each $t = 0, 1, \ldots, g - 1$, the value $x_t = u \cdot (b \,\text{DIV}\, g) + t \cdot (n \,\text{DIV}\, g)$ is a solution to (2.2).

2.1.1 Drawing Random Coprime Elements

Some systems, such as Rivest-Shamir-Adleman (RSA) encryption and signatures, call for a random value x that is coprime to another given value y. There is a simple algorithm for this:

1. Draw a random integer x.
2. Set $x \leftarrow x \,\text{DIV}\, \gcd(x, y)$.
3. If $\gcd(x, y) = 1$ then return x; otherwise go back to step 2.

Note that the loop is unavoidable, since dividing out the gcd only once would not necessarily yield coprime numbers. As an example, try the setting in which $x = p^4 \cdot q$ and $y = p \cdot r$, when p, q, r are all primes.

2.1.2   Computing Inverse Elements Modulo a Prime

Fact 2.1 is the key to doing divisions modulo a prime number p, since in that case the inverse a^{-1} of an element a is unique (note that WLOG, $a < p$ can be assumed, for otherwise we can put $a \leftarrow a \operatorname{MOD} p$ to achieve this). Looking for an element a^{-1} such that $a \cdot a^{-1} \operatorname{MOD} p = 1$ exactly means solving the respective congruence for the inverse a^{-1} in the role of the unknown x. For a prime p, the sought inverse a^{-1} satisfying $a \cdot a^{-1} \equiv 1 \pmod{p}$ is computed by the extended Euclidian algorithm via $\operatorname{EEA}(a, p)$ returning $(1, a^{-1}, b)$, where the value b can be abandoned, and the gcd is always 1, since p is a prime.

2.1.3   Computing Negative Powers Modulo a Prime

Computing positive powers of the form $a^k \operatorname{MOD} p$ is easy by the well-known square-and-multiply algorithm (see [1, Algorithm 2.143] or Chapter 6). Computing a negative power $a^{-k} \operatorname{MOD} p$ is thus a humble computation of $a^k \operatorname{MOD} p$, with a final inversion as described before. Notice that this makes sense only when p is a prime, since otherwise, the inverse element is no longer unique.

2.1.4   Getting (Large) Primes

Choosing large primes is mostly done by choosing large random numbers and testing for primality. Again, many mathematical programming libraries and software development kits (SDKs) of common programming languages provide the respective routines (further pointers are given in Chapter 6). However, often we need primes of a very specific form, such as $p = u \cdot q + 1$ where q is another prime, and u is an integer. For $u = 2$, the resulting primes of the form $p = 2q + 1$ are called *safe primes*.

   Generating such primes is done by first generating a prime (divisor) q and then testing if $p := u \cdot q + 1$ is prime for the given (chosen) u. In general, whenever a prime p with known factorization of $p - 1$ is required, the only feasible way is to generate the factors $q_1, \ldots, q_k$ and testing $p := 1 + (q_1 q_2 \cdots q_k)$ for primality. The reverse approach of choosing a large prime p and factoring $p - 1$ is usually intractable!

2.1.5 Quadratic Residues, Legendre Symbol, and Jacobi Symbol

Definition 2.2 (Quadratic (non)residue). Given integers $n, x \in \mathbb{N}$, we call x a *quadratic residue* if there is an integer y such that $x \equiv y^2 \pmod{n}$; that is, "x has a square-root modulo n." Otherwise, x is called a *quadratic nonresidue*. The set of all quadratic residues modulo n is denoted as QR_n.

Testing for the existence of a quadratic residue is feasible if n is prime, and intractable if n is composite, unless the factorization of n is known (see Definition 2.26).

Definition 2.3 (Legendre symbol). The *Legendre symbol* of a and p, hereafter denoted as $L(a, p)$, is defined as

$$L(a, p) := \begin{cases} 0, & \text{if } p | a, \\ 1, & \text{if } a \in QR_p \\ -1, & \text{if } a \notin QR_p, \end{cases}$$

where QR_p is the set of quadratic residues modulo p.

The Legendre symbol thus lets us *test* whether a value is a quadratic (non)residue modulo a prime p. This test is efficient, since we have a direct formula,

$$L(a, p) = a^{(p-1)/2} \operatorname{MOD} p.$$

For composite integers n, the respective generalization is the Jacobi symbol:

Definition 2.4 (Jacobi symbol). Let $n \geq 3$ be an odd integer with prime factorization $n = p_1^{e_1} p_2^{e_2} \cdots p_k^{e_k}$. Then, the *Jacobi symbol*, hereafter denoted as $J(a, n)$, is defined as

$$J(a, n) := L(a, p_1)^{e_1} L(a, p_2)^{e_2} \cdots L(a, p_k)^{e_k}.$$

Remark 2.1. Notice that unlike the Legendre symbol, the Jacobi symbol *cannot* be used to decide whether a number is a quadratic residue modulo a composite n. Indeed, if $a \in QR_n$, then $J(a, n) = 1$. The converse conclusion, however, would be wrong: $J(a, n) = 1$ does *not* imply $a \in QR_n$. In that case, we call a a *pseudosquare*.

Computing the Jacobi symbol according to this definition requires the factorization of the integer n, which is intractable to obtain when n is large. Remarkably, however, there is an algorithm (see below) that can compute the Jacobi symbol recursively *without* knowing the factorization of n.

Remark 2.2. It is important to notice that our notation of the Legendre and Jacobi symbols differs from the usual notation in the literature. Unfortunately, most references use *the same* notation $\left(\frac{a}{b}\right)$ to denote the Legendre symbol $L(a, b)$ or the Jacobi symbol $J(a, b)$. We avoid this notational clash here by writing $L(a, b)$ and $J(a, b)$ instead.

A recursive algorithm to compute the Jacobi symbol (and hence also the Legendre symbol) is as follows: upon input a, n with an odd integer $n \geq 3$ and $0 \leq a < n$, perform the following steps (see [1]):

1. If $a = 0$ then return $J(a, n) = 0$.

2. If $a = 1$ then return $J(a, n) = 1$.

3. Write $a = 2^e a_1$, where a_1 is odd.

4. If e is even, then set $s \leftarrow 1$. Otherwise, set

$$s \leftarrow \begin{cases} 1, & \text{if } n \operatorname{MOD} 8 \in \{1, 7\} \\ -1, & \text{if } n \operatorname{MOD} 8 \in \{3, 5\} \end{cases}$$

5. If $n \operatorname{MOD} 4 = 3$ and $a_1 \operatorname{MOD} 4 = 3$, then set $s \leftarrow -s$.

6. Set $n_1 \leftarrow n \operatorname{MOD} a_1$.

7. If $a_1 = 1$ then return $J(a, n) = s$; otherwise return $s \cdot J(n_1, a_1)$.

2.2   RINGS, GROUPS, FIELDS, AND LATTICES

In general, an algebraic structure is a set S with one or more operations $\circ$ that map two elements from S to another element in S. Depending on the properties of the operator $\circ$, different algebraic structures arise, denoted as $(S, \circ)$ or simply as S if the operations are clear from the context. Useful structures with two operations are *rings* and *fields*, denoted as $(R, +, \cdot)$ and $(F, +, \cdot)$, or commonly shorthanded as R or F. We define these below, since the definition rests on the properties of the respective operations, which we consider first.

Definition 2.5 (Neutral and inverse elements). Let an algebraic structure S with an operation $\circ$ be given. An element $n \in S$ is called *neutral*, if $n \circ x = x \circ n = x$ for all $x \in S$. If for given $x \in S$ we can find another element $x^{-1} \in S$ so that $x \circ x^{-1} = x^{-1} \circ x = n$, then we call x^{-1} the *inverse of* x. Elements that possess inverses are called *units*.

Fact 2.2. Let an algebraic structure $(S, \circ)$ be given.

- If a neutral element with regard to $\circ$ exists, then it is unique.
- If an element $x \in S$ possesses an inverse element x^{-1}, then the inverse is unique.

Definition 2.6 (Commutativity, associativity, distributivity). Let an algebraic structure with one operation $(S, \circ)$ be given. We say that $\circ$ is

- *Associative*, if for any $x, y, z \in S : (x \circ y) \circ z = x \circ (y \circ z)$.
- *Commutative*, if for any $x, y \in S : x \circ y = y \circ x$.

Let an algebraic structure with two operations $(S, +, \cdot)$ be given. We say that $\cdot$ is *distributive with regard to* $+$, if for any $x, y, z \in S : x \cdot (y + z) = x \cdot y + x \cdot z$ and $(x + y) \cdot z = x \cdot z + y \cdot z$.

Notice that the definition of distributivity explicitly requires both conditions to hold, unless the multiplication $\cdot$ is commutative (in which case either of the two implies the other). In noncommutative structures, the two conditions are called *left* and *right distributivity*.

Depending on whether one or two operations are defined on the structure and what properties the operations have, different algebras are distinguished. We summarize the respective definitions as overview in Table 2.1. It is important to remark that groups are found in the literature using the additive notation $(G, +)$, such as for elliptic curve groups, or in the multiplicative notation $(G, \cdot)$, as is common for modulo groups. We will use both notations in the sequel.

Among the most important structures used in cryptography are residue class groups, and finite fields and their multiplicative groups.

Definition 2.7 (Residue class groups $\mathbb{Z}_n$). The group $(\mathbb{Z}_n, +)$ is defined as $\mathbb{Z}_n = \{0, 1, 2, \ldots, n - 1\}$, with the addition $x + y := (x + y) \mathrm{MOD}\, n$, where the right-hand side is evaluated using standard integer arithmetic. The neutral element with regard to $+$ is (the integer) 0. The inverse element to x is simply $-x$, or after a modulo reduction, $(-x + n)$. A commutative ring with 1 $(\mathbb{Z}_n, +, \cdot)$ uses the same addition, and multiplication done as $x \cdot y := (x \cdot y) \mathrm{MOD}\, n$, again over the integers. The neutral element with regard to $\cdot$ is (the integer) 1.

It is a trivial task to check that the inverse of x with regard to addition is simply $n - x$ in $\mathbb{Z}_n$, since $x + (n - x) \mathrm{MOD}\, n = n \mathrm{MOD}\, n = 0$, hence it equals the neutral element. The difference to the field is the requirement of inverse elements to exist, which, by Fact 2.1, is the case if and only if all elements $\{1, 2, \ldots, n - 1\}$

Table 2.1

Definitions of Common Algebraic Structures

		Group	Commutative / Abelian Group	Ring	Ring with 1	Commutative Ring with 1	Field
Add (+)	Associative	✓	✓	✓	✓	✓	✓
	Commutative		✓			✓	✓
	Neutral Element	✓	✓	✓	✓	✓	✓
	Inverse Elements	✓	✓	✓	✓	✓	✓
Mult (·)	Associative	operation undefined	operation undefined	✓	✓	✓	✓
	Commutative					✓	✓
	Neutral Element				✓	✓	✓
	Inverse Elements						✓
Distributivity				✓	✓	✓	✓
Common examples			$(\mathbb{Z}, +)$			$(\mathbb{Z}, +, \cdot)$	$\mathbb{R}$

are coprime to n. In turn, this is the case if and only if n is a prime. For general (composite) numbers, an inverse for x in $\mathbb{Z}_n$ exists if and only if $\gcd(x, n) = 1$ (see Fact 2.1). The respective substructure is called the *group of units*:

Definition 2.8 (Group of units $\mathbb{Z}_n^*$)**.** The set $\mathbb{Z}_n^* := \{x \in \mathbb{Z}_n \,|\, \gcd(x, n) = 1\}$ is the set of all elements for which an inverse in $\mathbb{Z}_n$ exists.

In the case of n being a prime, we obviously have $\mathbb{Z}_p = \{0, 1, 2, \ldots, p - 1\}$ and $\mathbb{Z}_p^* = \{1, 2, \ldots, p - 1\}$.

In some cases (e.g., for Diffie-Hellman key exchange or many elliptic curve cryptosystems) it is mandatory to work in a substructure of a group:

Definition 2.9 (Subgroup, subring, extension field)**.** A subgroup $(U, \circ)$ of a group $(G, \circ)$ is a subset $U \subset G$ that is itself a group with regard to the $\circ$ operation (whether $\circ$ is an addition or multiplication). The same holds for subrings (i.e., the subset $R' \subset R$ is again a ring with regard to both operations on R). If $F' \subset F$ for two fields F, F', then F is called the *extension field* of F'.

Notice that the definition of a subgroup or subring in particular implies that any operation done on elements in the substructure will result in another element of the substructure (the set is said to be *closed* under the operation).

In a given group $(G, \circ)$, we define the nth power of an element $x \in G$ as the n-fold $\circ$-product of x with itself; that is,

$$x^n := \underbrace{x \circ x \circ x \ldots \circ x}_{n \text{ times}}.$$

Of particular interest are groups whose elements arise as powers of a particular element. If so, then we can define a logarithm function on such a group.

Definition 2.10 (Cyclic group, generators and discrete logarithm). Let a group $(G, \circ)$ be given. If an element $g \in G$ exists such that every $x \in G$ can be written as some power of g (i.e., $x = g^k$ for some integer k), then we call g a *generator* of the group G, and G itself is called *cyclic*. The value k in that case is called the *discrete logarithm of x with regard to the base (generator) g*, and denoted as $\log(x)$.

Definition 2.11 (Order). The *order* of an algebraic structure S (group, ring, field) is the number of elements in it, denoted as $|S|$. If the order is finite, then S is called finite. The *order* of an element $x \in S$, denoted as $ord(x)$, is the smallest exponent k such that x^k equals the neutral element, where the power is defined in terms of the group operation ($+$ or $\cdot$) or ring/field multiplication $\cdot$. If no such k exists, then x is said to have infinite order.

If the order of an algebraic structure is a finite number, then we call the structure itself *finite*. Throughout this book, all relevant fields, rings, and groups are finite.

Fact 2.3. Let a group $(G, \circ)$ be given.

- For a given element $g \in S$, its *generated subgroup* is defined and denoted as $\langle g \rangle := \{g^0, g^1, g^2, \ldots\} \subseteq S$. The order $|\langle g \rangle|$ of this subgroup equals the order $ord(g)$ of the generating element g. This is always a cyclic group.

- The order of any subgroup of G divides the group order $|G|$ (*Lagrange's theorem*).

- The group of units $\mathbb{Z}_p^*$ when p is prime is always cyclic.

For their initialization, many cryptographic primitives require a generator or an element with a prescribed order, or even impose constraints on the group order itself. For that matter, Fact 2.4 becomes handy, since it characterizes exactly the cases when a generator exists, and how it can be found (see [1]). It rests on the next definition.

Definition 2.12 (Euler's totient function). The function $\varphi(n)$ counts the integers $x \leq n$ that are coprime to n. If the prime-factorization of n is known as $n = p_1^{e_1} p_2^{e_2} \cdots p_k^{e_k}$, then

$$\varphi(n) = n \cdot \prod_{i=1}^{k} \left(1 - \frac{1}{p_i} \right).$$

Notice that without the factorization of n, it is infeasible to compute $\varphi(n)$. Indeed, computing $\varphi(n)$ is equivalent to breaking an RSA-encryption without knowing the secret key (details follow later).

Fact 2.4 ([1]). (Generators of $\mathbb{Z}_n^*$)

1. $\mathbb{Z}_n^*$ is cyclic (has a generator) if and only if $n = 2, 4, p^k$ or $2p^k$ for p being an odd prime and $k \geq 1$.

2. If g is a generator of $\mathbb{Z}_n^*$, then $\mathbb{Z}_n^* = \{ g^i \bmod n | 0 \leq i \leq \varphi(n) - 1 \}$.

3. If g is a generator of $\mathbb{Z}_n^*$, then $b = g^i \bmod n$ is also a generator of $\mathbb{Z}_n^*$ if and only if $\gcd(i, \varphi(n)) = 1$. It follows that the number of generators is exactly $\varphi(\varphi(n))$.

4. The element $g \in \mathbb{Z}_n^*$ is a generator if and only if $g^{\varphi(n)/p} \bmod n \neq 1$ for all prime divisors p of $\varphi(n)$.

Fact 2.4 is the key to solving the following sequence of tasks that frequently occur when setting up a cryptosystem.

2.2.1 Finding a Generating Element

If a group $\mathbb{Z}_p$ with p being prime is given, for which a generator of $\mathbb{Z}_p^*$ is required, then first observe that $\varphi(p) = p - 1$, so that we ought to construct the prime p such that the factorization of $p - 1$ is known (see Section 2.1.4), say $q_1, \ldots, q_k$. Next, we choose an element g within $2 \leq g \leq p - 1$ at random, and test whether $g^{(p-1)/q_i} \bmod p \neq 1$ for all known prime divisors q_i of $p - 1$. If so, then g is the sought generator.

In general, if the group order n is not a prime, then we require the factorization of its order as $|\mathsf{G}| = p_1^{e_1} p_2^{e_2} \cdots p_k^{e_k}$. With this, we choose a random element $g \in \mathsf{G}$ and test if $g^{n/p_i} \neq 1$ for all prime divisors p_i of n. If so, then g is the sought generator, otherwise we draw a new g and retry.

2.2.2 Groups of Quadratic Residues

It is easy to see that the product of any two quadratic residues a, b modulo n, with representation as $a = x^2 \text{ MOD } n$ and $b = y^2 \text{ MOD } n$ forms again a quadratic residue by the properties of powers, since $a \cdot b \equiv (x^2)(y^2) \equiv (xy)^2 \pmod{n}$, hence the set QR_n of quadratic residue modulo n forms itself a group with regard to the multiplication modulo n.

Finding a generating element α for $(QR_n, \cdot)$ is easy if a generator g for $\mathbb{Z}_n^*$ is known: simply put $\alpha := g^2 \text{ MOD } n$.

2.2.3 Constructing a Subgroup

If the group order $n = |G|$ is known and G is cyclic, then the order q of a subgroup must divide the group order (see Fact 2.4) and the subgroup must also be cyclic. We seek an element α whose order is a divisor of the group order. We call this a *qth root of unity*, since $\alpha^q = 1$ in G and α generates a (proper) subgroup of order q.

So, the task of setting up a subgroup of prescribed size (e.g., prime order and minimal bitlength) boils down to finding a qth root of unity within the group G. Finding a *qth root of unity* can be performed as follows when given a generator g of G. Simply compute $\alpha := g^{n/q}$ and α is the sought qth root of unity.

Furthermore, if we are given an element α and want to determine the order q of the subgroup $\langle \alpha \rangle$ generated by the element α, this can be obtained if the factorization of the group order $n = |G| = p_1^{e_1} p_2^{e_2} \cdots p_k^{e_k}$ is available. If so, we can compute the order q of α by the following steps [1]:

1. Set $q \leftarrow n$
2. For $i = 1, 2, \ldots, k$, do:
   - 2.1. Set $q \leftarrow q \operatorname{DIV}(p_i^{e_i})$.
   - 2.2. Compute $a_1 \leftarrow a^q$.
   - 2.3. While $a_1 \neq 1$, compute $a_1 \leftarrow a_1^{p_i}$ and set $q \leftarrow q \cdot p_i$.
3. Return q

Hence, groups and subgroups should be constructed so that their order, or more precisely the factorization of their order, is known.

2.2.4 Constructing General Finite Fields

Finite fields are either of the form $\mathbb{Z}_p$ for p being a prime, or are otherwise denoted as F_{p^n} for an integer $n \geq 1$. In that case, p^n is the order of the field, and finite fields exist *only* for orders of the form p^n, where p is a prime and $n \geq 1$. Fields with $p = 2$ are also called *binary fields*.

Arithmetic in a finite field F_{p^n} works in much the same way as in $\mathbb{Z}_p$, except that we add and multiply polynomials with coefficients from $\mathbb{Z}_p$ and reduce the results modulo an irreducible polynomial $f(x)$. Details follow:

Definition 2.13 ((Monic) Irreducible polynomial). A polynomial $f(x)$ is called *irreducible*, if it cannot be written as the product of two other nontrivial polynomials of lower degree. By convention, it is assumed that the coefficient of the largest power in $f(x)$ is 1, in which case we call $f(x)$ *monic*.

In this way, a monic irreducible polynomial $f(x)$ behaves much like a prime number, since no other polynomial except for 1 and $f(x)$ itself divides $f(x)$. Having an irreducible polynomial, the field takes the following form:

- An element $\alpha \in F_{p^n}$ is a polynomial $\alpha(x) = a_0 + a_1 x + a_2 x^2 + \cdots + a_{n-1} x^{n-1}$ of degree $n - 1$ and with n coefficients $a_i \in \mathbb{Z}_p$ for $i = 0, 1, \ldots, n$.

- Arithmetic is done modulo a fixed monic irreducible polynomial $f(x) = f_0 + f_1 x + f_2 x^2 + \cdots + f_{n-2} x^{n-2} + x^{n-1}$ that is part of the field representation. Adding and multiplying polynomials must be done symbolically, where computations on the coefficients happen in the field $(\mathbb{Z}_p, +, \cdot)$.

Testing a polynomial for irreducibility is much easier than testing a prime, and can be done by the following procedure: given a prime p and a monic polynomial $f(x)$ of degree m with coefficients from $\mathbb{Z}_p$.

1. Set $u(x) \leftarrow x$
2. For $i = 1, 2, \ldots, \lfloor \frac{m}{2} \rfloor$, do:
   2.1. Compute $u(x) \leftarrow u(x)^p$ MOD $f(x)$ symbolically.
   2.2. Compute $d(x) = \gcd(f(x), u(x) - x)$, using the Euclidian algorithm with symbolic computations (polynomial divisions) inside.
   2.3. If $d(x) \neq 1$, then return "reducible."
3. Otherwise, return "irreducible."

If a generator of the field is required, then it is useful to choose $f(x)$ as a *primitive* polynomial, which is an irreducible polynomial with the additional property that the simple polynomial $g(x) = x$ is a generator of F_{p^n} modulo $f(x)$. Testing a given irreducible polynomial $f(x)$ of degree $n - 1$ over $\mathbb{Z}_p$ to be primitive works analogously to Fact 2.4: given the prime divisors $q_1, q_2, \ldots, q_k$ of $p^n - 1$ (again, presuming that $p^n - 1$ is constructed from a priori chosen prime factors; see

Section 2.1.4), we test if $x^{(p^n-1)/q_i} \text{ MOD } f(x) \neq 1$ for all $q_1, \ldots, q_k$. If so, then $f(x)$ is primitive, and $g(x) = x$ is a generator of $\mathsf{F}_{p^n}^*$.

So, the steps to work with a general finite field can roughly be summarized as follows:

1. Choose an irreducible polynomial $f(x)$ according to the procedure above. Any irreducible polynomial works, since all finite fields of the same order p^n are isomorphic, so all that changes is the (visual) representation of its elements.

2. Do arithmetic by symbolic computations (polynomial addition, multiplication and division with remainder; especially within the Euclidian algorithm) modulo $f(x)$.

3. If a generator is needed, then check if $f(x)$ is primitive. If so, then $g(x) = x$ is the sought generator, and all elements of $\mathsf{F}_{p^n}^*$ can be formed via $x^k \text{ MOD } f(x)$ for $k = 0, 1, 2, \ldots, p^n - 1$. Otherwise, try a different irreducible polynomial (again, they all work equally well).

Definition 2.14 (Characteristic). Given a finite field with p^n elements, the prime p is called the field's *characteristic*.

Remark 2.3. The characteristic can be defined also for rings. For both fields and rings, it is the smallest number of times by which we can add the multiplicative neutral to itself so that the additive neutral element arises. Formally, if p denotes a fields's or ring's characteristic, then

$$\underbrace{1 + 1 + \cdots + 1}_{p \text{ times}} = 0,$$

when 1 is the multiplicative neutral, and 0 is the additive neutral element. This definition is as well consistent with the convention that $p := 0$ for all infinite fields, like the rational, real of complex numbers, since in no such structure, adding 1s will ever sum up to 0.

2.2.5 Homomorphy and Isomorphy

If we map elements from one algebraic structure $(\mathsf{S}_1, \circ)$ to another structure $(\mathsf{S}_2, *)$ via a function $f : \mathsf{S}_1 \to \mathsf{S}_2$, then it is interesting to check if operations done in S_1 "propagate" through the function f. This is the idea of homomorphy.

Definition 2.15 (Homomorphy and isomorphy). Let two algebraic structures $\mathsf{S}_1, \mathsf{S}_2$ be given. Let $\circ$ be an operation defined on S_1, and let $*$ be an operation defined on

S_2. If a mapping $f : S_1 \to S_2$ satisfies

$$f(x \circ y) = f(x) * f(y),$$

for all elements $x, y \in S_1$, then we call f a *homomorphism*. If f is invertible, and the inverse f^{-1} is as well a homomorphism, then we call f an *isomorphism*, and write $S_1 \simeq S_2$.

Notice that Definition 2.15 requires compatibility of f with both the addition and multiplication in case of rings and fields; that is, we need $f(x + y) = f(x) \oplus f(y)$ and $f(x \cdot y) = f(x) * f(y)$, for a mapping from one group/field $(S_1, +, \cdot)$ to another algebra $(S_2, \oplus, *)$.

An isomorphism f allows us to *convert* between different representations of basically the same elements. Intuitively, two structures that are isomorphic are essentially identical and only differ in the notation of their elements.

2.2.6 Elliptic Curves

An elliptic curve E over the finite field F_q is a plane algebraic curve (i.e., a set of points (x, y) that satisfy the Weierstrass equation)

$$E : y^2 + a_1 xy + a_3 y = x^3 + a_2 x^2 + a_4 x + a_6 \tag{2.3}$$

where $a_1, a_2, a_3, a_4, a_6 \in \mathsf{F}_q$ (see the bold curves in Figure 2.1 for an example). The set $E(\mathsf{F}_q)$ of points $(x, y) \in \mathsf{F}_q^2$ satisfying (2.3) plus the point at infinity $\mathcal{O}$, which is the neutral element, forms an additive Abelian group (see Table 2.1). Fields F_q of interest are those of characteristic 2 (binary fields), characteristic 3 (ternary fields), or fields of prime characteristic $p > 3$ (prime fields). We restrict ourselves in the following to elliptic curves over prime fields. For prime fields, (2.3) simplifies to

$$E : y^2 = x^3 + ax + b \tag{2.4}$$

with $a, b \in \mathsf{F}_q$. However, not every equation of the form (2.4) actually defines an elliptic curve as it is required that the curve is nonsingular, which holds if the discriminant $\Delta := -16(4a^3 + 27b^2)$ is nonzero.

Elliptic curve cryptography (ECC) has the advantage that the parameters compared to RSA or standard discrete logarithm based cryptosystems can be chosen relatively small. For instance, according to the National Institute of Standards and Technology (NIST) [2] to preserve long-term security ($>$ year 2030), 256-bit security in the context of ECC is comparable to 3072-bit RSA or discrete logarithm-based cryptosystems on prime fields. When working in $\mathbb{Z}_p^*$ (or some prime order subgroup thereof), we have well-known subexponential-time algorithms to solve the discrete logarithm problem (e.g., the index calculus method) (see [1]). However, these methods fail on various classes of elliptic curve groups. Therefore, the curves have to be chosen accordingly in order to satisfy this criteria. For instance, one should not use *supersingular curves* (i.e., curves where the characteristic of the underlying field evenly divides the trace) (see Fact 2.5) or other elliptic curves of trace 2, because they are susceptible to attacks (Menezes-Okamoto-Vanstone (MOV) reduction [3]).

Group Law (Chord-and-Tangent Method)

Since the group of points $E(\mathsf{F}_q)$ forms an additive group, the group operation is the addition of points $P, Q \in E(\mathsf{F}_q)$ with $P \neq Q$ to obtain a third point $R = P + Q \in E(\mathsf{F}_q)$. Furthermore, due to constraint in point addition, one is interested in point doubling; that is, computing $2P$ given $P \in E(\mathsf{F}_q)$. Since the latter is more efficient than addition, this then gives rise to application of an additive version of the square-and-multiply algorithm to efficiently compute $kP \in E(\mathsf{F}_q)$ given $k \in \mathbb{Z}_q$ and $P \in E(\mathsf{F}_q)$ instead of using repeated additions.

An intuitive way to illustrate the above-mentioned basic operations is by using the geometric interpretation. Let P and Q be two distinct points on $E(\mathsf{F}_q)$. An *addition* happens by drawing a line through P and Q that intersects the elliptic curve in another point $-R$. The reflection of this third point over the x-axis results in the sum $R = P + Q$. The *doubling* of a point $P \in E(\mathsf{F}_q)$ can be thought of as drawing a tangent to the elliptic curve on point P. This tangent intersects the elliptic curve in another point, where the reflection of this point over the x-axis results in the point $R = 2P$. Figure 2.1 shows an illustration on a continuous curve (over $\mathbb{R}$), whereas cryptography is only done over discrete curves (over finite fields). If the line does not intersect the curve, such as is the case for $P + (-P)$, then we may think of it "intersecting at infinity," which justifies why $\mathcal{O} = P + (-P)$ is called the "point at infinity" (see Figure 2.1c).

From this geometric interpretation, we can derive explicit formulas for computing the respective operations, which we present for elliptic curves satisfying (2.4) using affine coordinates below (more on different types of coordinates later). Therefore, let $P = (x_1, y_1)$ and $Q = (x_2, y_2)$ be two points on $E(\mathsf{F}_q)$ different from $\mathcal{O}$ and note that $P + \mathcal{O} = \mathcal{O} + P = P$ for all $P \in E(\mathsf{F}_q)$.

Point inversion: The inverse of $P = (x_1, y_1)$ is $-P = (x_1, -y_1)$.

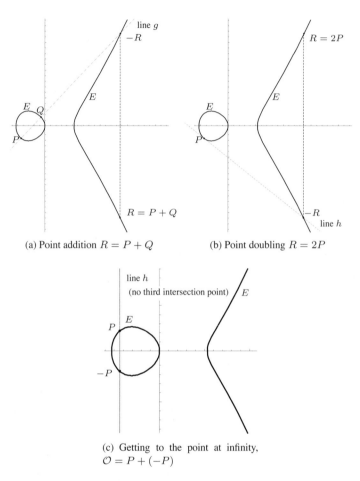

(a) Point addition $R = P + Q$ (b) Point doubling $R = 2P$

(c) Getting to the point at infinity,
$\mathcal{O} = P + (-P)$

Figure 2.1 Illustration of operations on a continuous elliptic curve E over $\mathbb{R}$.

Point addition: The coordinates of the point $P + Q = (x_3, y_3)$ for $P \neq \pm Q$ are
defined as

$$x_3 = \left(\frac{y_2 - y_1}{x_2 - x_1} \right)^2 - x_1 - x_2 \text{ and } y_3 = \left(\frac{y_2 - y_1}{x_2 - x_1} \right)(x_1 - x_3) - y_1.$$

Point doubling: The coordinates of the point $2P = (x_3, y_3)$ for $P \neq -P$ are defined as

$$x_3 = \left(\frac{3x_1^2 + a}{2y_1}\right)^2 - 2x_1 \text{ and } y_3 = \left(\frac{3x_1^2 + a}{2y_1}\right)(x_1 - x_3) - y_1.$$

We note that there are several ways to represent a point on an elliptic curve. Besides the already used affine coordinates (x, y), one can also use projective coordinates $(X : Y : Z)$ to represent points, where the conversion is achieved by $x = X/Z$ and $y = Y/Z$. Another important way to represent points is by using Jacobian coordinates, which are represented like projective coordinates with conversion $x = X/Z^2$ and $y = Y/Z^3$. Depending on the underlying field (binary, ternary, or prime), different types of coordinates have different advantages and disadvantages. Affine coordinates, for instance, require an inversion for every addition and doubling, but fewer multiplications than projective coordinates and Jacobian coordinates allow for faster point doubling. For a more detailed treatment and different methods for scalar multiplications, we refer the reader to [4, 5].

Generating Suitable Curves

It is important to choose elliptic curve groups of suitable (prime) order, denoted as $|E(\mathsf{F}_q)|$. A theorem due to Hasse gives bounds for the order of elliptic curve groups:

Fact 2.5. Let E be an elliptic curve defined over F_q, then

$$q + 1 - 2\sqrt{q} \leq |E(\mathsf{F}_q)| \leq q + 1 + 2\sqrt{q}$$

Alternatively, we can state Fact 2.5 as $|E(\mathsf{F}_q)| = (q + 1) + t$, with $|t| \leq 2\sqrt{q}$ and t is called the *trace*.

In cryptographic applications, one typically requires subgroups that are of known prime order and the question is how to find such subgroups efficiently. Therefore, one may generate suitable curves verifiably at random (see [4, 5]). But if one does not require special curves like pairing friendly elliptic curves, it is advisable to use standardized curves such as those proposed by NIST [6].

2.2.7 Pairings

Pairings used in cryptography are bilinear maps between cyclic groups on elliptic curves mapping to some cyclic multiplicative subgroup of an extension field. We note that not all ordinary elliptic curves are suitable for pairings (pairing friendly), but there are some well-known classes of pairing friendly curves.

Definition 2.16 (Bilinear map). Let $(G_1, +), (G_2, +)$ and $(G_T, \cdot)$ be cyclic groups of the same prime order p, where G_T is called the (multiplicative) target group. We call the map $e : G_1 \times G_2 \rightarrow G_T$ a *bilinear map* or *pairing*, if the following conditions hold:

Bilinearity: For all $P_1, P_2 \in G_1$ and $P_1', P_2' \in G_2$ we have:

- $e(P_1 + P_2, P') = e(P_1, P') \cdot e(P_2, P')$ for all $P' \in G_2$,
- $e(P, P_1' + P_2') = e(P, P_1') \cdot e(P, P_2')$ for all $P \in G_1$.

Nondegeneracy: If P is a generator of G_1 and P' a generator of G_2, then $e(P, P')$ is a generator of G_T, i.e., $e(P, P') \neq 1$ (multiplicative neutral) in G_T.

Efficiently computable: e can be computed efficiently.

If $G_1 = G_2$, then e is called *symmetric* and *asymmetric* otherwise. The former type is also called *Type-1* pairing, whereas in case of the latter we distinguish between *Type-2* and *Type-3* pairings. For Type-2 pairings there is an efficiently computable isomorphism $f : G_2 \rightarrow G_1$ and for Type-3 pairings, such an efficiently computable isomorphism f is not known to exist [7].

We note that sometimes in the context of cryptographic protocols, the groups G_1 and G_2 are also often written multiplicatively (although they are additive groups) in order to make the protocols easier and more intuitive to read and understand. We will also encounter this several times in the sequel.

Another important issue in the context of pairing-based cryptography is the so-called *embedding degree*. We typically have G_1 being a prime order p subgroup of $E(F_q)$ (denoted as $E(F_q)[p]$) and G_2 is typically a p order subgroup of an elliptic curve defined over an extension field of F_q. Furthermore, let $G_T = F_{q^k}^*[p]$, which is an order p subgroup of $F_{q^k}^*$. Then the *embedding degree* k is defined as $k = \min\{\ell \in \mathbb{N} | p \text{ divides } (q^\ell - 1)\}$ and is determined by the curve type. Symmetric pairings $e : G_1 \times G_1 \rightarrow G_T$ are only known for supersingular elliptic curves having a small embedding degree $k = 2$ in case of prime fields. Since such curves are susceptible to attacks [3], their security parameter κ needs to be chosen quite large (i.e., $\kappa \geq 1024$ bit), which requires working on at least 1024-bit elliptic curve groups to preserve security. Asymmetric parings are much more efficient and a very good choice at the moment are Type-3 pairings over a Baretto-Naehring (BN) curve (having $k = 12$). For instance, using a BN curve with $|p| = 256$ bit gives us 3072-bit security in $F_{q^k}^*$, which represents state-of-the-art security in elliptic curves and finite fields. For a classification of pairing friendly elliptic curves, we refer the reader to [8].

We note that most well-known pairings are the Weil and the Tate pairings, but there are several other types and optimizations known for different curve types today. Basically, they all use variants of Miller's algorithm for the computation of the pairing, whose complete description is beyond our scope here. We refer the interested reader to [9] for a sound treatment of pairings.

2.2.8 Lattices

Let a set of m vectors $\mathbf{b}_1, \mathbf{b}_2, \ldots, \mathbf{b}_m \in \mathbb{R}^m$ be given. We call these *linearly independent*, if the linear combination $\lambda_1 \mathbf{b}_1 + \lambda_2 \mathbf{b}_2 + \cdots + \lambda_m \mathbf{b}_m \neq 0$ whenever any of the coefficients λ_i's nonzero. Alternatively, the vectors are linearly independent if the rank of the matrix

$$
\mathbf{M} := \begin{pmatrix} \mathbf{b}_1 \\ \mathbf{b}_2 \\ \vdots \\ \mathbf{b}_m \end{pmatrix}
$$

is m, where each vector makes up another row in $\mathbf{M}$. This criterion is especially useful, as we can apply Gaussian elimination [10] to $\mathbf{M}$ and check if the resulting matrix contains a line of all zeros. If not, then the vectors $\mathbf{b}_1, \ldots, \mathbf{b}_n$ are linearly independent.

Definition 2.17. Given a set $B = \{\mathbf{b}_1, \ldots, \mathbf{b}_m\}$ vectors in $\mathbb{R}^n$, a *lattice* L is the set of all integer linear combinations of the vectors in B. That is, every point $x \in L$ has a representation as $\alpha_1 \mathbf{b}_1 + \alpha_2 \mathbf{b}_2 + \ldots + \alpha_m \mathbf{b}_m$, where $\alpha_i \in \mathbb{Z}$ for each index $i = 1, 2, \ldots, m$. The set B is called the *basis* of the lattice.

Lattices give rise to a rich variety of presumably intractable problems, some of which form the fundament of modern *postquantum* cryptography.

It is important to remark that the term *lattice* also refers to sets S on which a *partial* ordering relation $\prec \subseteq S \times S$ exists. The partial ordering means that there are elements that cannot be related to each other in the sense of $\prec$. Consequently, there are elements that are incomparable by $\prec$. If for any two elements $x, y \in S$ either $x \prec y$ or $y \prec x$ holds, we call this ordering *total*. We will only need such partially ordered structures in Section 3.3.1.

2.3 CODING

Codes enlarge a given piece of information by adding redundancy, so that if parts of the so-called code word get lost or modified, the remaining intact portions can be used to recover from the error. In the simplest case of the *repetition code* over the finite field $F_2 = \{0, 1\}$, a single bit is copied for, say $n \geq 3$ times. When some bits flip, a majority decision among the 0s and 1s of the (erroneous) received code word is made to determine the original information. This is the simplest example of a linear block code. The general idea of these codes is roughly the following:

1. The given information is represented as a tuple of k elements from a finite field F. In case of bitstrings, this is a vector with elements from $F_2 = \{0, 1\}$.

2. The *code* of length n is a subset $C \subset F^n$, so that any two elements $x, y \in C$ differ in at least d coordinates. This is called the *Hamming distance* of the code, and measures the maximal number of entries in a code word that may change until another valid code word is created. Formally, the Hamming distance of two words $\mathbf{v}, \mathbf{w} \in F^n$ is $d_H(\mathbf{v}, \mathbf{w}) = |\{i | v_i \neq w_i\}|$ and $d := \min_{\mathbf{v}, \mathbf{w}} d_H(\mathbf{v}, \mathbf{w})$.

3. The *encoding* maps a given information word onto a code word by adding check symbols (e.g., parity bits). If the information word appears in the code word in plain, then we call the code *systematic*, otherwise it is *nonsystematic*.

4. The *decoding* maps the given (erroneous) word $\mathbf{w}'$ to the closest code word $\mathbf{w}$ in terms of the Hamming distance (i.e., the code word $\mathbf{w}$ that differs from $\mathbf{w}'$ in the smallest number of coordinates (*nearest-neighbor decoding*)). Intuitively, this implements the idea that more errors are less likely than few ones, so we decode into the information word that is most similar to the received one. For the aforementioned repetition code, this is exactly a majority decision. For more general codes, more sophisticated procedures are known; see [11]. If the distribution of errors is known, in the sense that some changes can be classified as more likely than others, an alternative is to look for the code word $\mathbf{w}$ that most likely changed into the given code word $\mathbf{w}'$. This is called *maximum likelihood decoding*.

Figure 2.2 illustrates the concepts of Hamming distance and nearest-neighbor decoding using a geometric representation of the repetition code with length $n = 3$ for a single information bit ($k = 1$). The Hamming distance for this code is $d = 3$, and the black circles represent the only (two) valid words in this code, as opposed to erroneous words given as white circles.

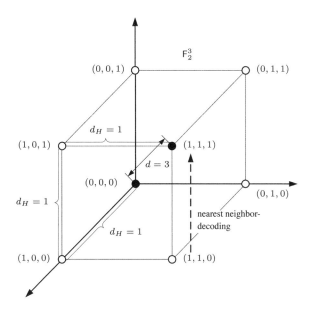

Figure 2.2 Graphical illustration of a $(3, 1, 3)$-repetition code over F_2.

In general, a linear (n, k, d)-block code is interpreted as a subset $C \subset \mathsf{F}^n$, so that code words are n symbols wide and encapsulate $k < n$ symbols of information. The redundancy is $n - k$ symbols and any two code words differ by at least d coordinates. This implies that there are two (specific) code words $\mathbf{v}, \mathbf{w}$ that differ in exactly d coordinates, and changing these d coordinates in $\mathbf{v}$ accordingly would lead to the valid code word $\mathbf{w}$. Furthermore, changing more than $d/2$ coordinates will render the erroneous code word $\tilde{\mathbf{v}}$ closer to the code word $\mathbf{w}$ than to the true origin $\mathbf{v}$. Hence nearest-neighbor decoding can detect up to $d - 1$ errors and will always produce a code word, but the result will be correct if and only if less than $(d - 1)/2$ symbols are erroneous (for otherwise, we mistakenly decode into the closer yet wrong code word). These observations can be summarized as follows:

Fact 2.6. Let an (n, k, d)-block code be given.

- Any number of up to $d - 1$ errors (changed symbols) can be detected.

- Any number of up to $\lfloor \frac{d-1}{2} \rfloor$ errors can be corrected using nearest-neighbor decoding.

Block codes can be constructed over any finite field, but common choices are the Reed-Solomon code based on $\mathbb{Z}_p$ for a prime p, or the BCD code, occasionally constructed over $\mathsf{F}_2 = \{0, 1\}$. Both of these codes can be designed to have a desired distance d and hence to provide the needed correction power. Both can correct any pattern of erroneous symbols, but since the Reed-Solomon code uses symbols from $\mathbb{Z}_p$, it is more suitable for burst-error correction of chunks of $\log_2 p$ bits (simply because a symbol being an element in $\mathbb{Z}_p = \{0, 1, 2, \ldots, p - 1\}$ has $\log_2 p$ bits). On the contrary, the BCD code (which is a generalization of the Reed-Solomon code) is able to correct single-bit errors of arbitrary scattering. It can be shown, however, that polynomial secret-sharing (see Section 2.5.6 and [12]) is equivalent to Reed-Solomon encoding [13]. It follows that we can do error correction in a secret-sharing scheme using techniques known from coding theory, such as the Welch-Berlekamp algorithm [14]. This may become handy in some applications, since error-correction algorithms (in software and hardware) are widely available.

2.4 COMPUTATIONAL COMPLEXITY

Assume that some *language* $L \subseteq \Sigma^* = \{0, 1\}^*$, merely being an infinite set of predefined strings, is given (note that the choice of $\Sigma = \{0, 1\}$ as the alphabet is arbitrary and without loss of generality). A general *decision problem* is to tell whether a given word $w \in \{0, 1\}^*$ belongs to L. Complexity theory is concerned with how much effort in terms of time and space it takes to decide $w \overset{?}{\in} L$. For that matter, let an algorithm $\mathsf{A} : \{0, 1\}^* \to \{0, 1\}$ be available that computes

$$\mathsf{A}(w) = \begin{cases} 1, & \text{if } w \in L; \\ 0, & \text{if } w \notin L. \end{cases}$$

that is, we say that the algorithm A *decides* the language L.

Definition 2.18 (Time and space complexity). Let a language $L \in \{0, 1\}^*$ and a word $w \in \{0, 1\}^*$ be given, and assume that an algorithm A decides L. If $n = |w|$, then let $T(n) = T(|w|)$ count the number of steps taken by A to decide $w \in L$. Likewise, let $S(n) = S(|w|)$ count the total storage required throughout the entire computation of $\mathsf{A}(w)$. We call $T(n)$ the *time complexity*, and $S(n)$ the *space complexity* of A.

We call an algorithm *efficient* if it's running time is *polynomial* in the length of the input word w, shorthanded as $T(n) = \mathrm{poly}(n)$, where $\mathrm{poly}(n)$ denotes a (not further specified) polynomial in n.

A more general class of problems are *search problems*, such as sorting, or *computational problems*, such as computing a discrete logarithm (see Definition 2.29), intractable examples of which play fundamental roles in cryptography. In general, problems of either class can be modeled as computing a function $f : \{0,1\}^* \to \{0,1\}^*$ using some algorithm A. The definition of time and space complexity remains unchanged.

For modeling reasons, it is often useful to give A an auxiliary input string $v \in \{0,1\}^*$ besides the input word $w \in \{0,1\}^*$. In this generalized version, the algorithm computes $f(w) = A(w, v)$, by virtue of the auxiliary string v. Depending on how v is used, we distinguish several classes of algorithms:

Definition 2.19. Let an algorithm A compute some function $f : \{0,1\}^* \to \{0,1\}^*$. Let the given input be w.

- If the auxiliary string v is *not needed at all*; that is, if $f(w) = A(w)$, then we call A *deterministic*.

- If for all w, there *exists* an auxiliary string v of length $|v| \leq \text{poly}(|w|)$ such that $f(w) = A(w, v)$, then we call A *nondeterministic*.

- We call A *probabilistic*, if its internal control flow makes use of random numbers (internal coin tosses), usually derived from the auxiliary input v, for example, by seeding a pseudorandom number generator with v, of length $|v| \leq \text{poly}(|w|)$.

Deterministic algorithms are the most widely found ones, as their output is determined only by the input values, and identical input values yield identical outputs. Examples are hash functions, or the textbook RSA encryption algorithm.

Nondeterministic algorithms are very convenient for modeling purposes, but cannot be implemented, since some unknown auxiliary string v has to be provided in advance to disambiguate the execution flow. Without v, there would be a point in the execution where several legitimate next steps would be possible, and the input w is by itself insufficient to make this choice. For modeling, we often let the nondeterministic algorithm "guess" certain information that we use for further (deterministic) computations. Practically, this auxiliary information v is often the *solution* to the computational problem $f(w)$ itself, and the remaining (deterministic) part of the algorithm is only concerned with *verifying* whether $A(w, v) \overset{?}{=} f(w)$ holds.

For example, the problem of factoring an integer n is nowadays intractable for large n, yet easily solvable by a nondeterministic algorithm as follows: let the algorithm (*nondeterministically*) guess a factorization $n = p \cdot q$, then (*deterministically*) compute $p \cdot q$, and check if the result is equal to n.

The crux of a probabilistic algorithm is to make it work correctly with high probability, for *any* uniformly random auxiliary string v. For this reason, probabilistic algorithms are hardly specified with an explicit auxiliary input, but mostly use an internal random number generator (i.e., make fair coin tosses) to reach their result. Hence the result and/or running time and/or storage requirements of the algorithm are determined by the internal random coins, and only the *expected (average) running time*, as well as the probability for a correct result are specified practically. The downside of knowing the expected running time only, however, is that such an algorithm may be very fast for some inputs but very slow for other inputs, since its runtime guarantees hold only on average. Such algorithms can be implemented with (strong cryptographic) pseudorandom number generators whenever random values are required internally.

Definition 2.20 (Classes P and NP). Let w denote a word.

- The class P is the set of all decision problems (languages) L for which the problem $w \overset{?}{=} L$ can be solved in $T(|w|) = \text{poly}(|w|)$ steps by a *deterministic* algorithm.

- The class NP is defined as P, except that the decision $w \overset{?}{=} L$ is made by a *nondeterministic* algorithm in $\text{poly}(|w|)$ steps.

An equivalent definition characterizes NP as the set of all decision problems, for which a given solution can be (deterministically) *verified* in polynomially many steps. Occasionally, this is the more useful definition.

When comparing problems in terms of their difficulty, *reductions* are a convenient tool. In short, a *reduction* from problem L_2 to problem L_1 is done by constructing an algorithm that solves L_2 and may call a solver (called *oracle*) for L_1 as a subroutine along the way, which takes only a single step in time. Having found such an algorithm, we can assert that problem L_2 cannot be harder than problem L_1, since knowing how to solve L_1 immediately tells us how to solve L_2 as well. We denote this either as $L_2 \leq_p L_1$ or $L_2 \leq_T L_1$, depending on how (often) we query the oracle for L_1 when working on L_2. Figure 2.3b illustrates the idea. Specifically, when proving that a cryptosystem is secure, one often provides a reduction to some problem which is assumed to be intractable. We come back to this in Section 2.5.1.

Of particular interest in complexity theory are the hardest problems in NP, in the sense of being at least as difficult than any other problem in NP:

Definition 2.21 (NP-hardness and NP-completeness). We call L_c NP-*hard*, if $L \leq_p L_c$ for all problems in NP. If L is NP-hard and $L \in NP$, then we call it NP-complete.

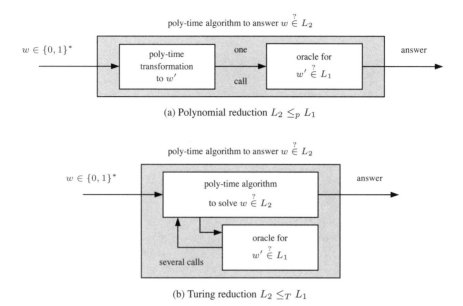

(a) Polynomial reduction $L_2 \leq_p L_1$

(b) Turing reduction $L_2 \leq_T L_1$

Figure 2.3 Two common types of reductions.

Famous examples of such problems are the NP-hard traveling salesperson problem or satisfiability of Boolean formulas, which is NP-complete. A comprehensive account with a vast number of examples is found in [15].

2.4.1 Computational Intractability

A fundamental prerequisite for public key cryptography and modern cryptography in general is one-way functions (i.e., functions that are easy to evaluate but hard to invert). More precisely, one requires that the probability of successfully inverting the function is a negligible function of a security parameter κ.

Definition 2.22 (Negligibility). We call a function $\nu(\kappa)$ *negligible* if for every constant $c > 0$, there is an integer $N_c > 0$ such that $\nu(\kappa) \leq \frac{1}{\kappa^c}$ for all $\kappa \geq N_c$.

Informally, Definition 2.22 states that a function is negligible, if it vanishes faster than the inverse of any polynomial. For example, the function $\nu(k) = 2^{-\kappa}$ is negligible. Throughout this book, we abbreviate a (not further specified) negligible function as $\mathrm{negl}(\kappa)$. Concerning a probability p, we call it *overwhelming* if $1 - p$ is negligible.

Definition 2.23 (One-way function). A mapping $f : \{0,1\}^* \to \{0,1\}^*$ is called a *one-way function* if the following properties hold:

- There exists a polynomial-time algorithm, which on input $x \in \{0,1\}^*$ outputs $f(x)$ in $\mathrm{poly}(|x|)$ steps.

- For every efficient algorithm, which is given only $y = f(x)$ for a randomly sampled $x \in \{0,1\}^\kappa$, the probability of determining z such that $f(z) = y$ is negligibly small in κ.

Intuitively, this means that the number of preimages is exponentially large in κ (there are 2^κ preimages to consider) and any algorithm that is limited to a polynomial number of probings will have negligibly small success probability. Hence, one-way functions are easy to compute, but in practice it will be intractable to find the preimage x for a given image $y = f(x)$, if the security parameter κ is sufficiently large. Another important class of functions are so-called trapdoor one-way functions. A *trapdoor one-way function* f is hard to invert as long as some additional information is unknown. More precisely, there exists an efficient algorithm A and an additional information t (the trapdoor), such that given an image $y = f(x)$, one can efficiently compute x as $x = \mathtt{A}(y, t)$. A prominent example for a trapdoor one-way function is the RSA encryption function [16].

Subsequently, we review problems that are considered to be intractable and which we will encounter throughout the book in various cryptographic constructions.

2.4.2 Factorization-Related Assumptions

The RSA cryptosystem [16] (see Section 4.2.1.1) proposed back in 1978 has been the first cryptosystem that is based on one of what we call today RSA (related) assumptions. Henceforth, we call a composite number $n = pq$, being the product of two distinct κ-bit primes p and q, an *RSA modulus*.

Definition 2.24 (Factoring problem). Given an RSA modulus n, the *factoring problem* is the task of finding two integers $p', q' > 1$ such that $n = p'q'$.

The *factoring assumption* states that for all efficient algorithms, the success probability for solving the factoring problem is negligible in the security parameter κ, where n is a 2κ-bit modulus.

Definition 2.25 (RSA problem). Let $n = pq$ be an RSA modulus, $e \geq 3$ an RSA public exponent and $c \in \mathbb{Z}_n^*$. The *RSA problem* is the task of finding an integer m satisfying $m^e \equiv c \pmod{n}$.

The *RSA assumption* states that for all efficient algorithms, the success probability for solving the RSA problem is negligible in the security parameter κ, where n is a 2κ-bit modulus. Loosely speaking, the RSA problem describes the task of inverting the RSA function (i.e., extracting eth roots modulo a composite integer). Another common and related problem is the so-called *strong RSA problem*, which is similar to the RSA problem, but does not fix the public exponent e (i.e., the algorithm trying to solve the strong RSA problem is allowed to choose $e \geq 3$ on its own). The intractability assumption based on the strong RSA problem is denoted as the *strong RSA assumption*.

It is obvious that the RSA problem cannot be harder than the factoring problem. Since knowledge of the prime factors p and q enables us to compute d such that $ed \equiv 1 \pmod{\varphi(n)}$ and thus provides the ability of inverting the RSA function. However, up to now it is unknown whether the reverse is true (i.e., whether a solver for the RSA problem helps to construct an efficient solver for the factoring problem).

Definition 2.26 (Quadratic residuosity problem). Given an RSA modulus n and a random element $x \in \mathbb{Z}_n^*$ such that $J(x, n) = 1$, decide whether $x \in QR_n$.

The *quadratic residuosity assumption* states that for all efficient algorithms, the success probability for solving the above problem differs from $1/2$ by a magnitude that is negligible in the security parameter κ.

Let $p = 2p' + 1$ and $q = 2q' + 1$ be two safe primes and $n = pq$ be an RSA modulus. Let g be a generator of the order $p'q'$ cyclic subgroup of quadratic residues QR_n of the group $\mathbb{Z}_n^*$. Then, the KEA-1 assumption [17] is defined as follows:

Definition 2.27 (KEA-1 assumption). For any algorithm A getting input (n, g, g^s) and returning elements (c, y) such that $y \equiv c^s \pmod{n}$, there exists another efficient algorithm A' that given the same input as A, outputs x such that $c \equiv g^x \pmod{n}$.

Finally, we briefly discuss a problem that is underlying the Paillier encryption scheme (see Section 4.2.1.3). Let n be an RSA modulus and we consider the group $\mathbb{Z}_{n^2}^* \simeq \mathbb{Z}_n \times \mathbb{Z}_n^*$ and instead of quadratic residues we are now interested in higher and in particular nth residues. We thereby say that a number $y \in \mathbb{Z}_{n^2}^*$ is an *nth residue*, if there exists an $x \in \mathbb{Z}_{n^2}^*$ with $y \equiv x^n \pmod{n^2}$. The corresponding problem can be seen as a generalization of the quadratic residuosity problem in $\mathbb{Z}_n^*$.

Definition 2.28 (Decisional composite residuosity problem). Given an RSA modulus n and a random element $x \in \mathbb{Z}_{n^2}^*$, decide whether x is an nth residue or not.

The *decisional composite residuosity assumption* states that for all efficient algorithms, the success probability for solving the above problem differs from $1/2$ by a magnitude that is negligible in the security parameter κ.

2.4.3 Discrete-Logarithm-Related Assumptions

Another famous class of intractability assumptions is concerned with problems related to discrete logarithms (DLs) in finite fields, which are for instance the basis of the Diffie-Hellman key exchange protocol [18] and its noninteractive application in the ElGamal encryption scheme [19] (see Section 4.2.1.2). Subsequently, we present a compact formulation of the most important discrete-logarithm-related problems based on a group G of prime order p and a random generator $g \in$ G.

Definition 2.29 (Discrete logarithm problem (DLP)). Given a cyclic group G, a generator g, and an element $h \in$ G, find an integer $a \in \mathbb{Z}_p$, such that $h = g^a$ holds.

Given the hardness of computing discrete logarithms, we provide the next definition, which is the basis for the famous Diffie-Hellman key agreement protocol.

Definition 2.30 (Computational Diffie-Hellman problem (CDHP)). Given G, a generator g, g^a, and g^b for $a, b \in \mathbb{Z}_p$, find an integer c, such that $g^c = g^{ab}$ holds.

It is obvious that the CDHP cannot be harder than the DLP, since an efficient solver for the DLP will yield a and b and g^{ab} can be efficiently computed.

Definition 2.31 (Decisional Diffie-Hellman problem (DDHP)). Given G, a generator g, elements g^a, g^b, and g^c for $a, b, c \in \mathbb{Z}_p$, decide whether $c \equiv ab \pmod{p}$ holds.

Given an efficient solver for the CDHP, we can compute g^{ab} and afterward check whether $g^{ab} = g^c$ holds. Consequently, the DDHP cannot be harder than the CDHP. The respective assumptions state that for all efficient algorithms the success probability for solving the respective problem is negligible in κ with $\kappa = \lceil \log p \rceil$. We can subsume that the DDH is a stronger assumption than CDH, which in turn is stronger than the assumption than the DLP is hard in suitable groups.

Equivalently, we can formulate the discrete logarithm problem for elliptic curve groups $E(\mathsf{F}_q)$.

Definition 2.32 (Elliptic curve discrete logarithm problem (ECDLP)). Let $E(\mathsf{F}_q)$ be an elliptic curve over a prime field F_q and $P \in E(\mathsf{F}_q) \setminus \{\mathcal{O}\}$ a point of large prime order r. Given Q and P, find an integer k such that $Q = kP$ holds.

Finally, we discuss discrete-logarithm-related problems in the context of pairings, where we state the problems in the context of symmetric pairings and then discuss how they can be transferred to the Type-2 and Type-3 setting [7]. Let G be a prime order p group and P be a generator of G. Note that when using pairing friendly elliptic curves together with a pairing $e : \mathsf{G} \times \mathsf{G} \to \mathsf{G}_T$, then G represents a so-called *gap Diffie-Hellman group*, which means that the CDHP in G is hard, while the DDHP in G is easy. The latter is due to the fact that the pairing e can be used as a DDH oracle; that is, given $aP, bP, cP \in \mathsf{G}$ one can check whether $e(aP, bP) = e(cP, P)$ and if this holds, we have $ab \equiv c \pmod{p}$, which allows efficiently solving the DDHP in G. Nevertheless, the following problem is assumed to be hard.

Definition 2.33 (Bilinear Diffie-Hellman problem (BDHP)). Let G, G_T be prime order groups, P a generator of G, and $e : \mathsf{G} \times \mathsf{G} \to \mathsf{G}_T$ a bilinear map. Given P, $P_1 = aP$, $P_2 = bP$, and $P_3 = cP$ for $a, b, c \in \mathbb{Z}_p^*$, compute $e(P, P)^{abc}$.

For the asymmetric setting $e : \mathsf{G}_1 \times \mathsf{G}_2 \to \mathsf{G}_T$, let P and P' be generators of G_1 and G_2, respectively. For Type-2 pairings, the problem instance for the so-called BDHP-2 is (aP, bP', cP') and for Type-3 pairings the problem instance for the so-called BDHP-3 is (aP, bP, cP, bP', cP'). We note that there are different variations of the input parameters of these problems, which can be shown to be equivalent and refer the interested reader to [7]. The respective decisional version (DBDHP) of (BDHP) is defined analogously to the BDHP.

2.4.4 Lattice Assumptions

Lattices allow formulations of various problems that are assumed to withstand even quantum computing power. Common examples are the *closest* or *shortest vector problems*; however, our main interest in the sequel lies on the following problem:

Let $n \geq 1$ and $q \geq 2$ be integers and χ be an "error" probability distribution on $\mathbb{Z}_q$. Let $F_{\mathbf{s}, \chi}$ on $\mathbb{Z}_q^n \times \mathbb{Z}_q$ be the probability distribution obtained by choosing a vector $\mathbf{a} \in \mathbb{Z}_q^n$ uniformly at random, choosing $e \in \mathbb{Z}_q$ according to χ, and outputting $(\mathbf{a}, \langle \mathbf{a}, \mathbf{s} \rangle + e)$, where additions are performed in $\mathbb{Z}_q$.

Definition 2.34 (Learning with errors (LWE) problem). The $\mathrm{LWE}_{q, \chi}$ problem is for any given vector $\mathbf{s} \in \mathbb{Z}_q^n$ and given access to an arbitrary number of independent samples from $F_{\mathbf{s}, \chi}$ to output $\mathbf{s} \in \mathbb{Z}_q^n$.

The $LWE_{q,\chi}$ assumption states that for all efficient algorithms, the success probability for solving the above problem is negligible. Essentially, the problem is to learn a secret vector s given a sequence of "approximate" random linear equations in s. This problem can also be viewed from a lattice perspective as a random distance bounded decoding problem in lattices, and its version for $q = 2$ is known as the learning parity with noise problem and the LWE has been introduced in the context of cryptography in [20]. There are various versions of this problem used in cryptography, and we refer the reader to [21] for a recent survey.

2.5 CRYPTOGRAPHIC PRIMITIVES AND SECURITY MODELS

In this section we briefly recap standard cryptographic primitives along with their respective security models. For a full-fledged formal treatment of this content, we refer the reader to [22] or [23].

2.5.1 Reductionist Security

Traditionally, cryptographic schemes were designed and their security analysis covered (convincing) arguments that these schemes were not vulnerable to attacks known at the time of design. Nowadays, security is commonly "proved" by describing a reduction by which a problem, for which strong evidence for intractability exists, could be solved, if the cryptosystem were insecure according to some well-defined model. More precisely, one assumes that there is an efficient algorithm A_{break} to break the cryptosystem at hand, and using this algorithm as an oracle describes another efficient algorithm A_{solve} that solves an otherwise intractable problem. Then, as long as the problem remains intractable, the reduction is tight (in the sense of efficiency), and the security model is reasonable, the cryptosystem is said to be *computationally secure* (or simply *secure*). Figure 2.4 displays the idea as a schematic (see Figure 2.3b).

An example is the Rabin cryptosystem [24], where encryption is squaring modulo an RSA modulus n and decryption amounts to computing square roots modulo n, which is efficiently possible, when knowing the factorization (the secret key). The security provided by Rabin encryption is equivalent to factoring large integers in the sense that:

1. If large integers could be factored, then Rabin encryption is insecure (trivial),

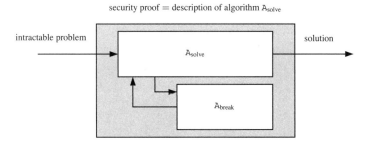

security proof = description of algorithm A_{solve}

Figure 2.4 Schematic of a security proof by reduction.

2. If one could decrypt a Rabin ciphertext without knowing the private decryption key, then this person (algorithm) could as well factor large integers (this is the reduction).

Hence, Factorization $\leq_T$ Rabin, and Rabin encryption is secure, since breaking it is at least as difficult as factoring an RSA modulus. We note that it is not known whether such a reduction exists for RSA, and it seems unlikely [25].

We, however, want to mention that provable security in the sense of reductionist security is a highly nontrivial and error-prone approach. Although it seems to be the only way to provide mathematical evidence that cryptosystems satisfy some meaningful security notions, some leading cryptographers urge that this approach needs to be handled with care [26].

2.5.2 Random Oracle Model and Standard Model

The *random oracle model* (ROM) was formalized by Bellare and Rogaway in [27] and the basic idea is to assume the existence of a publicly accessible ideal random function (an oracle O), which can be queried by all parties – good and bad alike. The oracle $O : \{0,1\}^* \rightarrow \{0,1\}^n$ is a blackbox (function) that provides truly random answers to queries, and identical queries result in identical answers. The idea behind the ROM is to find a formal definition of a problem including such random oracles, devise an efficient protocol π from this definition, prove that this protocol π satisfies the definition, and obtain a protocol π' by replacing the random oracles by a "heuristically secure" cryptographic hash function H. Although the last step is heuristic in nature, security proofs in the ROM are widely adopted, since they typically provide more efficient constructions than in the standard model. Security proofs of widely used cryptographic schemes as the RSA optimal asymmetric encryption padding (RSA-OAEP) [28] public key encryption scheme and the RSA probabilistic signature scheme (RSA-PSS) [29] are based on the ROM. But it is still a highly debated question whether proofs of security in the ROM are adequate (see [30]).

In the *standard model*, one bases security solely on complexity theoretic assumptions (e.g., factoring of integers, computing discrete logarithms, or the Diffie-Hellman problem family), which are widely believed to be intractable for properly chosen instances. Hence, it does not rely on the existence of idealized primitives such as truly random functions, as in the case of the random oracle model. Security in the standard model is generally considered stronger than under the ROM; however, the respective standard model schemes are in general much less efficient than those provably secure in the ROM.

2.5.3 Cryptographic Hash Functions

A hash function, generally denoted by H, maps strings of arbitrary length to hash values (digests) of fixed length. While many cryptosystems use very specific sets or even algebraic structures (some of which are described in more detail below), standardized hash functions such as the NIST recommendation SHA-2 or the recent alternative SHA-3 (Keccak [31]) map from $\{0,1\}^*$ to $\{0,1\}^\ell$, where typically $\ell \in \{224, 256, 384, 512\}$. Those are widely available in cryptographic programming libraries, and are essential building blocks for specialized hash functions such as the ones to follow. The following properties are of interest in the context of hash functions.

1. *Preimage resistance:* Given y, it must be computationally infeasible to find x such that $y = H(x)$. This property is also called one-wayness.

2. *Second preimage resistance / weak collision resistance:* Given y and x such that $y = H(x)$, it must be computationally infeasible to find $x' \neq x$ such that $y = H(x')$. In other words, when fixing one preimage, it is infeasible to find a second preimage that maps to the same value.

3. *(Strong) Collision resistance:* It must be computationally infeasible to find distinct x and x' such that $H(x) = H(x')$.

Hash functions that satisfy properties 1 and 2 are called *one-way hash functions* and those satisfying 1–3 are known as *collision-resistant hash functions*. We emphasize that collision-resistant hash functions are stronger than one-way hash functions, since the collision resistance is a weaker assumption than the second preimage resistance.

2.5.4 Hashing to Algebraic Structures

Subsequently, we briefly discuss some important constructions of hash functions, which are required in later parts of the book.

Hashing to $\mathbb{Z}_n^*$

Hash functions that map to $\mathbb{Z}_n^*$ for arbitrary n are typically denoted as *full-domain hash functions* (FDHs). In [27, 29] the authors provide some approaches for constructing such a FDH $H' : \{0,1\}^* \to \mathbb{Z}_n^*$ based on any cryptographic hash function H, where we briefly review the simplest construction. Therefore, take a hash function $H : \{0,1\}^* \to \{0,1\}^\ell$ such as SHA-3 and the value $H'(x)$ is taken as the appropriate-length prefix (e.g., the prefix of size 1024 bits if $n = 1024$) of the string

$$H(c\|\text{enc}(0)\|x)\|H(c\|\text{enc}(1)\|x)\| \ldots,$$

where $\text{enc}(i)$ is some suitable encoding of i and c is an arbitrary but fixed constant.

Hashing to QR_n

Consider a full-domain hash function $H : \{0,1\}^* \to \mathbb{Z}_n^*$ as for instance defined above. Then, a hash function $H' : \{0,1\}^* \to QR_n$ can be constructed as:

$$H'(x) = H(x)^2 \,\text{MOD}\, n.$$

The output of H' is by construction an element of QR_n.

Hashing into Order q Subgroups of $\mathbb{Z}_p^*$

Let G be a multiplicative subgroup of $\mathbb{Z}_p^*$ of prime order q that is generated by g. In order to map an arbitrary string x to G, one can construct a hash function $H' : \{0,1\}^* \to$ G, using a hash function H as above (i.e., interpret the hash value as an integer in $\mathbb{Z}_p$ or use a FDH that maps to $\mathbb{Z}_p$). Then, to ensure that the resulting hash value $H'(x)$ represents an element in G (note that G contains only elements of order q and the identity), one computes

$$H'(x) = H(x)^{(p-1)/q} \,\text{MOD}\, p,$$

which gives an element in G (see Section 2.2.3).

Hashing to Elliptic Curves

A naive way to construct a hash function $H' : \{0,1\}^* \to E(\mathsf{F}_q)$ mapping into an elliptic curve group $E(\mathsf{F}_q)$ of order N generated by some point P is to use a FDH $H : \{0,1\}^* \to \mathbb{Z}_N$, and then to compute the hash value for some string x as

$$H'(x) = H(x) \cdot P$$

resulting in another point in $E(\mathsf{F}_q)$. However, this simple construction is to be treated with caution, as it may make cryptographic protocols insecure due to the knowledge of the discrete logarithm between P and $H'(x)$. In particular, with this construction one needs to consider the knowledge of the discrete logarithm in a proof of security of a scheme using this construction, and, thus it *must* not be used if this knowledge is not explicitly allowed. Consequently, it is advisable *not* to use this construction in general and to use other approaches. We will present an alternative approach below. Therefore, let

$$E : y^2 = x^3 + ax + b$$

be an elliptic curve over the finite field F_q with a characteristic $q > 3$ and $E(\mathsf{F}_q)$ an elliptic curve group of some order N. Then we can hash into $E(\mathsf{F}_q)$ by following the subsequent approach (which is also denoted as the *try and increment method*):

1. For $i = 0$ to $k - 1$ do

    1.1. Set $x \leftarrow u + 1$.

    1.2. If $x^3 + ax + b$ is a quadratic residue in F_q (test with the Legendre symbol; see Section 2.1.5), then return $Q = (x, (x^3 + ax + b)^{1/2})$.

2. End For

3. Return $\perp$ (*failure*)

We note that this algorithm fails to return a point for a fraction of 2^{-k} of the inputs and the number of operations is not constant. For an overview of algorithms for computing square roots in finite (extension) fields, which are required in step 1.2; see for instance [32]. For a more detailed treatment and alternative more sophisticated constructions of hash algorithms, we refer the reader to [33].

Hashing for Pairings

Typically, efficient pairing-based protocols employ asymmetric (Type-2 or Type-3) pairings $e : G_1 \times G_2 \rightarrow G_T$ with $G_1 \neq G_2$. As already mentioned in Section 2.2.7, asymmetric parings and in particular Type-3 pairings are the recommended choice nowadays [7].

Hashing into G_1 can be performed as we have discussed it above in the context of elliptic curves, as we have G_1 being an order r subgroup of $E(F_q)$. However, hashing into G_2 is somewhat different, since G_2 is typically instantiated as an order r subgroup of a group of points with coordinates in some extension field on a twisted curve $E'(F_{q^d})$, where d divides the embedding degree k.

A standard strategy for hashing into G_2 is to choose a random point Q in $E'(F_{q^d})$ (like above by using a try and increment method) and multiplying Q with the cofactor $c = \left| E'(F_{q^d}) \right| / r$, which gives a point cQ in the order r subgroup of $E'(F_{q^d})$. However, the scalar c can be quite large and several improvements have been proposed recently [34, 35], which, however, are out of scope of this book. We furthermore refer the interested reader to [36] for limitations of hashing into groups required for different types of pairings.

2.5.5 Merkle Trees

Merkle trees [37] are a technique for hashing large data chunks that can be (made) tree-structured (e.g., XML-documents). The idea is to assign the data to the leaves of a binary tree from left to right, and do the hashing recursively upward, starting from the lowest level in the tree. The intuition is to have only $\mathcal{O}(\log n)$ hashing operations to update the overall hash, if one out of n parts of the document changes.

Definition 2.35 (Merkle tree). A *Merkle tree* is a complete binary tree, together with a cryptographic hash function $H : \{0,1\}^* \rightarrow \{0,1\}^\ell$ and an assignment $\phi : N \rightarrow \{0,1\}^\ell$, where N is the set of nodes of the tree. The assignment ϕ for the label of the nodes is recursively defined by expression (2.5), where v_P is the parent node and v_L and v_R the left and right child, respectively. Furthermore, x is a string that is assigned to a leaf.

$$\phi(v_P) := \begin{cases} H(\phi(v_L)||\phi(v_R)) & \text{if } v_P \text{ has two children;} \\ H(\phi(v_L)) & \text{if } v_P \text{ has one child;} \\ H(x) & \text{if } v_P \text{ is a leaf.} \end{cases} \tag{2.5}$$

Additionally, we define the *authentication path* $A_v = \{a_i | 0 < i \le h\}$ of a leaf v as the set containing all values a_i. The value a_i at height i is defined to be the label of the sibling of the node of height i at the unique path from v to the root.

A toy example of a Merkle tree is shown in Figure 2.5. The root hash v_R is computed by first hashing the leaves, and then working our way upward by hashing the concatenation of child nodes for each inner node, level by level. This requires $\mathcal{O}(n)$ hash operations for a total of n data blocks (leaves). Observe that block d_3 can be authenticated by recomputing the authentically known root hash. This only requires $\mathcal{O}(\log n)$ hash operations and knowledge of the hashes of all siblings along the nodes on the (dashed) path from d_3 up to the root. This path is called d_3's authentication path. It is represented by the hashes of the aforementioned sibling nodes, which are $\{v_{11}, v_0\}$ for d_3. It is easy to see that these suffice to recompute the root hash without having to re-create the entire tree.

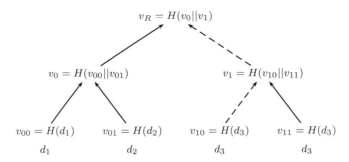

Figure 2.5 A Merkle tree for values d_1, d_2, d_3, and d_4.

Put differently, a Merkle tree can be used to release a part of some data along with the corresponding authentication path, and everybody is able to verify if this part belongs to the entire data but does not learn the remaining data. However, this does not ensure a real hiding of the remaining data, and we refer to Section 3.3.2 for a discussion in the context of redactable signatures.

2.5.6 Secret-Sharing

Shamir's polynomial secret-sharing [12] allows us to securely distribute a secret $v \in \mathsf{F}_q$ among n parties, addressed as $1, 2, \ldots, n$, such that whenever at least k shares are given, reconstruction of v is possible. Figure 2.6 illustrates an abstract description of such a threshold secret-sharing scheme. In the concrete setting of

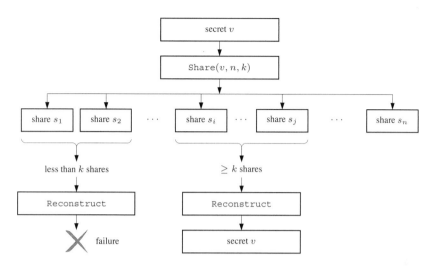

Figure 2.6 Schematic of k-out-of-n secret-sharing.

Shamir's scheme, let v be the constant term of an otherwise randomly chosen $k-1$ degree polynomial

$$p(x) = v + a_1 x + \ldots + a_{k-1} x^{k-1}$$

over some finite field F_q. The Share algorithm computes a share s_i as $s_i = p(i)$ for party i, $1 \leq i \leq n$. However, the indices may be chosen arbitrarily. Given any set S of cardinality at least k, let us denote the set of indices corresponding to shares in S by I_S. Then, one can use Lagrange interpolation as Reconstruct algorithm to compute s as

$$v = \sum_{j \in I_S} \lambda_j p(j),$$

where

$$\lambda_j = \prod_{i \in I_S \setminus \{j\}} j(j-i)^{-1},$$

and all computations happen in $(\mathsf{F}_q, +, \cdot)$. The confidentiality guarantees of this threshold scheme are information-theoretic; that is, any $k-1$ shares do not provide any information about v (indicated as "failure" in the figure), independently of the attacker's computational power.

We stress that the parameters k and n cannot be chosen independently of each other. In its plain form, secret-sharing is vulnerable to cheating and active manipulation of shares [38]. A number of at most $\lfloor (n - k)/2 \rfloor$ corrupted shares can, however, be recovered using the Welch-Berlekamp algorithm (see [13, 14]). Nevertheless, a symmetry argument reveals the scheme remains secure only against a collusion of at most $t < \min \{n/2, k\}$ attackers.

2.5.7 Public Key Cryptography

While symmetric key encryption requires two parties to safely exchange a common secret in advance, public key (asymmetric) encryption solves this problem elegantly by using different keys for the encryption and decryption. For symmetric encryption, authentication is thus implicit, since besides the receiver, there is only one other entity knowing the secret key, hence the origin is clear. However, this implies that no third party can be convinced about the message's origin, since from the third party's perspective two origins are possible (as the key is shared between two parties). For public key encryption, anyone knowing the public key can encrypt, so message authentication requires explicit action via digital signatures. Contrary to symmetric encryption, the signature can only come from the (one and only) entity that knows the signature key. Hence, a digital signature *does* provide a proof of origin to a third party. When using public key cryptography in practice one requires a public key infrastructure (PKI) – i.e., some means to guarantee that the public keys of all parties are available in an authentic fashion (i.e., bound to their identities) to all participants. Thereby, PKIs based on X.509 certificates (PKIX) [39] are the most prevalent model in practice today. A known alternative to public key cryptography today is identity-based cryptography; see [40] for an introductory book. However, in practice it is questionable whether it represents a better alternative [41], with the additional drawback for the requirement of a trusted secret key generation authority that knows the secret keys of all parties (distributed generation of secret keys is a possibility to mitigate this problem, which, however, in practice does not seem to be efficiently manageable).

2.5.8 Public Key Encryption

A public key encryption (PKE) scheme is composed from three algorithms, whose interplay is depicted in Figure 2.7. Notice that KeyGen and Encrypt can be deterministic or probabilistic, but Decrypt is normally deterministic. The security parameter κ passed to KeyGen usually controls the size of the keys.

Security of public key encryption is generally defined against passive attackers (trying to extract useful information off-line from a given ciphertext) or active

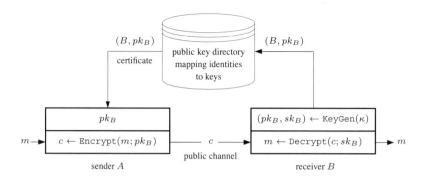

Figure 2.7 Schematic of (probabilistic) public key encryption.

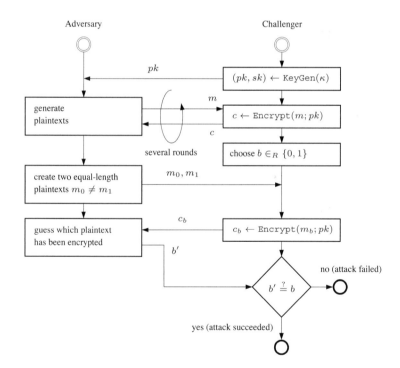

Figure 2.8 Chosen plaintext attack.

adversaries. An active attacker may interact with an honest owner of the private decryption key (called *challenger*) in an attempt to gain information about the plaintext or the keys. Depending on the way in which this interaction happens, we distinguish several levels of security, listed below in sequence of increasing strength. In all these cases, the attacker's goal is to get "the least" information from a ciphertext; that is, his or her sole modest goal is to *distinguish* two encrypted plaintexts that he or she can even provide themselves. Having no a priori information, an uninformed guess whether m_0 or m_1 has been encrypted into the given ciphertext c would succeed with chance $1/2$. It is easy to imagine (though nontrivial to prove) that no detailed information about an unknown message can be obtained, if not even a priori known messages can be told apart based on the ciphertext only.

IND-CPA security: An attacker interacts as shown in Figure 2.8, and has a chance of winning that is only negligibly better than $1/2$; that is,

$$\mathbf{Adv} := \left| \Pr[\text{attack succeeded}] - \frac{1}{2} \right| \leq \text{negl}(\kappa),$$

when κ is the security parameter, and $\mathbf{Adv}$ is called the attacker's *advantage*.

IND-CCA1 security: An attacker interacts as shown in Figure 2.9, except that the attacker does not have access to the Decrypt oracle in the second challenge-response cycles (after receiving the challenge c_b). The attacker's advantage $\mathbf{Adv}$ is defined as for IND-CPA, and is negligible.

IND-CCA2 security: An attacker interacts as shown in Figure 2.9, with negligible advantage $\mathbf{Adv}$ (as for IND-CPA).

Remark 2.4. Only *probabilistic* encryption algorithms can ever be IND-CPA secure or stronger, although not necessarily so; for example, standard ElGamal encryptions hide the plaintext m, but testing whether m is a quadratic residue is nevertheless possible using the ciphertext only, so some information does leak out. Deterministic encryption can never be IND-CPA secure (nor stronger).

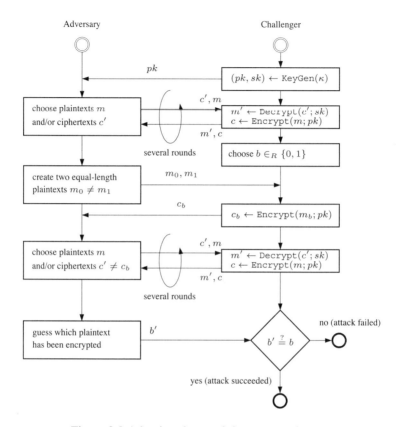

Figure 2.9 Adaptive chosen ciphertext attack.

2.5.9 Digital Signature Schemes

Digital signatures provide (message) authentication in the public key setting via the assurance that whoever created a signature for a given message m that verifies under a public key pk must have done this using the corresponding secret key sk and for message m. A digital signature scheme is composed from three (probabilistic) algorithms (KeyGen, Sign, Verify), whose interplay is depicted in Figure 2.10. In practice, the Sign and Verify algorithms will use a hash value $H(m)$ instead of m to operate on constant size strings, which is also known as the *hash-then-sign* paradigm.

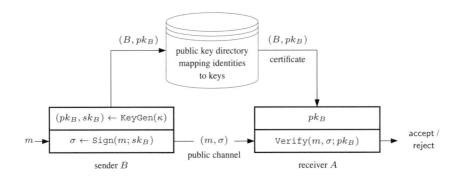

Figure 2.10 Schematic of digital signatures.

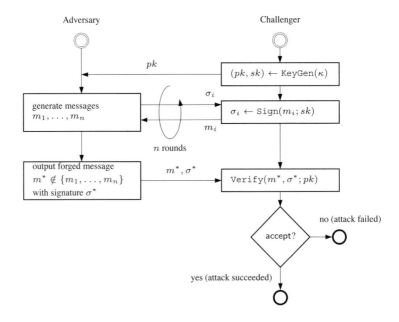

Figure 2.11 Existential forgery attack with chosen messages.

Security is defined in only a negligible chance of forging a signature under the attack scenario as shown in Figure 2.11. Here, we demand that

$$\mathbf{Adv} := \Pr[\text{forged signature is accepted}] \leq \text{negl}(\kappa),$$

when κ is the security parameter that goes into `KeyGen` during initialization of the system. For a *universal forgery*, the attacker is free to choose a meaningful message m^* (subject to not having obtained a valid signature for it beforehand), whereas for *existential forgery*, the attacker wins if he or she outputs any (not necessarily meaningful) message whose signature verifies under pk. Figure 2.11 refers to existential forgery.

2.5.10 Commitment Schemes

A commitment scheme [42, 43] is an interactive protocol between a sender (prover) and a receiver (verifier) that runs in two phases. In the first phase, the sender is committed to ("deposits") a secret s from some finite set S by computing a commitment c and sending it to the receiver. Security for the sender requires the receiver to remain unable to figure out the value s hidden in the commitment c (*hiding*) unless the sender explicitly allows to open the commitment. If so, then the sender transmits an open information o, which reveals s to the receiver. The *binding* assures security for the receiver by preventing the sender from submitting a chosen open information that makes the receiver disclose some other value than the initial choice s. Thus, a commitment scheme is a pair (`Commit`, `Open`) of polynomial-time algorithms, whose interplay is depicted in Figure 2.12.

Hereby, the `Open` algorithm outputs either $s \in S$ or $\perp$ to indicate success or failure, and we stress that `Commit` may be probabilistic. The commitment is called *correct*, if for any $s \in S$, we have $\text{Open}(\text{Commit}(s)) = s$. Besides, the correctness of a commitment scheme (i.e., every honestly generated commitment (c, o) to a value s will return s when using o), it needs to satisfy the *hiding* and *binding* property already discussed above. These properties come in two flavors, namely unconditional or computational, but both cannot be unconditional at the same time. Unconditional binding commitments can be obtained from injective one-way functions and prominent examples for unconditional hiding commitments are Pedersen commitments [44] for groups of known order and Fujisaki-Okamoto commitments [45] for groups whose order is unknown (*hidden order groups*). In order to support larger messages as input to the `Commit` algorithm, it is common to use the so-called *hash-then-commit* approach.

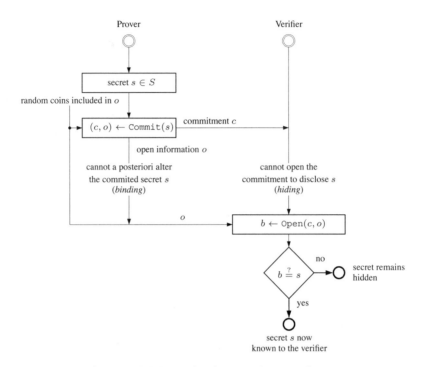

Figure 2.12 Schematic of a commitment scheme.

2.5.11   Zero-Knowledge Proofs

Zero-knowledge proofs are interactive protocols between two parties, a *prover* and a *verifier*. The prover seeks to convince the verifier that either

- The prover knows a secret; or
- Some claim holds because of reasons that only the prover knows.

The proof is usually done by the verifier challenging the prover to solve some problem based on a commitment to some secret information (the *witness*) that the prover provides in the first step. Based on this, the verifier submits a *challenge*, to which a correct *response* is expected (three-pass protocol; see Figure 2.13 for an illustration). The most important features of such an interactive (zero-knowledge) proof are the following:

- The prover can cheat, if he or she correctly guesses the challenge in advance. For most proof protocols, the challenge space C is rather small; for example, the challenge is a single bit, so there is a chance of cheating of approximately $\Pr[\text{mistakenly accept}] = \alpha \approx \frac{1}{|C|} \leq \frac{1}{2}$. Consequently, the protocol has to be *repeated* for n rounds to lower the cheating probability down to $\leq 2^{-\mathcal{O}(n)}$.

- The proof must be *complete* and *sound*, which means:

  Completeness: If the prover knows the secret, then the verifier will accept the proof with overwhelming probability; that is, the chance of rejecting it is negligible in the security parameter κ that went into the initialization algorithm of the proof protocol, similar to KeyGen for a public key encryption or signature scheme.

  Soundness: If the prover does not know the secret, then there is only a negligible chance of the verifier to accept.

- For the interactive proof to be *zero-knowledge* [46], there must be a way to efficiently simulate it in the sense of a poly-time algorithm being able to output a sequence of triples $(w_1, c_1, r_1), \ldots, (w_n, c_n, r_n)$ that make up a transcript that cannot be distinguished from a real transcript by any poly-time probabilistic algorithm. This has two important effects:

  1. If a "real-looking" transcript can be simulated by a machine that does not possess the secret, then the transcript cannot contain and hence does not leak any information about the secret (it is said to be "zero-knowledge").

  2. Showing a real transcript to a third party, however, cannot be used to convince anyone that the protocol actually happened, since the third party can reject the transcript on doubts of it coming from the simulator.

- Since the proof requires several rounds, in all of which a correct response must be computed, this kind of protocol can be time-consuming. However, it is *not* advisable to run the rounds in parallel, since the security guarantees may deteriorate. The number of rounds can also be reduced by increasing the challenge space. However, the zero-knowledge property as defined gets lost if the challenge space becomes exponentially large, as this precludes efficient poly-time simulations.

In the case of increasing the challenge space, the zero-knowledge property boils down to the weaker notion of *honest verifier zero-knowledge proofs* (HVZKP), since in the absence of the simulator we must trust the verifier to refrain from extracting information from the transcript beyond the certificate of knowledge that the proof provides. This class is known as Σ-protocols [47] and Example 2.1 presents an HVZKP of a discrete logarithm taking the challenge space to be $\mathbb{Z}_p$.

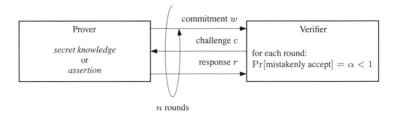

Figure 2.13 Schematic of a zero-knowledge proof.

Example 2.1. Let G be a group of prime order p generated by an element g. The prover P wants to convince the verifier V that it knows x representing the discrete logarithm of $y = g^x$.

- P chooses $k \in_R \mathbb{Z}_p$, computes $r = g^k$, and sends r to V.
- V chooses $c \in_R \mathbb{Z}_p$ and sends it to P.
- P computes $s = k + cx \operatorname{MOD} p$ and sends s to V.
- V checks accepts if $g^s = ry^c$ holds and rejects otherwise.

In the context of anonymity, it is interesting to prove knowledge of one out of n secrets (e.g., if we seek to prove membership to a group without exhibiting who we actually are). Such proofs are known as Σ-OR proofs, and loosely speaking, work as follows:

1. Create a (real) proof for the secret in possession.

2. Use the simulator to create "fake proofs" for all other (unknown) secrets.

3. The verifier will accept all proofs, but since the simulated transcripts cannot be distinguished from the real one, he or she cannot tell which secret is actually known to the prover.

Table 2.2 gives an overview of different assertions that can be proved in zero-knowledge, with many more found in the literature (see for instance [48] for an overview of basic proofs). Any HVZKP can be made *noninteractive* by applying the Fiat-Shamir heuristic [54]:

1. Generate a witness (commitment) w.

2. Extract the challenges from the hash $H(w)$ and compute the correct response for the challenge.

Table 2.2

Examples of (Interactive) Zero-Knowledge Proofs

Proof	Reference
Knowledge of a DL x (i.e., the content of a DL-commitment g^x)	Example 2.1, [49]
Knowledge of a DL representation $x_1, \ldots, x_n$ based on $\prod_{i=1}^{n} g_i^{x_i}$	Example 2.1, [49]
Proof that a number is the product of two safe primes	[48]
And/or composition of single proofs	[50]
Proving that an unknown integer x lies within a specific interval (i.e., $a \leq x \leq b$)	[51, 52]
Solution to any NP-complete problem (i.e., graph coloring)	[53]

Provided that the hash function is one-way, this construction may convince the verifier that the prover could not know the challenges in advance, since they were obtained from a hash value whose result could neither be predicted nor preconstructed.

In [55], Groth and Sahai proposed a noninteractive zero-knowledge proof system based on pairings. Proofs based on this system can be seen as the second large class of proof systems besides Σ protocols discussed above, which are used in many recent cryptographic protocols and applications. In contrast to Σ protocols, these proof systems, however, are *malleable*. Thereby, a proof system is called malleable if it allows a prover to derive proofs of statements not just from witnesses for their truth, but also from proofs of related statements. We do not require such proof systems in the following and refer the interested reader to study [56, 57].

References

[1] A. Menezes, P. C. van Oorschot, and S. A. Vanstone, *Handbook of Applied Cryptography*. CRC Press, 1996.

[2] "Cryptographic Key Length Recommendation." http://www.keylength.com, 2013.

[3] A. Menezes, T. Okamoto, and S. A. Vanstone, "Reducing Elliptic Curve Logarithms to Logarithms in a Finite Field," *IEEE Transactions on Information Theory*, vol. 39, no. 5, pp. 1639–1646, 1993.

[4] D. Hankerson, A. J. Menezes, and S. Vanstone, *Guide to Elliptic Curve Cryptography*. Springer, 2003.

[5] J. Silverman, *The Arithmetic of Elliptic Curves*, vol. 106 of *Graduate Texts in Mathematics*. Springer, 1986.

[6] P. Gallagher and C. Furlani, "FIPS PUB 186-3 Federal Information Processing Standards Publication Digital Signature Standard (DSS)," 2009.

[7] S. Chatterjee and A. Menezes, "On Cryptographic Protocols Employing Asymmetric Pairings – The Role of ψ Revisited," *Discrete Applied Mathematics*, vol. 159, no. 13, pp. 1311–1322, 2011.

[8] D. Freeman, M. Scott, and E. Teske, "A Taxonomy of Pairing-Friendly Elliptic Curves," *J. Cryptology*, vol. 23, no. 2, pp. 224–280, 2010.

[9] I. F. Blake, G. Seroussi, and N. P. Smart, eds., *Advances in Elliptic Curve Cryptography*. London Mathematical Society Lecture Note Series, Cambridge University Press, 2005.

[10] W. H. Press, S. A. Teukolsky, W. T. Vetterling, and B. P. Flannery, *Numerical Recipes in C*. Cambridge University Press, second ed., 1992.

[11] W. Huffman and V. Pless, *Fundamentals of Error-Correcting Codes*. Cambridge University Press, 2003.

[12] A. Shamir, "How to Share a Secret," *Communications of the ACM*, vol. 22, no. 11, pp. 612–613, 1979.

[13] R. McElice and D. Sarwate, "On Sharing Secrets and Reed-Solomon Codes," *Communications of the ACM*, vol. 24, no. 9, pp. 583–584, 1981.

[14] E. Berlekamp and L. Welch, "Error Correction of Algebraic Block Codes, US Patent No. 4,633,470," Dec. 30, 1986.

[15] M. R. Garey and D. S. Johnson, *Computers and Intractability*. Freeman, 1979.

[16] R. Rivest, A. Shamir, and L. Adleman, "A Method for Obtaining Digital Signatures and Public-Key Cryptosystems," *Communications of the ACM*, vol. 21, no. 2, pp. 120–126, 1978.

[17] G. Ateniese, R. Burns, R. Curtmola, J. Herring, O. Khan, L. Kissner, Z. Peterson, and D. Song, "Remote Data Checking Using Provable Data Possession," *ACM Trans. Inf. Syst. Secur.*, vol. 14, pp. 12:1–12:34, June 2011.

[18] W. Diffie and M. E. Hellman, "New Directions in Cryptography," *IEEE Transactions on Information Theory*, vol. IT-22, no. 6, pp. 644–654, 1976.

[19] ElGamal, Taher, "A Public-Key Cryptosystem and a Signature Scheme Based on Discrete Logarithms," in *CRYPTO*, vol. 196 of *LNCS*, pp. 10–18, Springer, 1984.

[20] O. Regev, "On Lattices, Learning with Errors, Random Linear Codes, and Cryptography," in *STOC*, pp. 84–93, ACM, 2005.

[21] O. Regev, "The Learning with Errors Problem (Invited Survey)," in *IEEE Computational Complexity*, pp. 191–204, IEEE, 2010.

[22] J. Katz and Y. Lindell, *Introduction to Modern Cryptography*. Chapman and Hall/CRC Press, 2007.

[23] W. Mao, *Modern Cryptography: Theory and Practice*. Prentice Hall Professional Technical Reference, 2003.

[24] M. O. Rabin, "Digitalized Signatures and Public-Key Functions as Intractable as Factorization," Tech. Rep. MIT/LCS/TR-212, MIT, 1979.

[25] D. Boneh and R. Venkatesan, "Breaking RSA May Not Be Equivalent to Factoring," in *EUROCRYPT*, vol. 1403 of *LNCS*, pp. 59–71, Springer, 1998.

[26] N. Koblitz and A. Menezes, "Another Look at Provable Security." http://anotherlook.ca/, 2013.

[27] M. Bellare and P. Rogaway, "Random Oracles Are Practical: A Paradigm for Designing Efficient Protocols," in *CCS*, pp. 62–73, ACM, 1993.

[28] M. Bellare and P. Rogaway, "Optimal Asymmetric Encryption," in *EUROCRYPT*, vol. 950 of *LNCS*, pp. 92–111, Springer, 1994.

[29] M. Bellare and P. Rogaway, "The Exact Security of Digital Signatures - How to Sign with RSA and Rabin," in *EUROCRYPT*, vol. 1070 of *LNCS*, pp. 399–416, Springer, 1996.

[30] G. Leurent and P. Q. Nguyen, "How Risky Is the Random-Oracle Model?," in *CRYPTO*, vol. 5677 of *LNCS*, pp. 445–464, Springer, 2009.

[31] G. Bertoni, J. Daemen, M. Peeters, and G. Van Assche, "Keccak." http://keccak.noekeon.org/, 2013.

[32] G. Adj and F. Rodríguez-Henríquez, "Square Root Computation over Even Extension Fields," *IACR Cryptology ePrint Archive*, vol. 2012, p. 685, 2012.

[33] T. Icart, "How to Hash into Elliptic Curves," in *CRYPTO*, LNCS, pp. 303–316, Springer, 2009.

[34] M. Scott, N. Benger, M. Charlemagne, L. J. D. Perez, and E. J. Kachisa, "Fast Hashing to G_2 on Pairing-Friendly Curves," in *Pairing*, vol. 5671 of *LNCS*, pp. 102–113, Springer, 2009.

[35] L. Fuentes-Castañeda, E. Knapp, and F. Rodríguez-Henríquez, "Faster Hashing to $\mathbb{G}_2$," in *SAC*, vol. 7118 of *LNCS*, pp. 412–430, Springer, 2011.

[36] S. D. Galbraith, K. G. Paterson, and N. P. Smart, "Pairings for Cryptographers," *Discrete Applied Mathematics*, vol. 156, no. 16, pp. 3113–3121, 2008.

[37] R. C. Merkle, "A Certified Digital Signature," in *CRYPTO*, vol. 435 of *LNCS*, pp. 218–238, Springer, 1989.

[38] M. Tompa and H. Woll, "How to Share a Secret with Cheaters," *Journal of Cryptology*, vol. 1, no. 2, pp. 133–138, 1988.

[39] D. Cooper, S. Santesson, S. Farrell, S. Boeyen, R. Housley, and W. Polk, "RFC 5280 – Internet X.509 Public Key Infrastructure Certificate and Certificate Revocation List (CRL) Profile." http://tools.ietf.org/html/rfc5280, May 2008.

[40]   L. Martin, *Introduction to Identity-Based Encryption*. Artech House, 2008.

[41]   Y. Desmedt and M. Burmester, "Identity-Based Key Infrastructures (IKI)," in *SEC*, pp. 167–176, Kluwer, 2004.

[42]   M. Blum, "Coin Flipping by Telephone," in *CRYPTO*, pp. 11–15, ECE Report No 82-04, 1981.

[43]   G. Brassard, D. Chaum, and C. Crépeau, "Minimum Disclosure Proofs of Knowledge," *J. Comput. Syst. Sci.*, vol. 37, no. 2, pp. 156–189, 1988.

[44]   T. P. Pedersen, "Non-Interactive and Information-Theoretic Secure Verifiable Secret Sharing," in *CRYPTO*, vol. 576 of *LNCS*, pp. 129–140, Springer, 1992.

[45]   E. Fujisaki and T. Okamoto, "Statistical Zero Knowledge Protocols to Prove Modular Polynomial Relations," in *CRYPTO*, vol. 1294 of *LNCS*, pp. 16–30, Springer, 1997.

[46]   S. Goldwasser, S. Micali, and C. Rackoff, "The Knowledge Complexity of Interactive Proof-Systems," in *STOC*, pp. 291–304, ACM, 1985.

[47]   R. Cramer, *Modular Design of Secure Yet Practical Cryptographic Protocols*. PhD thesis, CWI and University of Amsterdam, 1996.

[48]   J. Camenisch and M. Michels, "Proving in Zero-Knowledge that a Number is the Product of Two Safe Primes," in *EUROCRYPT*, vol. 1592 of *LNCS*, pp. 107–122, Springer, 1999.

[49]   C. P. Schnorr, "Efficient Identification and Signatures for Smart Cards," in *CRYPTO*, vol. 435 of *LNCS*, pp. 239–252, Springer, 1989.

[50]   R. Cramer, I. Damgård, and B. Schoenmakers, "Proofs of Partial Knowledge and Simplified Design of Witness Hiding Protocols," in *CRYPTO*, vol. 839 of *LNCS*, pp. 174–187, Springer, 1994.

[51]   F. Boudot, "Efficient Proofs That a Committed Number Lies in an Interval," in *EUROCRYPT*, vol. 1807 of *LNCS*, pp. 431–444, Springer, 2000.

[52]   J. Camenisch, R. Chaabouni, and A. Shelat, "Efficient Protocols for Set Membership and Range Proofs," in *ASIACRYPT*, vol. 5350 of *LNCS*, pp. 234–252, Springer, 2008.

[53]   O. Goldreich, S. Micali, and A. Wigderson, "How to Prove All NP-Statements in Zero-Knowledge, and a Methodology of Cryptographic Protocol Design," in *CRYPTO*, vol. 263 of *LNCS*, pp. 171–185, Springer, 1986.

[54]   A. Fiat and A. Shamir, "How to Prove Yourself: Practical Solutions to Identification and Signature Problems," in *CRYPTO*, vol. 263 of *LNCS*, pp. 186–194, Springer-Verlag, 1987.

[55]   J. Groth and A. Sahai, "Efficient Non-interactive Proof Systems for Bilinear Groups," in *EURO-CRYPT*, vol. 4965 of *LNCS*, pp. 415–432, Springer, 2008.

[56]   M. Belenkiy, J. Camenisch, M. Chase, M. Kohlweiss, A. Lysyanskaya, and H. Shacham, "Randomizable Proofs and Delegatable Anonymous Credentials," in *CRYPTO*, vol. 5677 of *LNCS*, pp. 108–125, Springer, 2009.

[57]   M. Chase, M. Kohlweiss, A. Lysyanskaya, and S. Meiklejohn, "Malleable Proof Systems and Applications," in *EUROCRYPT*, vol. 7237 of *LNCS*, pp. 281–300, Springer, 2012.

Chapter 3

Protection of Identifying Information

3.1 PRIVACY PRESERVING AUTHENTICATION

Contents in Brief

What is this? Methods to authenticate users and data.

What can it do? Prove authenticity or access rights without revealing the prover's identity.

How can it be used in cloud computing? Users can anonymously access cloud resources, with the cloud provider learning nothing but the fact that a *legitimate* user requested a service.

Privacy preserving or *anonymous authentication* apparently seems to be an oxymoron. This is due to the fact that authentication means proving one's identity to another party, whereas anonymity is concerned with hiding one's identity. However, anonymous authentication realizes these contradictory goals by requiring users to solely prove membership in a group of users, such that the exact identity of the authenticating user cannot be determined by the verifying party.

In the sequel, by U, we denote the set of authorized users seeking to authenticate themselves to a verifier (usually a service provider) V. This one in turn should accept the authentication of any legitimate user $u_i \in U$ (prover), and even a dishonest V should not be able to tell which particular user has actually conducted the proof.

This is the basic setting of anonymous authentication, which more precisely culminates in the following requirements:

Anonymity: A verifier, no matter whether cheating or not, should have no means to identify an authenticating prover (*full anonymity*). This may be relaxed; that is, the probability of identification may be slightly higher (*probabilistic anonymity*, see Section 3.1.2.2), in order to obtain more efficient protocols. Furthermore, the prover ideally should be able to choose the degree of anonymity (size of the anonymity set U') on his or her own and adaptively (i.e., for every single authentication independently from prior authentications, which we call *adaptive anonymity*).

Correctness: An honest prover (i.e., a member of the authorized set) should always pass an authentication in an anonymous fashion.

Unforgeability: Any party that does not belong to the set of authorized users must not be able to run an anonymous authentication protocol with the verifier such that the verifier accepts. This includes arbitrary sets of cooperating revoked users (one of the first approaches is a negiative example [1]).

Unlinkability: Verifiers must not be able to relate anonymous authentication protocol executions to one another (i.e., to tell if they were conducted by the same – yet unknown – prover).

Traceability: It may be necessary that a trusted third party should be able to revoke the anonymity of users in question, given the protocol transcript of the anonymous authentication.

No misattribution: Anonymous authentication protocols should provide mechanisms such that provers can plausibly report cheating verifiers but at the same time are unable to accuse honest verifiers of cheating.

Membership withdrawal: Anonymous authentication protocols should provide efficient mechanisms to exclude users from the set of authorized users.

As authentication usually rests on secrets like passwords; it is common to measure their quality by the difficulty to guess the authentication secret. This difficulty is measured in terms of *entropy*, which is a statistical measure of uncertainty. Given that elements are selected at random from a set $X = \{x_1, \ldots, x_n\}$ with likelihoods $p_1, \ldots, p_n$, the *entropy* (i.e., uncertainty about what element is chosen) is computed as

$$h := -\sum_{i=1}^{n} p_i \log p_i,$$

with the convention that $0 \cdot \log 0 := 0$. Its unit is usually bits if the logarithm is base-2. Roughly speaking, an entropy of h bits means an average need to correctly guess h bits to discover the (full) secret. Alternatively, if a secret of n bits has $h < n$ bits of entropy, then the remaining $n - h$ bits can (uniquely) be derived from h known bits.

In the following, we discuss various mechanisms for anonymous authentication, which can generally be separated into two classes. The first class covers anonymous authentication protocols, which require users only to remember (store) a quite short (potentially) low entropy secret, such as a human memorable password. These techniques, discussed in Section 3.1.1, are called *anonymous password authentication protocols* or more generally as anonymous password-based authenticated key exchange (APAKE) protocols. The second class covers anonymous authentication protocols, which require users to remember a quite long secret with high entropy (such as a secret key); various such mechanisms are discussed in Sections 3.1.2, 3.1.3, and 3.2.

We note that for the latter class, the use of trusted storage such as smart cards allows us to reduce the secret to be remembered by the user to a short string too. This is quite common today; however, it requires additional infrastructure such as smart card readers available at the users, which might not always be possible.

3.1.1 Anonymous Password Authentication and Authenticated Key Exchange

Contents in Brief

What is this? Anonymous authentication that uses short or low entropy strings (e.g., passwords) only.

What can it do? Prove that an individual belongs to a permitted group of users without revealing the active user's identity.

How can it be used in cloud computing? Clients can anonymously access a cloud resource, whereas the client machine only needs to remember a password.

Password-based authenticated key exchange (PAKE), proposed in [2] and later formalized in [3], is a popular method for user authentication in a setting where the user and the server only share a short low entropy secret (a password). This field has seen considerable interest and, starting with [4], such protocols have also been considered in the setting of anonymous authentication, which we are going to discuss now.

Short passwords let users easily remember a password, but for the same reason, the secret may be easy to brute force guess, for example, by dictionary attacks.

Those can be divided into online and off-line attacks. For an online attack, the adversary needs the assistance of the server (i.e., it engages in authentication protocols with the server using a guessed password). There are server-side countermeasures such as lockup accounts after a number of consecutive failed authentication attempts in the traditional setting, but in case of anonymous authentication (especially when unlinkability is desired) such attacks are unavoidable. In an off-line attack scenario, the adversary tries to extract or guess the password based on transcripts of prior authentication protocol executions, but without server interaction. Consequently, password-based (anonymous) authentication protocols should be designed in a way that off-line dictionary attacks are not efficiently feasible.

A general problem of any password-based authentication is that the server knows the user's secret information (password) or some derived value thereof, for example, a (keyed) hash value of the password. Consequently, the server hosting all the user's secrets is the most valuable target for an attacker.

Overview

The first approach to password-based anonymous authentication (or authenticated key exchange) presented in [4] is based on a Diffie-Hellman (DH) PAKE protocol [5] combined with 1-out-of-n oblivious transfer (OT; see Section 3.4.2.5). Thereby, OT can be seen as an (efficient) instantiation of a private information retrieval (PIR) protocol (see Section 3.4.2), and n denotes the numbers of users in the system. Besides the standard setting where a single user (i.e., $k = 1$) authenticates to a server, they also propose an k-out-of-n variant of the aforementioned protocol (i.e., k of n users need to cooperatively authenticate). The latter version, however, was shown to be susceptible to off-line dictionary attacks. This has been fixed in [6], who also propose an alternative protocol (NAPAKE) for the case $k = 1$. The latter is not based on 1-out-of-n OT, and is more efficient than previous proposals. A recent protocol in this line of work is the VEAP protocol proposed in [7], which is based on a particular blind signature scheme [8] (see Section 3.1.5 for general remarks on blind signatures). Subsequently, we are only going to discuss protocols for $k = 1$, since they seem to be the most relevant for the cloud computing setting.

In [9], Abdalla et al. consider anonymous password authentication as a three-party protocol between a user, an authentication server, and a gateway. In a so-called gateway-based PAKE (GPAKE), a user, with the aid of an authentication server, computes an authenticated session key shared between him or her and a gateway. Essentially, it is a slight modification of the protocol in [10] combined with an arbitrary symmetric PIR (SPIR) protocol (see Section 3.4.2). Since this type of construction is covered by a more general approach presented below, we will not discuss the anonymous password authentication version of GPAKE any further.

It is worth mentioning that a general problem of all above-mentioned protocols is that the server is required to be passive in order to ensure anonymity and unlinkability (i.e., the server is assumed to honestly follow the protocol specification). Furthermore, they are susceptible to online guessing attacks and always require computations of the server (and the user), which are linear in the number of registered users and therefore do not scale very well.

In order to mitigate these problems and to introduce other features such as anonymity revocation, another line of work under the name (practical) anonymous password authentication [11, 12] pursues a totally different approach. However, compared to the other approaches from before, these protocols are not password-based authentication protocols in the strict sense. In particular, they are protocols based on anonymous credentials (as will be discussed in Section 3.1.5 and Section 3.2) and use the passwords only to encrypt credentials in a way that off-line password guessing attacks are hard even if the encrypted credentials are known. Consequently, such encrypted credentials can be stored anywhere in an unprotected storage (e.g., in the cloud).

Despite those not being password-based authentication protocols in the strict sense, we will briefly present the ideas after the generic framework below.

A Generic Protocol and an Efficient Instantiation

First we present a generic construction for anonymous password-based authentication and key exchange, which covers a broad class of existing protocols [4,6,9,13]. Let us therefore first recall a simplified version of Diffie-Hellman key exchange: let G be a group of prime order p generated by g. For two parties A and B to compute a common secret, A chooses $a \in_R \mathbb{Z}_p$ computes $K_A = g^a \bmod p$ and sends K_A to B. B also chooses an element $b \in_R \mathbb{Z}_p$, computes $K_B = g^b \bmod p$ and sends it to A. Both can now compute a common secret as $K = g^{ab} \bmod p$ by computing $K = K_B^a \bmod p$ and $K = K_A^b \bmod p$, respectively, and this protocol is secure assuming that the CDHP in G is hard (see Definition 2.30). This simplified version is practically insecure, since it is susceptible to person-in-the-middle attacks (see [14] for an extensive treatment). Nevertheless, in our subsequent setting, we use it as one building of the generic construction to give an idea how this works. Furthermore we require additively homomorphic public key encryption, as it is going to be discussed in detail in Section 4.2.1. Let us write $\texttt{Encrypt}(m; pk)$ for the encryption of the plaintext $m \in M$ from a plaintext space M, and under the public key pk. Homomorphic encryption means that $\forall m_1, m_2 \in$ M:

$$\texttt{Encrypt}(m_1 + m_2; pk) = \texttt{Encrypt}(m_1; pk) \cdot \texttt{Encrypt}(m_2; pk)$$

and decrypting the "product ciphertext" with the corresponding sk gives $m_1 + m_2 \in$ M. Obviously, the plaintext and ciphertext spaces must be at least groups, rings, or fields for this to work. Furthermore, we require a PIR protocol that allows the user to retrieve exactly one item from a collection of n items, such that the server does not learn the index i of the queried item.

For the generic construction, let G be a group of order q with g being an element of large order. On this group, take an additively homomorphic encryption scheme ($\texttt{KeyGen}, \texttt{Encrypt}, \texttt{Decrypt}$) known to all parties, along with a cryptographic hash function $H : \{0,1\}^* \rightarrow \{0,1\}^k$ and a PIR scheme (see Section 3.4.2). Assume that every user $u_i \in U = \{u_1, \ldots, u_n\}$ shares a distinct password p_i, which is encoded into an element of G such that the additive homomorphism works and is denoted as pwd_i, with a server S. Let us for the ease of presentation assume that $pwd_i = g^{p_i}$ and that the homomorphism applies to the exponents. The server maintains a password file $P = (p_1, \ldots, p_n)$. Anonymous authentication then works as follows:

1. The user u_i generates a one-time key pair (sk, pk) running $\texttt{KeyGen}$ with a suitable security parameter. Then, u_i picks $x \in_R \mathbb{Z}_q$, computes $X = g^x$ as well as $c = \texttt{Encrypt}(pwd_i; pk)$, and sends (X, c, pk) to S.

2. On receiving (X, c, pk), S picks $y \in_R \mathbb{Z}_q$, and computes $Y = g^y$ and $A_S = H(Y\|X)$. Then, for every user $u_j \in U$, S chooses $r_j \in_R \mathbb{Z}_q$ and computes

$$\begin{aligned} c_j &= (c \cdot \texttt{Encrypt}(-pwd_j; pk))^{r_j} \cdot \texttt{Encrypt}(Y; pk) \\ &= \texttt{Encrypt}((pwd_i - pwd_j)r_j + Y; pk), \end{aligned}$$

where all "arithmetic" on the encoded passwords is done in the group G. Finally, S creates a collection $L = (L_j)_{j=1}^n$ with entries of the form $L_j = (c_j, A_S)$.

3. User u_i engages in a PIR protocol to obtain the ith entry in L; that is, $L_i = (c_i, A_S)$. From this entry, u_i computes $Y = \texttt{Decrypt}(c_i; sk)$, and checks whether $A_S \overset{?}{=} H(Y\|X)$ holds. If the verification succeeds, u_i computes the shared authenticated key $K = H(X\|Y\|Y^x \text{ MOD } p)$. Next, u_i computes and sends $A_U = H(X\|Y)$ to S.

4. Upon S receiving A_U, it checks whether $A_U \overset{?}{=} H(X\|Y)$ holds. If so, then S computes the shared authenticated key $K = H(X\|Y\|Y^x)$, and otherwise aborts the protocol.

It is quite easy to see that u_i knowing p_i and pwd_i, respectively, can only decrypt the ith entry in L to obtain Y, since in any other case $i \neq j$ the "difference" of the encoded passwords yields some group element that is blinded by a random value r_j. Consequently, if u_i uses PIR, then S does not learn the index i of the queried item L_i. We note that it is not really necessary to use a homomorphic public key encryption scheme as stated in [11], but homomorphic commitment schemes (e.g., Pedersen commitments [15]) are sufficient. This is for instance used in the construction of [4] together with a 1-out-of-n oblivious transfer protocol (to efficiently implement PIR).

As already stated in the overview, the problem with all these approaches is that the computational as well as communication costs are always linear in $n = |U|$ and S has to be passive in order to preserve anonymity and unlinkability. To see this, one may just think of S picking a distinct y for every user in U in the second step above (see Section 3.1.2). Membership revocation of u_j is straightforward, since S simply needs to remove pwd_j from P, but anonymity revocation (traceability), which is discussed in Section 3.1.4, is not possible.

Password-Protected Credentials

This approach is not a password-based authentication protocol in the strict sense, but builds upon anonymous credentials (to be discussed in Section 3.2). In particular, the approaches presented in [11, 12] are based on Camenisch-Lysyansaya (CL) signatures [16, 17] and Boneh-Boyen-Shacham (BBS) group signatures [18], respectively. Essentially, these signature schemes and the signature scheme underlying the latter construction are signature schemes satisfying the usual correctness and unforgeability properties, but possess special (additional) properties. Relevant for these constructions is that signatures can be *randomized*, meaning that anyone can take a signature and compute another signature for the same message such that the signatures are unlinkable, and that a holder of such a signature can use efficient zero-knowledge proofs to prove knowledge of a signature on committed messages.

The basic idea behind the initial construction [11] based on CL signatures [16] is that a user when registering at a server obtains a CL signature that is then split and password-encrypted in a clever way, such that off-line password guessing attacks become impractical. However, one inherent drawback of the construction in [11] is that a server cannot revoke a user (i.e., remove one of the users from U) since it cannot block issued credentials. Consequently, this scheme is impractical. The same authors therefore propose an improved version of the protocol in [12], which makes use of BBS signatures for the sake of more efficiency and uses dynamic accumulators for blocking (revoking) credentials, which are standard revocation mechanisms for anonymous credentials. Basically, a dynamic accumulator [19] allows us to compile a set of values into a compact representation, (supports updates of the accumulator when the set changes), and to generate a witness for each value of the set that allows us to prove (in zero-knowledge) that the the respective value was accumulated. In [12], a dynamic accumulator is used to represent the set U and every user u_i obtains a witness for the respective identity that is encrypted together with the signature. If a user gets revoked, then the accumulator and the witnesses are updated. Furthermore, [12] supports anonymity revocation of authentications, which is realized using a *virtual* TTP and involves cooperation of a set of users but is not going to be discussed here.

3.1.2   Anonymous Authentication from PKE

Contents in Brief
___

What is this? Anonymous authentication that uses off-the-shelf public key encryption (as a black box) only.

What can it do? Prove that an individual belongs to a permitted group of users, without revealing the active user's identity.

How can it be used in cloud computing? Client can anonymously access a cloud resource, whereas the client machine needs nothing beyond a conventional public key encryption suite.

Since there are well-known challenge-response authentication protocols based on public key encryption schemes (e.g., the Needham-Schroeder-Lowe protocol), it is natural to ask whether it is also possible to construct anonymous authentication schemes using those as a building block. It turns out that there are straightforward constructions, which were for the first time discussed in [20], although they are quite limited, since they require deterministic public key encryption schemes. This approach was refined in [21] and further improved and extended in [22] toward the efficient use of probabilistic public key encryption schemes. Besides the aforementioned results, we also present additional (efficient) construction ideas [23].

3.1.2.1 The Basic Idea

Call U a group of n users, whose public keys $pk_1, \ldots, pk_n$ are authentically known to a server (*verifier*) S. If a member $u \in U$ (*prover*) wishes to anonymously authenticate himself or herself, then S selects a random challenge r, encrypts r under all public keys, and sends the ciphertexts $c_1, \ldots, c_n$ to u. The prover decrypts the ciphertext referring to his or her own public key pk_i and responds with the (correct) value of r. Since S cannot determine which ciphertext has been decrypted, the prover u remains anonymous.

This simple scheme calls for care and needs some remarks: first, it must be assured that the encryption remains secure in this multiuser setting. Fortunately, this is the case of any IND-CPA or IND-CCA scheme [24] (but fails for textbook RSA, for instance, by Håstad's attack [25]).

Equally important is that anonymity only holds, if the verifier uses *the same* challenge r for each ciphertext. If S encrypts different challenges for each user, then u's identity is trivially discovered. Countermeasures are manifold and discussed below.

3.1.2.2 Using Probabilistic Encryption

In this case, S created the ciphertexts $c_1 = \texttt{Encrypt}(r; pk_1, \omega_1), \ldots, c_n = \texttt{Encrypt}(r; pk_n, \omega_n)$ by a probabilistic encryption using random coins $\omega_1, \ldots, \omega_n$. Upon receiving the correct response, S can provide these values to the prover, who can then reencrypt r under another (different) public key pk_j to check whether c_j as obtained from S equals $\texttt{Encrypt}(r; pk_j, \omega_j)$ (*trial reencryption*). If so, then S has behaved correctly. When using deterministic encryption this is trivial to perform, but when using probabilistic encryption as proposed in [21], this is a *two-round scheme*. Alternatively, u may publish a digitally signed compilation of all ciphertexts of r on a public bulletin board to have the other users in U verify their ciphertexts against r. This puts S into jeopardy of loosing the group's trust upon misbehavior (*postactive anonymity* [26]), hence making honest behavior his or her best option. This variant as well requires *two rounds* (where the second is for the publishing step).

Another alternative to reduce the computational burden for u is letting S publish a commitment to r and encrypt only the respective open information in the ciphertexts $c_1, \ldots, c_n$. The response r is then obtained by decrypting c_i and opening the commitment. If the commitment is unconditionally binding, then it is impossible for S to have different users open the commitment to distinct values. The best cheating strategy is to partition U into two sets, where only one half receives the open information, and the other half receives rubbish. If u checks only a single other ciphertext, then there is only a chance of 0.5 to detect the cheating. Therefore, either all $n - 1$ ciphertexts must be verified (*full anonymity*), or at least $k < n$ ciphertexts should be checked if we can live with *probabilistic anonymity*, leaving an exponentially small likelihood $\mathcal{O}(2^{-k})$ of undetected cheating.

3.1.2.3   Using Deterministic Encryption

Without random coins, identical plaintexts will yield identical ciphertexts, so u can straightforwardly do the trial reencryption and verify the other ciphertexts. This is a *one-round scheme*, which has to be implemented carefully, however.

Converting a Probabilistic into a Deterministic Encryption

Taking a probabilistic encryption function $\texttt{Encrypt}(m; pk, \omega)$, one may derive the random coins from the hash of m and the public key pk; that is, do the encryption as $\texttt{Encrypt}(m; pk, H(m \| pk))$. This approach is called *encrypt-with-hash* (EwH) [27]. In order to avoid disclosing the plaintext by trial encryptions, however, r must be chosen from a large set, whose size is usually determined by some security parameter κ. More specifically, the random variable X from which r is sampled must have high *min-entropy*. Given random plaintexts being κ-bit string values $r \in \{0, 1\}^\kappa$, we call the largest real number $\mu(\kappa)$ so that

$$\Pr[X = r] \leq 2^{-\mu(\kappa)} \tag{3.1}$$

holds, the *min-entropy* of X, denoted by $h_\infty(X)$ in the literature. Hence, $\mu(\kappa)$ is the largest number so that all plaintexts occur with probability $\leq 2^{-\mu(\kappa)}$. We say that the min-entropy is *high*, if

$$\lim_{\kappa \to \infty} \frac{\mu(\kappa)}{\log \kappa} = \infty, \tag{3.2}$$

that is, the min-entropy grows strictly faster than $\log(\kappa)$ in the security parameter. This technical requirement is to rule out plaintext discoveries by trial encryptions performed by outsiders (i.e., parties not in U). To see why, recall that by (3.1), any plaintext occurs no more frequent than in a fraction of $2^{-\mu(\kappa)}$ among all cases. Trial encryptions would thus need at least $2^{\mu(\kappa)}$ iterations until the first success (expectation of the geometric distribution). Since $\mu(\kappa)$ is "high" in the sense of

(3.2), we get for any constant $c > 0$ and sufficiently large security parameter κ,

$$\mu(\kappa) > c \cdot \log \kappa,$$

which further implies that

$$\Pr[X = r] \le 2^{-\mu(\kappa)} < 2^{-c \cdot \log \kappa} = \kappa^{-c}.$$

Therefore, a realistic (polynomially bounded) adversary who cannot run more than polynomially many trials, say κ^c, *cannot* succeed by trial encryptions, as strictly more trials are required if the min-entropy is high in the sense of (3.2).

To date it is, unfortunately, still open to show that the EwH construction is also secure in the multiuser setting. Bellare et al. [27] strongly conjecture that this is true, but do not explicitly provide a formal proof.

3.1.2.4 Minimal Costs of Anonymous Authentication

Anonymous authentication cannot be made arbitrarily efficient, and the least efforts are as follows:

Communication rounds: Since we have interactive protocols, they require at least two messages (one round). Hence, the deterministic EwH construction presented at last is round-optimal.

Bandwidth consumption: The verifier needs to transmit the encrypted challenge for every member of U and the prover at least needs to transmit the decrypted challenge. This can be made bandwidth-optimal, if the encryption reuses its random coins (see Section 4.2.1.2 for details on how this is done for ElGamal encryption).

Computational effort: The computational effort is at least $|U|$ encryptions for the verifier and at least one decryption for the prover. Furthermore, it requires additional effort to check whether the verifier behaves honestly. Within the latter aspect, improvements have been presented before.

3.1.3 Group and Ring Signatures

Contents in Brief

What is this? Digital signatures that link a signature to a group of potential signers rather than only a single individual.

What can it do? Create a digital signature whose verification tells nothing but the fact that a message/document has been signed by *one* person in a specific group, whereas the actual signer cannot be identified.

How can it be used in cloud computing? Client can submit an authenticated document or access credential on behalf of a group, without showing his identity to the cloud provider. Clients can thus authenticate anonymously.

Anonymous signature-based challenge-response authentication protocols allow any user u_i of a group $U = \{u_1, \ldots, u_n\}$ to produce a signature on behalf of the group U off-line, such that anybody who verifies the signature is unable to identify the signer. Consequently, the verifier solely learns that someone of U has produced the signature, but not who exactly. Additionally, all these signature primitives have also interactive counterparts.

We start with *CDS-type signatures* named after the authors [28], which are obtained from applying the Fiat-Shamir (FS) heuristic to an OR composition of honest-verifier zero-knowledge proofs of knowledge. These CDS-type signatures can also be considered as an instantiation of the second primitive called *ring signatures*. Such ring signatures can either be constructed from scratch [29] or can generically be obtained by applying the FS heuristic to so-called ad hoc group identification schemes [30, 31]. The third and last important class of primitives are state-of-the-art *group signatures* [18, 32]. They can also be obtained from their interactive counterparts by applying the FS heuristic to identity-escrow schemes [33]. See also [34] for an in-depth treatment of generic constructions and compilers.

3.1.3.1 Noninteractive OR Composition of Σ Protocols

By applying the FS heuristic to OR composition of honest-verifier zero-knowledge proofs (see Section 2.5.11), one constructs a signature scheme, which can be used for anonymous authentication in a standard challenge-response signature-based authentication protocol. The concept of such signatures is based on the work of [28]. They can also be generalized to different DL parameters per user (see [35]) as discussed below.

Generic CDS-Type Signature

Assume that every member of $U = \{u_1, \ldots, u_n\}$ has his or her own DL parameters; that is, two large primes p_i, q_i, and an element g_i, that generates a subgroup $\langle g_i \rangle \subseteq \mathbb{Z}_{p_i}^*$ of order q_i. Let $y_i = g_i^{x_i}$ for $x_i \in_R \mathbb{Z}_{q_i}$ and set $sk_i := x_i$ as the user's secret key. The user's public key is set to be $pk_i := (p_i, q_i, g_i, y_i)$. Furthermore, let $H : \{0,1\}^* \rightarrow \{0,1\}^\ell$, $\ell > \max_i\{|q_i|\}$ be a cryptographic hash function. A user u_i who owns the secret key $sk_i = x_i$ and wants to produce a signature on some challenge R from the verifier (the message to be signed) with respect to anonymity set U first simulates all remaining members of $u_j \in U$, $j \neq i$, by choosing $s_j, c_j \in_R \mathbb{Z}_{q_j}$ and computing

$$z_j = g_j^{s_j} y_j^{c_j} \operatorname{MOD} p_j$$

For his or her own index i $r_i \in_R \mathbb{Z}_{q_i}$ is chosen and the real proof is done as follows:

$$z_i = g_i^{r_i} \operatorname{MOD} p_i,$$
$$c = H(U\|R\|z_1\| \ldots \|z_n),$$
$$c_i = c \oplus c_1 \oplus \cdots \oplus c_{i-1} \oplus c_{i+1} \oplus \cdots \oplus c_n, \text{ and}$$
$$s_i = (r_i - c_i x_i) \operatorname{MOD} q_i.$$

Thereby, the random challenge c for the noninteractive proof is obtained by applying the hash function H (i.e., via the FS heuristic). The resulting signature $\sigma = (c_1, \ldots, c_n, s_1, \ldots, s_n)$ together with the description of U and the challenge R is given to the verifier and he or she can check whether the following equation holds (which can easily be verified for correctness):

$$c_1 \oplus \cdots \oplus c_n = H(U\|R\|g_1^{r_1} y_1^{s_1}\| \ldots \|g_n^{r_n} y_n^{s_n})$$

This construction can be seen as the first construction of a ring signature scheme, and a similar interactive construction using the RSA cryptosystem was proposed in [30].

3.1.3.2 Ring Signatures

A ring signature [29], like the construction above and anonymous authentication schemes from PKE, is ad hoc (in contrast to group signatures), meaning that the signer does not need the knowledge, consent, or assistance of the remaining ring members to produce a signature. Besides anonymity of the signer, different signatures of one signer with respect to the same ring must be unlinkable.

RST Construction

For the sake of clarity, we briefly review the idea of [29]: Therefore, the signer u_i, which we call s here for simplicity, when using n trapdoor one-way permutations on n values $x_1, \ldots, x_n$ denoted as $y_1 = f_1(x_1), \ldots, y_n = f_n(x_n)$ needs to noninteractively prove to a verifier that he or she is able to invert one among these n functions (i.e., compute $f_s^{-1}(y_s)$ for some index s) using the knowledge of the trapdoor information without revealing the index s. In other words, the verifier must be convinced that the signer possesses any of the anonymity set's (ring's) secret keys without learning which one. Note that when instantiating the above constructions with the RSA trapdoor permutation, then we have $f_i(x) := x^{e_i} \bmod n_i$ and $f_i^{-1}(y) := y^{d_i} \bmod n_i$ with d_i being the trapdoor information.

A core concept of [29] is the use of $C_{v,k}(y_1, \ldots, y_n) = z$ as a keyed combining function, which takes as input a key k (for a symmetric block cipher), an initialization value v; that is, $v = 0$ may be fixed, and inputs $y_i \in \{0, 1\}^b$ for some b (which is the common domain of the f_i's, details follow), and outputs a single value.

Definition 3.1 ([29]). A *combining function* needs to provide the following properties, for fixed k and v:

1. For each s, $1 \leq s \leq n$, and fixed y_i, $i \neq s$ the function $C_{v,k}$ is a one-to-one mapping from y_s to the output $z \in \{0, 1\}^b$.
2. For each s, given a b-bit value z and all values y_i except y_s, one is able to efficiently find a preimage y_s such that $C_{v,k}(y_1, \ldots, y_n) = z$ holds.
3. Given k, v, z and access to all f_i's, it is infeasible to solve the equation

$$C_{v,k}(f_1(x_1), \ldots, f_n(x_n)) = z$$

for $x_1, \ldots, x_n$, unless one inverts any of the trapdoor permutations $f_1, \ldots, f_n$.

The idea for a signer with index s is to fix z and compute all y_i, $i \neq s$, using the remaining trapdoor one-way permutations, i.e., $y_i = f_i(x_i)$, for randomly chosen x_i. Then he solves $C_{v,k}(y_1, \ldots, y_n) = z$ for y_s (which provides a unique solution due to property 1) and uses his trapdoor information to obtain $x_s = f_s^{-1}(y_s)$. One obvious problem is that the trapdoor permutations may be defined over different domains, e.g., different moduli in case of RSA. However, it is straightforward to extend the permutations to a common domain (cf. [29]), which we assume hereafter.

RSA-Based Construction Hash and XOR

Bresson et al. [36] present an improved and simplified version of the construction of [29], where their combining function uses the RSA function and a hash and XOR mechanism. The idea is as follows: the signer with index s chooses a random seed

r and random x_i, for $1 \leq i \leq n$, $i \neq s$, and computes the values $v_{s+1}, v_{s+2}, \ldots, v_s$ along the ring (see Figure 3.1) in one direction. To ease and clarify notation here, put $H(x_1, x_2, \ldots) := H(x_1 \| x_2 \| \cdots)$.

$$v_{s+1} = H(m, r)$$
$$v_{s+2} = H(m, v_{s+1} \oplus f_{s+1}(x_{s+1})) = H(m, H(m, r) \oplus f_{s+1}(x_{s+1}))$$
$$\vdots$$
$$v_s = H(m, v_{s-1} \oplus f_{s-1}(x_{s-1}))$$

Since we have $v_{s+1} = H(m, r) = H(m, v_s \oplus f_s(x_s))$, the signer is able to compute $f_s(x_s) = r \oplus v_s$ and using the knowledge of the trapdoor information, he or she is consequently able to compute x_s (see Figure 3.1). In order to hide his or her identity, the signer chooses $j \in_R \{1, \ldots, n\}$ and provides $(U, j, v_j, x_1, \ldots, x_n)$ together with the message m to the verifier (j may also be fixed, e.g., to 1).

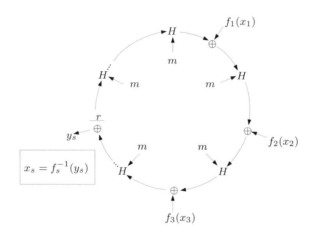

Figure 3.1 Graphical illustration of the ring signature construction of [36].

The verification is straightforwardly done by completing the ring (i.e., by checking the following equation to hold):

$$v_j = H(m, H(m, H(m, \ldots H(m, v_j \oplus f_j(x_j)) \oplus \ldots$$
$$\oplus f_{j-3}(x_{j-3})) \oplus f_{j-2}(x_{j-2})) \oplus f_{j-1}(x_{j-1})).$$

A proof of anonymity and unforgeability of these signatures along with threshold variants of the scheme can be found in [36].

Classes of Ring Signatures

Since the invention of ring signature schemes, a large number of schemes based on ElGamal variants [37], identity-based ring signatures [38, 39], and separable ring signatures [35], which use public keys from arbitrary signature schemes, as well as ring signatures provably secure in the standard model [40] (although rather of theoretical interest) have been proposed. We have only presented standard ring signatures here, but a lot of variants can be found in the literature. Below, we briefly present some major classes of ring signatures and refer the interested reader to a general survey on ring signatures to the article by Wang et al. [41].

Threshold and general access ring signatures: In a (t, n)-threshold ring signature scheme, each ring signature is a proof that at least t members of the anonymity set (ring) U of size n have signed the message; and this may also be applied to general access structures $\Gamma \subset 2^U$.

Linkable ring signatures: In a linkable ring signature scheme, anyone is able to determine whether two ring signatures were produced by the same anonymous signer. Clearly, this requires that signatures are produced with respect to the same ring U.

Verifiable ring signatures: A verifiable ring signature allows the actual signer to later expose himself or herself by proving to a verifier that he or she actually did create the signature.

Deniable ring signatures: In a deniable ring signature scheme, the signer of a message is able to prove to a verifier that a member of the anonymity set is authenticating a message without revealing who has issued the signature. Nevertheless, the verifier is unable to prove to another party that the message was indeed authenticated by a member of the anonymity set.

3.1.3.3 Group Signatures

The concept of group signatures was introduced by Chaum and Van Heyst in [42] and can be somewhat compared to ring signatures, although realizing distinct features. In particular, in contrast to ring signatures there exists a designated party, the so-called *group manager* (GM), who is responsible for managing the group of users (i.e., users need to run a join protocol with the GM to join the group and the GM is responsible for revoking users). Furthermore, the GM is able to open signatures (i.e., reveal the identity of the group member who has anonymously signed a message). Hence, in contrast to ring signatures, group signatures are neither ad hoc nor unconditionally anonymous. After joining, every group member can issue signatures for arbitrary messages anonymously on behalf of the group, whereas the GM is in possession of some trapdoor information, which enables him or her to reveal the identity of the group member who has anonymously signed a message in case of suspicion. Every party who is in possession of the public group verification key is able to verify that a signature for a given message is valid, but is only convinced that some member of the group has issued the signature and is not able to identify the particular signer.

For a discussion of state-of-the-art constructions of group signature schemes [18,32], we refer the reader to the literature and present only a generic construction principle below.

Generic Construction of Group Signatures

Every group member u_i is blindly issued a signature (see Section 3.1.5 for respective protocols) for a user chosen secret x_{u_i}, the so-called membership certificate $cert_{u_i}$, by the GM who maintains a list of group members. If u_i wants to issue a group signature, he or she proceeds as follows:

- u_i encrypts his or her membership certificate $cert_{u_i}$ for the GM and proves in zero-knowledge that the resulting ciphertext contains any valid membership certificate.
- Furthermore, u_i proves in zero-knowledge that he or she knows a secret x_{u_i} corresponding to a valid membership certificate without revealing which one.
- By making the zero-knowledge proofs noninteractive (using the FS heuristic), one can include a message "into" the proofs and thus obtain a signature scheme.

In case of suspicion, the GM is able to identify a signer by decrypting the encrypted membership certificate of a signature. In order to find all signatures issued by a suspicious signer, existing group signature schemes require the GM to open all signatures and thus violate the privacy of the remaining (well-behaving) users. In order to overcome this drawback and to introduce additional traceability features, the concept of *traceable signatures* was introduced [43] and refined [44].

Most importantly, it should be noted that managing dynamic groups and especially the revocation of users is still an open issue to achieve really practical group signature schemes. More precisely, group signature schemes require a mechanism to exclude users without the need for costly update of the group's public key or reissuing of membership certificates to remaining group members. State-of-the-art mechanisms to realize user revocation require signers to additionally prove in the course of signature generation that their membership certificate is not included in a certificate revocation list [45, 46], which is still quite expensive or to employ verifier local revocation (VLR), which outsources this computational task solely to the verifier [47].

3.1.3.4 Comparison of Different Approaches to Anonymous Authentication

Anonymous password authentication: Anonymous password authentication only requires the user to remember a simple password. However, this approach is not immune to cheating servers (which is, however, important in this context) and requires computations linear in the anonymity set.

Anonymous authentication from PKE: Anonymous authentication from public key encryption is apparently simple and can be deployed using existing PKIs. In contrast to ring signatures, they do not require computations linear in the number of users in the anonymity set when accepting only probabilistic anonymity guarantees.

CDS-type and ring signatures: Ring signatures provide unconditional anonymity (i.e., there is no anonymity revocation). However, using hardware security modules like smart cards, anonymity revocation can be integrated into ring signatures [48]. More importantly, in ring signature schemes, the user always needs to perform a number of operations that are linear in the size of the anonymity set.

Group signatures: Group signatures provide conditional anonymity (i.e., there is a GM who is able to revoke the anonymity of users). In contrast to the other approaches, efficient constructions only require a constant amount of computation not depending on the size of the anonymity set. However, compared to the other constructions, they usually involve more computationally expensive ZKPs.

Table 3.1 provides an overview of all discussed anonymous authentication methods and their involved computation and communication overhead as well as the support of some selected properties. Thereby, we abbreviate password-based authentication by PB. Likewise, $PKEB$ indicates public key encryption based approaches, and RSB, GSB stands for anonymous authentication from ring and group signatures, respectively. Furthermore, note that semitrusted means that the server behaves honestly but curiously (i.e., strictly follows the protocols without cheating), and malicious means that the server may deviate from the protocol specifications.

Table 3.1

Overview of Anonymous Authentication Methods

	PB	PKEB	RSB	GSB
Communication overhead				
Client $\rightarrow$ Server	$\mathcal{O}(1)$	$\mathcal{O}(1)$	$\mathcal{O}(n)$	$\mathcal{O}(1)$
Server $\rightarrow$ Client	$\mathcal{O}(n)$	$\mathcal{O}(n)$	$\mathcal{O}(1)$	$\mathcal{O}(1)$
Computation – semitrusted				
Server	$\mathcal{O}(n)$	$\mathcal{O}(n)$	$\mathcal{O}(n)$	$\mathcal{O}(1)$
Client	$\mathcal{O}(1)$	$\mathcal{O}(1)$	$\mathcal{O}(n)$	$\mathcal{O}(1)$
Computation – malicious				
Server	n.a.	$\mathcal{O}(n)$	$\mathcal{O}(n)$	$\mathcal{O}(1)$
Client	n.a.	$\mathcal{O}(n)$	$\mathcal{O}(n)$	$\mathcal{O}(1)$
Infrastructure – semitrusted				
PKI/TTP	$\times$	$\times$	$\times$	$\times$
Infrastructure – malicious				
PKI/TTP	n.a.	$\checkmark$	$\checkmark$	$\checkmark$
Properties				
User revocation	$\checkmark$	$\checkmark$	$\checkmark$	$\checkmark$
Anonymity revocation	$\times$	$\times$	$\times$	$\checkmark$
Impersonation	$\checkmark$	$\times$	$\times$	$\times$

We note that there are already some efforts of integration of anonymous authentication into the framework of PKIs based on X.509 certificates (PKIX) [49,50] and in Section 6.2 we also briefly comment on some standardization efforts.

3.1.4 Revocable Anonymity

Contents in Brief

What is this? Methods to dissolve anonymity in case of fraud.

What can it do? In case a client exhibited malicious behavior, revocable anonymity lets some party discover the misbehaving user's identity.

How can it be used in cloud computing? Provides assurance for the cloud provider that clients will behave honestly, for otherwise their anonymity can be revoked in order to take (legal) actions.

The ability to communicate and to perform actions anonymously is a double-edged sword and has its dark side. There are many analogies for anonymous service usage and usage of services in the real world, like buying goods with cash, suggestion boxes to drop criticism, and telephone tip lines to report information on criminal activities (and whistleblowing in general), which are widely accepted. Anonymity in the digital world seems to be reasonable and even mandatory in many cases. Nevertheless, criminals can benefit from anonymity, since anonymity prevents leaving traces for forensic investigators and people may misuse the cloud.

Consequently, integrating traceability may be required by law enforcement or it may be a desirable feature to provide the ability to revoke the anonymity of users and trace their behavior in case of misuse or fraud.

3.1.4.1   How to Trace

Basically, there are two major directions how anonymity revocation can be achieved.

1. *Traceability authority:* The system incorporates a (mutually trusted) party, the so-called traceability authority, which is able to revoke the anonymity of a user in case of suspicion. This party may be represented by a single entity or by a set of traceability authorities. For instance, in group signature schemes [32,42], the GM (or a separate entity called the revocation manager) is able to identify a signer, who has anonymously produced a signature on behalf of the group.

2. *Cooperative traceability:* Here, traceability does not rest with any central authority, but is performed in a distributed way by the users of the system themselves. This approach is for instance employed in [51] to realize traceability in the context of anonymous communication networks, or in [12] in the context of anonymous password authentication. Basically, the idea behind this distributed approach is to have a set Ω of possible tracers, and a so-called tracing policy $T \subseteq 2^{\Omega}$. Tracing occurs when all members of a tracing set $T \in \mathcal{T}$ agree.

We stress that it is usually hard to define what suspicion means and how to prove to another party that misuse has actually happened. It is quite straightforward for instance in case of double-spending of a coin in the e-cash setting, since the anonymity revocation is a protocol-inherent feature. However, if anonymity revocation or tracing is triggered by any out of bound action (i.e., some party claims that an anonymous user has conducted misuse), this is usually hard to verify.

3.1.4.2 What to Trace

For cloud computing, it seems most reasonable that tracing should be done by some trusted third party (TTP), since the cloud provider is not necessarily trusted. Every action conducted by a user results in some information available to the cloud provider (a transcript of the protocol) or some authorization information (some token) that needs to be provided to the cloud provider to authorize some action. Subsequently, we call all these kind of information *tokens*. For traceability, we have to consider two aspects:

i. *Tracing of single tokens:* Every token can be given to the TTP and the TTP can determine the user who has spent the token. This tracing can either be possible in any case, or only if certain conditions are satisfied (e.g., a token is shown more often than defined by a threshold k).

ii. *Linking of tokens:* If one token is given to the TTP, all other tokens spent by the same user can be efficiently identified. Ideally, this can be realized without revoking the anonymity of unsuspicious users (which is called *selective traceability*). Clearly, the trivial case amounts to opening all tokens and determining the links between tokens spent by the suspicious user, which, however violates the privacy of all other users.

3.1.4.3 How to Realize Traceability

In order to achieve traceability, the token itself or the protocol transcript needs to integrate some identifying information of the user, which can only be accessed by the TTP usually by means of some private trapdoor information given to the TTP. This process is in general called *identity escrow* [33]. Thereby, it is important to guarantee that this identity escrow has been performed correctly, since we cannot assume that all users will behave honestly (i.e., integrate their real identity). Basically, there are two paradigms to realize identity escrow:

i. *Proof of correct identity escrow:* The user proves during the showing of a token that the identity has been escrowed correctly. Typically, this involves ZKPs of some specific properties of the token (e.g., by means of verifiable encryption [52]). Due to ZKPs, this approach is usually more expensive than the approach below in terms of bandwidth and computational effort.

ii. *Enforcing correct identity escrow:* When the protocols allow or require the use of tamper-resistant devices like smart cards (possessed by users), this task can usually be achieved at tremendously lower cost. Such devices are assumed to be tamper proof (and trusted by the user), store identifying information of the user, and perform identity escrow on behalf of the user. Generally, identity escrow is thus reduced to encrypting identifying information for a TTP as for instance used in [22, 53].

3.1.4.4   Revocation within Anonymous Authentication

Note that standard password-based anonymous authentication and anonymous authentication from public key encryption do not support traceability. When using tamper-resistant devices like smart cards the latter approach can be adapted to integrated traceability [22]. In the design of ring signatures (Section 3.1.3.2), traceability is usually not desired. *Linkable ring signatures* [41] are explicitly designed to have this feature. Using smart cards, anonymity revocation can be integrated into standard ring signatures [48]. Group signatures have an inherent traceability feature, allowing the group manager to revoke the anonymity of signers whenever desired.

3.1.5   Blind Signatures for Anonymous Transactions

Contents in Brief

What is this? A method to obtain access credentials for anonymous service consumption.

What can it do? Provides an anonymous ticketing machine, with single-show or multishow tickets for anonymous service requests.

How can it be used in cloud computing? Lets a cloud provider enforce (fine-grained) access policies, depending on what tickets are valid for which services.

Within the next sections we discuss some generic approaches to realize anonymous and unlinkable token-based protocols. In particular, we present simple token-based anonymous transactions from *blind* and *partially blind* signatures in Section 3.1.5 and anonymous credential systems in Section 3.2. Before discussing them, we go into a brief classification of different existing approaches to make those topics more accessible.

The general idea behind all such approaches is that some party (e.g., the cloud provider or a trusted entity) issues tokens (also called *credentials*) to users such that they can be used to anonymously consume a service. Usually, it is desirable that the issuing and the showing of a token are unlinkable and the token does not reveal any information about the holder (anonymity).

Number of Showings

Some systems are designed for *single-show* tokens and others for *multishow tokens*. In the latter case this may be an unlimited number or some integer k (k-show tokens) (i.e., one is able to show a token at most k times in an anonymous and unlinkable fashion, but showing the token $k + 1$ times allows tracing of the user).

Single-show: A single-show token can be used exactly once and either k tokens are issued to the user prior to protocol runs (batch issuing) or refreshable tokens are used. This means that spending a single-show token triggers the issuing of a new token, whereas properties of the new token may depend on the currently spent token.

Tokens issued in a batch are usually independent of each other. In order to make them dependent, the concept of a *multicoupon* (MC) has been introduced, which represents a collection of coupons (or tokens) that are regarded as a single unit. The idea of privacy-preserving MC systems is relatively new [54–57] and can be seen as an enhancement of simple batch issuing of single tokens, since in an MC system coupons issued within one MC (comprised of k coupons) are tied together. The spending of single coupons can either only be performed in a sequential order or in arbitrary order [58]. However, all single showings are anonymous and unlinkable. Furthermore, each coupon within an MC may be of a different type and may also have a different validity period. An important property of MC systems is unsplittability. This means that users cannot split a multicoupon in a way so that single coupons can be given to other (unauthorized) users. Usually, MC systems realize *weak unsplittability*, which means that giving away a single coupon means giving away the entire MC. This approach is also known as all-or-nothing nontransferability.

Multishow: The most prominent representatives of multiple- and limited-show tokens (with $k > 1$) are anonymous credential systems, introduced in [59]. We discuss them later in Section 3.2.

Expressiveness

Single-show tokens in their simplest form do not provide any information besides that they were issued by some specific party. However, often one wants to include additional information in such tokens. In Section 3.1.5, we discuss how to realize this using partially blind signatures. However, this approach is limited to including some information in a token, which needs to be fully revealed during showing of a token. In contrast, anonymous credential systems (see Section 3.2) usually realize much more. Namely, they encode several attribute values into credentials and provide mechanisms to *selectively* prove several properties of these and relations among attributes to verifiers (in zero-knowledge).

We note that by ticket, token, coupon, and credential we essentially mean the same; we use the diverse naming for consistency with the literature.

Blind Signatures

Roughly speaking, a *blind signature* is a digital signature in which the signer *does not see* the document that he or she digitally signs. Unlike a conventional signature that is created by a single entity, a blind signature is an *interactive process* between two parties, namely the document owner and the signer. Let m be the document that will be signed, or more precisely its hash value to thwart existential forgery. In the cloud context, blind signatures may be used to authorize a transaction via a ticket. The ticket itself is digitally signed by the provider, while the blinding assures that the provider cannot recognize the ticket to establish usage profiles or link them to an identity.

A simple construction of a blind signature [60] is based on the RSA cryptosystem. Let p, q be two large primes, let $n = p \cdot q$ and e, d be two integers satisfying $e \cdot d \equiv 1 \pmod{\varphi(n)}$ (i.e., consider a standard instantiation of an RSA signature scheme using a full-domain hash function H). Call $pk = (n, e)$ the signer's public key that is authentically known to the document owner, and let $sk = (d, n)$ be the signer's private key. A blind signature for a document m can be obtained as follows:

1. The document owner selects a random integer r coprime to n and calculates the blinded message $\widetilde{m} = H(m) \cdot r^e \operatorname{MOD} n$, where H is any cryptographically secure hash function (to thwart existential forgery). He or she transmits $\widetilde{m}$ to the signer.

2. The signer calculates the digital signature for $\widetilde{m}$ as usual: $s = \widetilde{m}^d \operatorname{MOD} n$. Note that

$$\widetilde{m}^d \equiv (H(m) \cdot r^e)^d \equiv H(m)^d \cdot r^{e \cdot d} \equiv H(m)^d \cdot r \pmod{n},$$

so the signer, no matter how powerful in computational means, at no point gets to see the document's hash value $H(m)$, since it is either blinded by the factor r or a power of it. Since r is unknown to the signer and randomly chosen, the document remains perfectly secret.

3. The owner receives $s = H(m)^d \cdot r$ and can multiply with r^{-1}, which works since r is coprime to n.

The resulting signature $s' = s \cdot r^{-1} = H(m)^d \, \text{MOD} \, n$ is then valid for the document m, and public verification proceeds as usual for RSA signatures.

Besides unforgeability as for any standard signature, security of blind and partially blind signatures calls in addition for confidentiality of the document submitted for signature and the unlinkability of issuing and showing of a signature. Since the security model is very similar for both notions, we postpone its discussion until partially blind signatures have been introduced.

Partially Blind Signatures

In a blind signature scheme, the signer has no control whatsoever over the content of the document that he or she signs. This can be undesirable if the document is a ticket whose validity period is limited or if the ticket will facilitate certain access control regulations. Partially blind signatures [61] allow, besides the blinded document, a common information string $info$ to be included in the generation of a signature, in a way that $info$ needs to be input to the verification algorithm for signature verification. Of course, $info$ must not uniquely identify an entity when anonymity of the token holder is required. However, the common string $info$ can carry any nonidentifying additional attributes regarding the cloud service ticket (validity periods, etc.).

Assume that the document owner and the signer agreed on $info$ prior to the signature protocol (there is no prescribed way in which $info$ is to be negotiated, so it can be provided by the signer or by the document owner or interactively). A partially blind signature scheme consists of three algorithms:

KeyGen: Using a security parameter κ, the key generation algorithm outputs a secret key sk and a public key pk for the signer.

Sign: An interactive protocol between the document owner and the signer, which takes the message m and $info$, as well as the signer's secret key sk as input and outputs the tuple $(m, info, \sigma)$, where σ is the signature.

Verify: This algorithm uses the signer's public key pk to verify the signature σ for the pair $(m, info)$, i.e., the signature explicitly refers to both, the message and the common information, and would be invalidated if either is omitted or modified. The verification algorithm outputs either accept or reject.

Security for (partially) blind signatures is defined as resistance against the following attacks:

Attack 3.1 (Unblinding). The attacker sets up the system and chooses two messages m_0 and m_1 that he or she releases to two honest users. The honest users secretly agree on one of the two messages for which they request a blind signature. The attacker's goal is to correctly guess which document has been blindly signed.

Definition 3.2 ((Partial) blindness). A signature is *(partially) blind* if Attack 3.1 succeeds with negligible probability.

Attack 3.2 (Forgery). The attacker engages in a number of concurrent and interleaved blind signature protocols, allowing for chosen information strings and messages. The attack succeeds if he or she manages to use this data to output a new (forged) valid signature for a new document (that has not been blindly signed before) and either a new or previously used information string.

The attack description insofar it regards the information string $info$ applies only to partially blind signatures. In that case, however, the attack succeeds not only if a new valid signature has been released (after having seen a sequence of valid signatures), but also if the attacker was able to output a document including a completely new information string $info$ (forgery of the common information).

Definition 3.3 (Unforgeability of (partially) blind signatures). A (partially) blind signature is *unforgeable*, if Attack 3.2 succeeds with negligible probability.

An example of a partially blind signature that is secure in the sense of the above definition is the Schnorr-type signature scheme of Abe and Okamoto [62].

Application for Token-Based Anonymous Transactions

Blind signatures can conveniently be used to issue refreshable tokens for cloud services. The validity of the signature assures that the person presenting the token is authorized to request the service. The blindness of the signature assures that the service provider cannot recognize a previously issued token so as to associate it with some identity. In addition, it makes all transactions unlinkable so that usage profile recording is ruled out. For example, this is especially interesting in health care applications in the cloud, where the frequency of access to personal health records might get correlated with the state of health. Hence, the service provider should be prevented from collecting such information.

This can be realized as follows (see [63]): During the registration, the user receives an initial blindly signed token from the service provider that enables subsequent requests for services. Whenever a service is requested, the user passes his or her current signed token (t_i, σ_i) and a fresh yet unsigned and blinded token $\overline{t_{i+1}}$ to the provider, who

1. Validates the authorization of the user for the request attached to the token t_i by checking his or her own digital signature σ_i.

2. Issues and returns to the user a new blind signature for the blinded token $\overline{t_{i+1}}$ for subsequent requests. The server can then either blacklist the current token t_i to make it one-time usage only, or permit a certain number of reshowings to cover for connection problems.

Subletting a token is equal to a registered user acting on behalf of the person to which the token was sublet to, so reacting on this incidence is up to noncryptographic (contractual) means. In case of fraud or misuse, the blind signature prevents determining to whom the token has been issued, since the chain of transactions cannot be constructed due to the unlinkability of tokens.

For these reasons, it appears advisable to prescribe that *tracing information* (e.g., in the form of an encrypted pseudonym information) is included in each token. The association between the pseudonym and the identity can then be shifted to a trusted third party whose duty is establishing this link in case of evidence for a misuse reported by the service provider. The inclusion of this tracing information must be made in a way that precludes the user from omitting or modifying the tracing information. A quite straightforward method is to put the token generation process inside a tamper-proof smart card [64].

If the service provider wishes to implement a fine-grained access control over his or her resources, then the token issuing can use the defined access privileges in the common information string $info$ of a partially blind signature scheme. Unlinkability is preserved since the actual token still remains concealed. Anonymity is preserved as long as the particular set of access privileges does not allow the service provider to narrow down the set of candidate customers to a single identity.

3.2 ANONYMOUS CREDENTIAL SYSTEMS

Contents in Brief

What is this? (Anonymous) access control by issuing credentials to clients.

What can it do? Fine-grained access control by issuing tickets that reveal only a minimal and controllable amount of information to the service provider and do not reveal the holder's identity.

How can it be used in cloud computing? Cloud services can be consumed without revealing more information than required (e.g., an age over 18 years can be proved without telling the actual birthdate or age).

The most prominent representatives of multishow (and single-show) tokens are anonymous credential systems [59,65]. In an anonymous credential system, a user can obtain credentials from an organization, and then can prove to the organization or any other party that the user has been given appropriate credentials. The important point is that the user proves the possession of a credential without revealing anything more than the fact that the user owns such a credential and in particular does not reveal the identity. Furthermore, anonymous credentials are far more expressive than all other approaches discussed so far; since they allow us to encode arbitrary attributes into the credential and during the proof of possession of a credential, a user can selectively reveal values of attributes or prove that certain relations on attributes hold. For instance, a user may prove that for the attribute "birthdate" encoded in this credential the following holds: for the age of the holder based on attribute "birthdate" it holds that age > 18 without revealing anything about the attribute "birthdate" and any other attributes encoded in the credential.

Over the years, different approaches to design anonymous credential systems, providing quite different functionalities, have been proposed [17,65–70]. We will briefly present the two main classes and state-of-the-art anonymous credential systems. The system due to Camenisch and Lysyanskaya [67] is the representative for a multishow anonymous credential system. This approach is the foundation of the idemix system developed by IBM [71]. The second approach due to Brands [66] represents a single-show anonymous credential system and is implemented as U-Prove by Microsoft [72]. For both approaches common formats and high-level interface are developed within the Attribute-based Credentials for Trust (ABC4Trust) project (see https://abc4trust.eu/).

3.2.1 Camenisch-Lysyanskaya Credentials (Idemix)

Contents in Brief

What is this? Multishow ticket systems for (anonymous) access control at any chosen granularity.

What can it do? Prove possession of certain required attributes of a client in order to anonymously access a resource, without revealing any information beyond what is necessary.

How can it be used in cloud computing? Cloud service provider can validate access rights without violating a user's privacy by learning the client's identity or any information that is not relevant for the access permission.

In the Camenisch-Lysyanskaya credential system [67], every organization o has a public key pk_o, a special RSA modulus n_o, and five elements $(a_o, b_o, d_o, g_o, h_o)$ of the group of quadratic residues modulo n_o. Every user u in the system holds his or her private master secret key x_u. A pseudonym $N(u, o) = N_1||N_2$ of user u with organization o is a string consisting of a user-generated part N_1 and an organization-generated part N_2 and is tagged with a value $P(u, o)$. This so-called *validating tag* is of the form $P(u, o) := a^{x_u} b^{s(u,o)} \text{ MOD } n_o$, where $s(u, o)$ is a random string to which the user and the organization contribute randomness, but only known to the user. A credential issued by o to a pseudonym $N(u, o)$ is now represented by a tuple $(e(u, o), c(u, o))$ where $e(u, o)$ is a large prime number and $c(u, o)$ is such that $c(u, o)e(u, o) \equiv P(u, o)d_o \pmod{n_o}$. Assuming that the strong RSA assumption holds, such pseudonyms cannot be generated by an adversary. The showing of a credential is a proof of knowledge of a correctly formed tag $P(u, o)$ and a credential on it. This is done by publishing commitments to the validating tag $P(u, o)$ and the credential $(e(u, o), c(u, o))$, and proving relationships between these commitments. We note that the pseudonym can encode arbitrary attributes and corresponding values.

As already outlined above, there are several approaches to realize multishow credentials [16, 17, 67, 69], but the conceptually most elegant approach is due to the work of Camenisch and Lysyanskaya [16, 17]. They reduce the task of realizing an anonymous credential system to designing a signature scheme, which supports some specific functionalities. Namely, it is sufficient to have the following building blocks along with some efficient protocols:

- *Commitment scheme:* A commitment scheme and efficient protocols for proving the equality of two committed values.
- *Signature scheme:* A signature scheme and efficient protocols for obtaining a signature on a committed value (without revealing the value) and proving the knowledge of a signature on a committed value. Furthermore, the signature scheme must support randomization, meaning that anyone can take a signature and compute another signature for the same message such that the signatures are unlinkable.

A Very Simple Anonymous Credential System

Based on the above primitives, such a scheme can be realized as follows: A user u chooses a secret x_u and computes a commitment $c_u = \text{Commit}(x_u)$. Then, the user obtains a signature σ from the service provider on this commitment c_u. When the user wants to show the credential, the user rerandomizes the signature σ to

σ' (such that the signature parameters are no longer related) and provides a zero-knowledge proof that σ' is a valid signature computed by the service provider. If this signature scheme, as the ones proposed in [16, 17], supports the signing of tuples of messages, then besides x_u arbitrary (commitments to) attributes can be signed together with the commitment to the secret x_u. Then, showing a choice of the credential's attributes amounts to a proof of knowledge of a secret and proofs of knowledge of (relations among) attributes.

3.2.2   Brands Credentials (U-Prove)

Contents in Brief

What is this? One-show ticket systems for (anonymous) access control.

What can it do? Prove possession of attributes in order to gain access to a resource, while preventing the provider from establishing a link between different transactions.

How can it be used in cloud computing? Cloud provider can issue expressive tickets that are good for only one anonymous usage, since the client would reveal himself or herself (identity and transaction activities) upon showing a ticket multiple times.

Brands' credential system [66] realizes single-show anonymous credentials and thus allows users to prove the possession of a credential (properties of the respective attributes) exactly a single time and is built on *restrictive blind signatures* [73]. If the credential is shown twice, then the executions of the showings can be linked by the protocol transcripts. Restrictive blind signatures are somewhat related to partially blind signatures (see Section 3.1.5) in the sense that users can obtain blind signatures where the verifier has influence on the message to be signed.

In the setting of [66], the service provider (SP) specifies a set of ℓ attributes, which are represented as a tuple $(x_1, \ldots, x_\ell)$, whereas $x_i, 1 \le i \le \ell$ are elements of $\mathbb{Z}_p$. The SP needs to specify an appropriate encoding of the values of every attribute. It is convenient to use a prime order p subgroup of $\mathbb{Z}_q^*$, denoted as G subsequently.

To set up the system, SP chooses a generator $g_0 \in_R G$ and $x_0, y_1, \ldots, y_\ell \in_R \mathbb{Z}_p$ and computes $h_0 := g_0^{x_0}$ as well as $g_i := g_0^{y_i}, 1 \le i \le \ell$. SP's public key is $pk := (p, g_1, \ldots, g_\ell, h_0, g_0)$ and it's secret key is $sk := (y_1, \ldots, y_\ell, x_0)$. The basic idea is that a user u obtains a credential $h' := g_1^{x_{u,1}} \cdots g_\ell^{x_{u,\ell}} h_0^{\beta_1}$ for an attribute tuple $(x_{u,1}, \ldots, x_{u,\ell})$ and β_1 is a blinding factor solely known to user u. The credential is issued in a way that during the issuing both u and the SP agree on $(x_{u,1}, \ldots, x_{u,\ell})$, but the SP does not learn β_1 (and consequently h') during issuing a valid restrictive blind signature (c', r') for this credential. It should be noted that Brands also provides a credential issue protocol, which hides the attribute values [66]. The issuing of a credential is essentially a restrictive blind signature for the attributes $(x_{u,1}, \ldots, x_{u,\ell})$.

Brands provides a set of flexible showing protocol techniques for such digital credentials (see [66] also for a variant in an RSA like setting). They enable a holder of a credential h' and the corresponding signature (c', r') to selectively disclose properties about the respective attributes (i.e., proving arbitrary Boolean formulas connecting linear relations over the single attributes by AND, OR, and NOT operators).

Nontransferability

An inherent problem with anonymous credentials and digital tokens in general is that they can easily be copied and thus a user may give his or her credential along with the corresponding secret to another person. Note that this problem can be somewhat mitigated by storing the secret information inside a tramper-resistant device like a smart card. Nevertheless, the loan of this device can also not be prevented. In order to fully tackle this problem, the following techniques have been proposed:

PKI-assured nontransferability: The idea is to tie the user's secret to some "valuable" secret key from outside the system, such as the secret key that gives access to the user's bank account or the signing key of a digital signature scheme used for e-government purposes. Thus sharing a credential inevitably exposes some valuable secret key [65].

All-or-nothing nontransferability: The basic idea of this approach is that sharing *one* pseudonym or credential implies sharing *all* of the user's other credentials and pseudonyms in the system (i.e., sharing all of the user's secret keys inside the system [67]).

Biometrics-based nontransferability: The basic idea here is that before starting the proof of knowledge of a credential, the user's biometrics are checked [74]. This could be done with a smart card with embedded fingerprint reader or a so-called match-on-card system, where an external reader delivers the biometrics directly to the card.

Revocation of Anonymous Credentials

Revocation of credentials is in particular of importance in the context of multishow credentials, since those credentials can be shown an arbitrary number of times in an unlinkable fashion. In traditional credential systems such PKIX, revocation of credentials can be achieved by including the serial number of a revoked certificate in a blacklist (e.g., a certificate revocation list). However, for obvious reasons (e.g., the serial number must never be revealed to provide anonymity), this approach is not applicable to anonymous credentials. Major approaches to revocation are:

Limited validity: The credential encodes an attribute that represents an expiration date and every showing of a credential requires proving that the credential is not already expired. This attribute can then either be updated after expiration or a new credential is issued.

Proving membership in a whitelist: A whitelist consists of signatures on identifiers of valid credentials, and a user has to prove that the identifier in his or her credential is contained in this list without revealing the exact position in the list.

Proving nonmembership in a blacklist: A blacklist consists of revoked signatures on identifiers, and a user has to prove that the identifier in the credential does not correspond to a signature on the list without revealing the exact position.

In order to implement such proof protocols, either compositions of ZKPs can be employed or ZKPs together with (dynamic) accumulators [19] may be used. Cryptographic accumulators allow the compilation of a number of elements into a constant sized value and for each accumulated element a witness can be computed that allows (non)membership proofs of this value in the accumulator. For a more detailed presentation as well as pros and cons of different approaches to revocation of anonymous credentials, as well as results from an implementation, we refer the interested reader to [75].

3.3 PRIVACY PRESERVING DISCLOSURE OF DATA

Contents in Brief

What is this? Methods to anonymize data.

What can it do? Remove or modify information from a collection of records in a way that retains enough content for processing but destroys logical connections to identities of individuals.

How can it be used in cloud computing? Client can protect the privacy of customer data when handing over information for processing to a cloud provider. This protects against leakage of sensitive information about individuals either by direct access or by inference.

Whenever information is released for processing by a third party (e.g., a cloud provider), parts of it may be concealed in an attempt to protect an identity or to prevent reasoning about some individual. Replacing identities with pseudonyms is a straightforward method to protect an identity from *direct* access. Encrypting an identity is a simple solution that comes with the additional appeal of making the pseudonymization reversible in case of fraud attempts. Protection of sensitive information against *indirect* access via inference, however, requires more sophisticated information restriction techniques, which will receive attention next.

3.3.1 k-Anonymity, ℓ-Diversity, and t-Closeness

Contents in Brief

What is this? Anonymization techniques for database records.

What can it do? Remove or modify information from database records in order to prevent inference toward linking attribute values to individuals.

How can it be used in cloud computing? Client can anonymize a database table before submitting it for processing; protection is especially against disclosure of sensitive data by inference using information from other (different) clients of the cloud provider or publicly available information.

When a database is submitted to a cloud provider for processing, anonymization of its records can be done by *suppressing* or *generalizing* attributes so that no unique relation to an individual can be established. In the case of attribute suppression, consider a table T_{patients} of patient records from which the names have been removed for anonymity, but the birthdate, ZIP code, and gender are still available. Suppose that there exists a (external) voter's list T_{voters} available, perhaps publicly, which shares the latter three attributes along with the voter's name, address, and so forth. Then joining the anonymized table with the voter's list on the birthdate, ZIP code, and gender attributes will produce a view on the medical conditions of persons in the voter's table and likewise destroy the anonymity of T_{patients}. This example is due to [76], and shall illustrate the insufficiency of pure attribute suppression for proper anonymization. A recent study [77] discovered that the majority (more than 60%) of U.S. citizens could be uniquely identified only based on ZIP code, gender, and full date of birth. This empirically demonstrates the power of joining data sources to disclose sensitive information.

The problem cannot be solved by pure access control or access rights management, although many aggregation inference problems can be relieved by proper database design. Access control and cryptography can only protect against unauthorized data disclosure. However, they also cannot safeguard against data extraction via inference, such as by joining two tables, which on their own would not release any sensitive information. In a cloud, data is stored decentralized, scattered, and partially replicated across multiple hosts. More importantly, the user has limited control about where data items are stored, as this happens automatically and transparently. Consequently, query restrictions or access control based on the security classification of the data and the security clearance of the accessor are likely to fail in protecting the data owner's privacy. As the joining attack demonstrates, sensitive information can leak out if multiple sources of nonsensitive information are available to the same (cloud) provider.

To inhibit information leakage by joining (anonymized) tables, it is necessary to identify attributes admitting this kind of linking. The central tool for that matter will be a *quasi-identifier*. Remember that an *identifier* in a table is a set of attributes, which is unique *for every* record (i.e., no two records share the same values of the identifier's attributes). Similarly, a *quasi-identifier* (QID) is a set of attributes such that there is *at least one* record that has a unique setting for the QID attributes. In other words, while an identifier is distinct for each record in the table, a specific QID may be common to many records, but there is at least one record for which even the QID is unique.

Assumption 3.1. A data holder can identify attributes that coexist in his private data and in external databases, so that a QID can be defined accurately.

The identification of QIDs is a crucial issue and presents several difficulties [78]. Although some proposals for an automatic identification of QIDs exist [79], the actual task should remain with an expert of the field. Attributes commonly found in a QID are, for instance, age, gender, race, dates (birth, death, etc. [80]), and so forth. The uniqueness of a QID for at least one individual can be checked by issuing a SELECT COUNT(*) SQL query, which groups by the QID attributes. If at least one group comes back with a single element, a QID has been obtained. More sophisticated techniques in this regard are found in [81].

Now suppose that, grouping by a QID, the SELECT COUNT(*) query comes back with no value less than k. Then no join with any external resource will yield less than k records carrying particular QID values. Hence, any individual with these QID values remains anonymous among at least $k - 1$ other individuals. We call such a table k-*anonymous*, since any given combination of QID values is either not found in the table or is common to at least k records.

Definition 3.4. A table is called k-*anonymous*, if grouping on a quasi-identifier creates no group of size less than k records.

So, anonymization boils down to reducing the information carried by the QID attributes, for instance by:

1. Suppression of whole attributes: this may limit the value of the remaining data for processing.
2. Generalization of attributes: either by partial suppression (e.g., retaining only the first three digits of a ZIP code, or by replacing attribute values with more general terms).

Besides these two, it is also possible to swap values of attributes or to add noise to distort the value. Both techniques may create difficulties in subsequent processing stages. Table 3.2 shows an example of k-anonymization by suppression (attribute "nationality") and generalization (ZIP code and age).

Generalization aims at creating larger bins into which at least k QID incarnations of the table would fall. For a single attribute, we can replace a value by its more general concept. For example, if the attribute is "city," then it generalizes to "country," which in turn generalizes to "region," which in turn generalizes to "continent," and so forth. Figure 3.2a shows an example of such a *generalization hierarchy* (left side), with the tree on the right showing how attribute values are unified in the same bin under the more general value.

If the QID is composed from several attributes, say $QID = (A, B, \ldots)$, then we generalize *one attribute at a time* according to its individual generalization hierarchy. For example, let the ZIP code Z and gender S of a person make up a QID, and let Z_0, S_0 be its most specific form (i.e., lowest set in the hierarchy (Figure 3.2)).

More general versions of (S_0, Z_0) are (S_1, Z_0) and (S_0, Z_1). Both in turn generalize to (S_1, Z_1) but also to (S_2, Z_0) and (S_0, Z_2). Figure 3.3 displays the resulting *generalization lattice*. In general, a compound of three or more attributes $(A_i, B_i, C_i, D_i, \ldots)$ is generalized into

$$(A_{i+1}, B_i, C_i, D_i, \ldots),$$
$$(A_i, B_{i+1}, C_i, D_i, \ldots),$$
$$(A_i, B_i, C_{i+1}, D_i, \ldots),$$
$$(A_i, B_i, C_i, D_{i+1}, \ldots), \text{etc.}$$

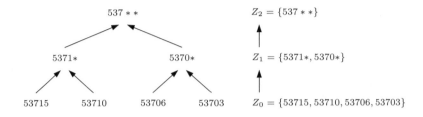

(a) Generalization of ZIP code

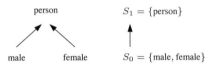

(b) Generalization of gender

Figure 3.2 Generalization hierarchy examples [82].

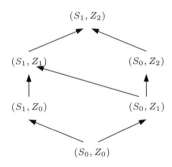

Figure 3.3 Example of generalization lattice for QID with two attributes [82].

Achieving k-Anonymity

According to Definition 3.4, k-anonymity holds if the QID attributes do not narrow down the table to less than k records. Consequently, a simple technique to achieve

k-anonymity is by working our way up the generalization lattice/hierarchy and replacing the QID attribute values accordingly, until grouping on the QID produces no group of size less than k. The desired generalization can be obtained by breadth-first searching from the bottom of the lattice upward, so as to find the "least" generalization providing k-anonymity. This basic technique along with various optimizations has been detailed as the Incognito algorithm [82]. Its correctness follows from the observation that k-anonymity is preserved under generalization (a property that is known as *monotonicity*).

Limits of k-Anonymity and Some Practical Advice

Any release of a k-anonymized table must in any future release be considered as available external information for joining. So, the QID must include all QIDs of previous table releases. Also, the records should be shuffled before releasing the table in order to avoid joining records only by their sequential number in the table. Failure to comply with these rules may lead to identifying information leaking out, as for example [76] demonstrates.

In its pure form, k-anonymity fails to protect against inference based on background knowledge or in cases where a sensitive attribute may be common to a group defined by a QID value. For example, consider Table 3.2a and its 4-anonymous version Table 3.2b. In the latter, three groups are formed by the generalized/suppressed quasi-identifier attributes $QID = ($"ZIP code," "age," "nationality"$)$.

Table 3.2 is 4-anonymous, since every group contains at least four records. However, observe that the sensitive attribute "medical condition" takes only a single value in the third group, and the diagnosis "cancer" is not found in the first group. Therefore, if external information lets us put an individual into the third group with certainty, the medical condition is clear (*homogeneity attack*). Similarly, if external knowledge tells that a person is in the first group and, by his or her ethnicity, has a low risk of heart diseases, then the medical condition is discovered with high probability (*background knowledge attack*). Countermeasures against such disclosures require attributes within a group to be represented with certain frequencies so as to avoid inference based on values that appear too often, too infrequently, or not at all within a group.

ℓ-Diversity

Adhering to the scientific literature, let us refer to a group of records all having the same QID values q^* as a q^*-*block*. Assume that in a table, we have identified

Table 3.2

Example of k-Anonymity (and its shortcomings) due to [83]

(a) Example medical records table

	Nonsensitive data			Sensitive data
	ZIP code	**Age**	**Nationality**	**Condition**
1	13053	28	Russian	Heart disease
2	13068	29	American	Heart disease
3	13068	21	Japanese	Viral infection
4	13053	23	American	Viral infection
5	14853	50	Indian	Cancer
6	14853	55	Russian	Heart disease
7	14850	47	American	Viral infection
8	14850	49	American	Viral infection
9	13053	31	American	Cancer
10	13053	37	Indian	Cancer
11	13068	36	Japanese	Cancer
12	13068	35	American	Cancer

(b) 4-anonymous version of it

	Nonsensitive data			Sensitive data
	ZIP code	**Age**	**Nationality**	**Condition**
1	130**	< 30	*	Heart disease
2	130**	< 30	*	Heart disease
3	130**	< 30	*	Viral infection
4	130**	< 30	*	Viral infection
5	1485*	≥ 40	*	Cancer
6	1485*	≥ 40	*	Heart disease
7	1485*	≥ 40	*	Viral infection
8	1485*	> 40	*	Viral infection
9	130**	3*	*	Cancer
10	130**	3*	*	Cancer
11	130**	3*	*	Cancer
12	130**	3*	*	Cancer

a *sensitive attribute (SA)*, which we seek to keep unlinkable to an identity such as medical condition.

ℓ-diversity calls for the SA within each q^*-block to be "well-represented." Depending on what this exactly means, different forms of ℓ-diversity are known. A table is said to enjoy the respective ℓ-diversity property if all q^*-blocks have the same ℓ-diversity property. Two example variants are *entropy ℓ-diversity*, demanding the distribution of the sensitive attribute within a q^*-block to have at least $\log \ell$ bits of entropy (based on relative frequencies within the q^*-block; see Figure 3.4a and Figure 3.4b). This criterion implies at least ℓ distinct values for the SA in each q^*-block, and at least $\log \ell$ bits of entropy for the entire table. More involved is *recursive (c, ℓ)-diversity*: let $n_1 \geq n_2 \geq \ldots \geq n_m$ count the occurrences of all m distinct SA values in the given q^*-block in decreasing order. Recursive $(1, 2)$-diversity requires that the most frequent value s_1 does not constitute the majority (i.e., $n_1 < n_2 + n_3 + \cdots + n_m$). Recursive $(c, 2)$ diversity calls for $n_1 < c \cdot (n_2 + n_3 + \cdots + n_m)$. Recursive (c, ℓ)-diversity demands that after removing the most frequent attribute, a recursively $(c, \ell - 1)$-diverse q^*-block remains. Formally, we demand $n_1 < c \cdot (n_\ell + n_{\ell+1} + \cdots + n_m)$ and require this to hold recursively after n_1 is removed and so on. For example, for $m = 7$ attribute values, recursive $(2, 3)$-ℓ-diversity digests into the following set of conditions:

$$n_1 \leq 2(n_3 + n_4 + n_5 + n_6 + n_7)$$
$$n_2 \leq 2(n_4 + n_5 + n_6 + n_7)$$
$$n_3 \leq 2(n_5 + n_6 + n_7)$$
$$n_4 \leq 2(n_6 + n_7)$$
$$n_5 \leq 2n_7$$

ℓ-diversity targets a homogeneous representation of the sensitive attribute's values within a group that shares a common QID. Several other variants and extensions of the above two instantiations of ℓ-diversity are known, and can be found in the respective literature [83]. A criticism that applies to any of these criteria is their lack of accounting for possibly skewed distributions of the SA (that is, the unconditional likelihood for a certain sensitive attribute value is not necessarily reflected within a q^*-block, even if it is ℓ-diverse). Consequently, background knowledge may still rule out certain values of the SA based on frequencies that are known independently of the table data. For example, if ℓ-diversity causes a generally rare medical condition to appear unexpectedly often within a q^*-block, then this condition can still be ruled out with high probability simply because it is known to be uncommon. In case that the distribution is skewed so that its entropy drops below $\log \ell$, entropy ℓ-diversity is impossible.

t-Closeness

Unrealistic distributions of sensitive attributes can be avoided if the relative frequencies of the SA within a q^*-block are required to approximate the relative frequencies of the SA over the whole table. Let the quality of this approximation be measured in terms of a chosen distance function between two probability distributions. If the distance between the distribution of the SA within each q^*-block and the whole table is no more than a threshold t (see Figure 3.4d for an illustration), then the table is said to enjoy *t-closeness*. Figure 3.4c displays a distribution that adheres to entropy ℓ-diversity within the q^*-block, but violates t-closeness. The choice of distance metric is up to a domain expert, since it must take care of semantic similarities between distributions. The inventors of t-closeness proposed the *earth-mover distance* as preferred choice, especially since it yields explicit formulas and simple algorithms to evaluate the goodness of approximation (see [84] for details). However, other choices exist and there is no general guideline on which metric on the space of distributions one should use.

Achieving ℓ-Diversity or t-Closeness

Observe that neither ℓ-diversity nor t-closeness are linked to k-anonymity. However, like k-anonymity, both are preserved under generalizations, so that any algorithm for k-anonymity can be cast into an algorithm for ℓ-diversity or t-closeness. The bottom-up breadth-first search procedure that we sketched for k-anonymity can accordingly be rephrased for ℓ-diversity or t-closeness.

Some Critical Remarks on ℓ-Diversity and t-Closeness

Both concepts refer to a *single* sensitive attribute, and neither concept is easy to generalize to multiple SAs. For ℓ-diversity, one may treat each SA in a q^*-block separately, but must put all remaining SAs into the QID when checking the diversity condition [83] (otherwise, examples demonstrate that inference toward the correct value of an SA is possible). For t-closeness, the generalization toward multivariate SAs needs a distance measure over the space of multivariate distributions, which may be nontrivial on both the theoretical and computational level.

Both concepts work only if an attribute is not both sensitive *and* quasi-identifying. In that case, an alternative approach is offered by [85], which splits the

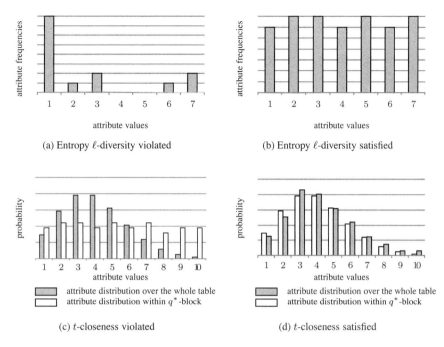

Figure 3.4 Examples of ℓ-diversity and t-closeness.

table into one containing only the QID and the other containing only the sensitive attributes. The logical link is established by a common artificial linking attribute, so that neither table releases any sensitive information by itself. This attribute can be set to yield k-anonymity, ℓ-diversity, or t-closeness upon a joining of the two tables.

Some useful heuristic guidance on how to anonymize data is found in [80]. Alternatives and extensions are found in [78, 86–88].

3.3.2 Redactable and Sanitizable Signatures

Contents in Brief

What is this? Signature schemes that permit document modifications of signed documents without invalidating the digital signature.

What can it do? Document parts can be blacked out, for example to anonymize documents, while retaining a valid digital signature without interaction with the original signer.

How can it be used in cloud computing? Sensitive information can be removed from documents before submitting them for archiving or processing to a cloud provider.

Digital signatures link an identity to a document, thus providing a proof of the document's authenticity to anyone in possession of the signer's public key. Subsequent manipulation of the document (e.g., for anonymization by removing identifying or sensitive information) will necessarily invalidate the digital signature. For example, if the document is a health record from which the patient's name and birthdate (plus any additional identifying attributes) will be deleted, then the original digital signature of the doctor who signed the document would become invalid. Unless the doctor is available and willing to sign the document in its anonymized form again, such changes need to be done "off-line" without interaction with the original signer and in a way that retains a valid digital signature. This is not possible when using conventional digital signatures, but indeed possible when using a redactable or sanitizable signature scheme. In a cloud computing environment, suppose that the cloud serves as a database of medical conditions and diagnoses. For this, we can expect several thousand documents to be anonymized yet remain authentic to properly serve for statistical and differential diagnostic purposes. In such scenarios, getting the digital signature for each document by calling back the original signer is very likely to be infeasible.

Subsequently, we present two types of signature schemes that permit such modifications on signed documents and make the aforementioned example entirely practical.

Redactable Signatures

The general representation of a redactable signature scheme consists of the following algorithms:

KeyGen: An algorithm taking a security parameter as input and outputs a public/secret key pair.

Sign: An algorithm that takes a message and a secret key as input and outputs a digital signature for the given document.

Redact: An algorithm that takes a message and corresponding signature as input and permits removing parts of the document (*without* any need for the private signing key or interaction with the original signer of the document). It outputs the modified document and a valid digital signature for it.

Verify: An algorithm that takes a potentially redacted document, its signature, and the signer's public key. It outputs either accept or reject, depending on whether or not the signature of the document verifies under the signer's public key.

To prevent existential forgery of a signature, the application of a hash function prior to the document before signing it is mandatory. The *hash-then-sign* paradigm is thus intended to prevent computing a signature for some message from scratch or by deriving it from a given message/signature pair (existential forgery). Provided that the used hash function is second preimage resistant, the signature scheme preserves security.

The idea behind redactable and sanitizable signatures is thus a mere replacement of the hash function so that certain second preimages can be found efficiently, while the hash remains secure in general (see Section 2.5.3). Therefore, the KeyGen, Sign, and Verify algorithms come from a conventional signature scheme of choice, and it remains to specify the computation of the hash value and the redaction operation only. We present a very simple technique intended to convey the idea only, and refer to the literature for efficient and practical schemes.

A Simple Scheme Supporting Redaction

Consider a message $m \in \{0,1\}^*$, which we partition into n blocks $m = m_1\|m_2\|\cdots\|m_n$. Let us apply a cryptographic hash to each block, and a final hash to the concatenation of all subhashes. That is, we define the hash to be $H^*(m) := H(H(m_1)\|H(m_2)\|\cdots\|H(m_n))$. Here, H is any cryptographic hash function such as SHA-3. In addition, assume that each block carries a flag that indicates whether it has been hashed already, so that the outer hash will not redigest any marked blocks. The function H^* is, due to the outer hash H, still preimage-resistant given a hash value $H(m)$ only. However, for a given preimage m, we can easily find a second preimage $m' \neq m$ by replacing a subblock by its hash value and marking the block accordingly. For example, $m' = m_1\|H(m_2)\|m_3\|\cdots\|m_n$, with the second block properly marked, is a second preimage to $H^*(m)$. This is already the basic idea behind redactable signatures, since the hash value $H(m_2)$ hides the content of block m_2 thanks to the preimage resistance of H. After the hashing, *any* secure digital signature scheme can be used to generate the final signature. The verification is easy by rehashing the document, where redacted parts go directly into the outer digest and all remaining message blocks are hashed first. This leaves the original message digest unchanged by the redaction, so that the signature verification function will indicate authenticity.

More Sophisticated Schemes

This simple scheme is insecure if the redacted document parts are small or easy to guess and thus open to a brute force preimage search. For example, if m_2's content is the birthdate of a person, then hashing the birthdates over the last 100 years leaves a space of no more than $100 \times 365.25 = 36525$ entries in the search space for the preimage of $H(m_2)$. In order to prevent such brute force attacks, each block must be augmented with a *salt* value, so as to increase the uncertainty about the preimage. Then, the hash value can be seen as a commitment that hides the message. Hence, we would choose a *root salt* r_0 and compute a sequence of random values $r_1, r_2, \ldots, r_n$ for each document block $m_1, m_2, \ldots, m_n$, and do the redaction of, say m_i, by publishing the redacted document

$$m^* = (m_1, \ldots, m_{i-1}, H(m_i \| r_i), m_{i+1}, \ldots, m_n)$$

along with its signature s and all but the ith salt value. The salts are needed to let the verifier correctly reconstruct the hash value(s), while in the ith block it prevents m_i from discovery by brute force. This scheme is suboptimal in terms of the signature containing $\mathcal{O}(n)$ salt values for n blocks. A more efficient scheme taking only $\mathcal{O}(\log n)$ salt values for n blocks is based on Merkle trees and found in [89, 90]. Figure 3.5 shows the construction where redacted blocks are circled by gray boxes.

The redaction happens by replacement of the leaf or subtree hash within the document. Without any redactions, the document signature contains only one salt value for the root R from which all other salts can be derived. For a redaction, we retract the root salt from the signature, and extend the signature by a list L of salts parallel to the path from the redacted node up to the root (dashed line; *authentication path*), so that all salt values for the remaining parts can be reconstructed (dotted lines in Figure 3.5). Obviously, the signature is then of size $\mathcal{O}(\log(n))$ for n document parts. The scheme is especially useful for XML documents.

The following generalizations and extensions to the above and other schemes are possible:

- *Nonredactable document parts:* Redactable signatures usually allow for any part of the document to be blacked out. Restricting this ability to a set of

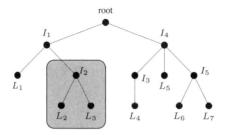

(a) Document tree.

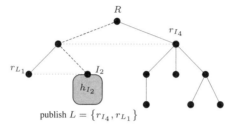

publish $L = \{r_{I_4}, r_{L_1}\}$

(b) Published information after redaction.

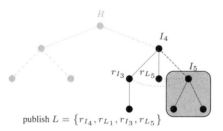

publish $L = \{r_{I_4}, r_{L_1}, r_{I_3}, r_{L_5}\}$

(c) Further redaction of the subtree rooted at I_5.

Figure 3.5 Illustration of a redaction process.

designated document portions is the subject of *sanitizable signatures* that we will discuss later.

- *Redactions changing the document structure:* In a tree-structured document, redacting leaf nodes is easy by replacing them with their respective hash values (see Figure 3.5). When removing an inner node, we must take care of dangling nodes and must specify where to connect these nodes after their (common) parent disappears. One solution (see [91]) is to create copies of redactable parts at potential alternative positions when their parents are redacted. The redaction process then removes all but one of these structural alternatives until the desired structure is obtained. Figure 3.6 displays two examples. Suppose that the inner node X will be redacted only, and that its child node Y will be relocated to either hang under X's sibling Z or to be *level-promoted* to become a child of the root node. These possible relocations are denoted through the dashed edges in the tree displayed in Figure 3.6a. The signer thus "clones" the child Y into (recognizable) copies Y', Y''. He then creates and signs a modified structure as shown in Figure 3.6b, so that the redacter can prune the tree until it has the desired form. The signature can be rejected upon the detection of clones, which enforces the redacter to prune the structure properly.

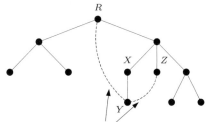

possible new positions for child node Y after redaction of X

(a) Structural change options.

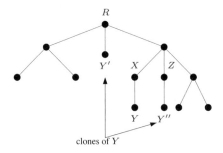

clones of Y

(b) Modified structure that is redactably signed.

Figure 3.6 Illustration of structural modifications.

- *Hiding the redaction event:* If there are no indications that anything has been deleted, we call the redactable/santizable signature scheme *transparent* or *hiding*. The aforementioned simple replacement of content by hash values is not transparent as the redaction is evident from the replacement. To achieve hiding, we compile the redactable document parts into an *accumulator hash* [92], which has the following properties: (i) it is collision- and preimage resistant in the same sense as a normal hash function would be, and (ii) it allows for testing whether or not a certain value has been included in the hash (i.e., is a cryptographic representation of a *set*). Notice that Bloom filters [93] are *insecure* in this cryptographic application. The accumulator then takes the role of the hash value in a normal signature process, whereas the verification tests for membership of all document parts in the accumulator. Redactions then boil down to the plain deletion of document contents without any replacement.

- *Restricting or redacting the ability to redact:* The document may include a redaction policy that is digitally signed along with the document itself. This redaction policy must be nonredactable and is checked by the verification algorithm. Sanitizable signatures offer a way of excluding certain parts of a document from redactions while leaving others open for manipulations. Redacting the ability to redact can be done by removing (redacting) the permission flag to do further redactions (according to the policy).

- *Allowing only for specific replacements during redaction:* If the redaction is such that only a set of admissible replacements are allowed, then another accumulator can be used to test the redacted (i.e., replaced) parts of the document for validity and reject the signature otherwise. Admissible replacements can be derived using generalization/suppression techniques as for k-anonymization, for instance [94]. The document would then be modified to contain all admissible replacements for the attribute so that the redacter can delete all but the one he desires.

- *Reversible redactions:* Simply replace a redacted block with a hash value *and* an encrypted version of the contents so that the process is reversible by revealing the respective decryption key.

Sanitizable Signatures

Sanitizable signatures permit only a *designated* party to arbitrarily modify *designated* parts of a document, whereas a redactable signature allows arbitrary parts of a document to be removed by any third party.

The general representation of a sanitizable signature scheme consists of the following algorithms:

KeyGen: An algorithm taking a security parameter as input and outputs a public/private signature key pair pk_{sign}, sk_{sign} and sanitization key pair pk_{sanit}, sk_{sanit}.

Sign: This is an algorithm that takes a message, a private signature key sk_{sign}, the sanitizer's public key pk_{sanit} and a list of blocks admissible for sanitization as input and outputs a digital signature for the given message.

Sanitize: This is an algorithm that takes a digitally signed message, the sanitizer's secret key sk_{sanit} and the list of blocks admissible for sanitization as input and permits modifying parts of the message (*without* any need for the private signing key sk_{sign} or interaction with the original signer of the message). It outputs the modified message with a valid digital signature.

Verify: This is an algorithm that takes a potentially sanitized message, its signature, the signer's public key pk_{sign} and the sanitizer's public key pk_{sanit}. It outputs either accept or reject, depending on whether or not the signature of the message verified under the signer's public key.

Judge: This is an algorithm that helps to decide whether or not a signed message has been sanitized. It relies on an auxiliary algorithm Proof, which takes as input the private signature key sk_{sign}, the public key pk_{sanit}, and at least one pair of message and signature to output a proof information. This information is fed as additional input into the Judge algorithm, besides the public keys of both parties, when this procedure is invoked to decide a past sanitization on a given message and signature. It outputs either Signer or Sanitizer to indicate the creator of the message/signature-pair.

Similar as for redactable signatures, the only modification is *inside the hash function* before the actual signature is computed. A sanitizable signature can therefore be constructed from any standard signature scheme. A general construction is sketched in Figure 3.7. Consider a document m with some immutable parts and designated parts that will be sanitizable (*mutable*). Any *immutable* portion of the document goes into a cryptographic hash function H as usual. However, any *mutable* part of the document first goes through a *chameleon hash* function CH using the sanitizer's public key pk_{sanit} before entering the overall document hashing algorithm H. The hash function H can be any standardized cryptographic hash function, such as a member of the SHA family or similar. The signature is created as usual, by invoking a conventional digital signature scheme with the signer's private signing key sk_{sign}.

The *sanitizer* can replace the mutable parts of the document by using his or her secret key sk_{sanit} to efficiently construct a collision for the chameleon hash function. The so constructed second preimage for the chameleon hash then becomes the substitute portion for the mutable part in the sanitized document. The only requirement is that the mutable and the substitute parts yield the same chameleon hash value so that the overall document hash remains unchanged.

Notice that the sanitizer cannot play this trick on immutable parts of the document, as this would call for efficiently finding second preimages for H, which is ruled out by the choice of H. However, the sanitizer, by virtue of his or her secret key sk_{sanit}, can produce a value $m_i' \neq m_i$ such that

$$CH_{pk_{\text{sanit}}}(m_i) = CH_{pk_{\text{sanit}}}(m_i')$$

for the chameleon hash. It is essential that m_i' can be chosen "freely" by the sanitizer (however, this implies that CH must take some additional parameters for the hashing, or alternatively, only parts of the preimage can be reset arbitrarily). Thus, the constructed collision eventually yields identical hash values for the original and the sanitized documents, so that the digital signature for the original document remains intact and valid for the sanitized document, too. The substitute for m_i in the original document is m_i' in the sanitized document.

Not all chameleon hashes are suitable for constructing a sanitizable signature, since some candidates may unwillingly reveal the sanitizer's secret key (*key-exposure problem*; see [95]). The chameleon hash function presented below due to [95], however, *is* a suitable choice.

Let us define the chameleon hash function $CH : \{0,1\}^* \to \mathbb{Z}_q$, mapping strings of arbitrary length to integers in $\mathbb{Z}_q$ (bitlength determined by the size of the prime q) and let m the message to be hashed. Then, we can define the corresponding algorithms as follows:

Setup: Given a security parameter pick two large primes p, q such that $p = u \cdot q + 1$ according to the security parameter, and select a generator g of the subgroup of squares of order q. Pick a random secret key $sk \in \{\mathbb{Z}\}_q^*$ and define the public key to be $pk = g^{sk} \bmod p$. Choose a secure cryptographic hash function $H : \{0,1\}^* \to \{0,1\}^\tau$ with $\tau \geq \lceil \log_2 p \rceil$.

Hash: Choose two random values $\rho, \delta \in \mathbb{Z}_q$ and compute $e = H(m\|\rho)$ and compute the chameleon hash as

$$CH_{pk}(m, \rho, \delta) \equiv \rho - (pk^e g^\delta \bmod p) \pmod{q}.$$

FindCollision: Let $C = CH_{pk}(m, \rho, \delta)$ be the known output for which we seek a second preimage. Pick an arbitrary value $m' \neq m$ and a random number

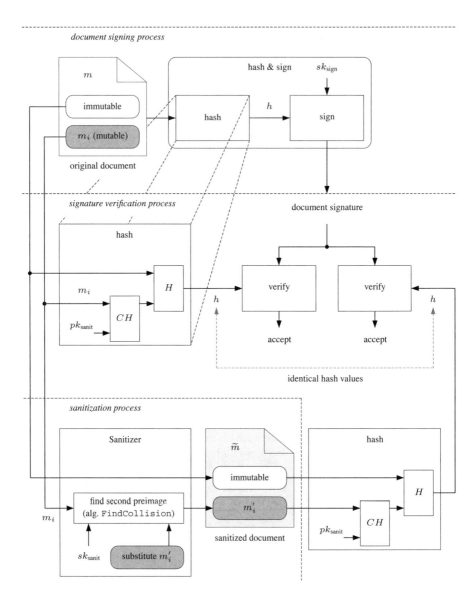

Figure 3.7 Sanitizable signature – example construction.

$k \in \mathbb{Z}_q^*$. Compute the values $\rho' \equiv C + (g^k \operatorname{MOD} p) \pmod{q}$, $e' = H(m' \| \rho')$ and $\delta' \equiv k - e' \cdot sk \pmod{q}$. The sought collision is found at (m', ρ', δ'), since

$$
\begin{aligned}
CH_{pk}(m', \rho', \delta') &\equiv \rho' - (pk^{e'} g^{\delta'} \operatorname{MOD} p) \pmod{q} \\
&\equiv C + (g^k \operatorname{MOD} p) - \left(g^{sk \cdot e'} g^{\delta'} \operatorname{MOD} p\right) \pmod{q} \\
&\equiv C = CH_{pk}(m, \rho, \delta).
\end{aligned}
$$

The above construction will only illustrate the basic ideas, while we refer the reader to references [95, 96] for a more detailed treatment and construction. To complete the picture here, there is no need to dig into the details about the actual signature creation and verification procedures since those come with the chosen digital signature scheme.

It remains to speak about how the judging and proof algorithms work, which are used to decide a document's origin to be either from the signer or the sanitizer. In the construction of [96], the proof algorithm basically searches for a nontrivial hash collision among a given auxiliary sequence of signed documents and the document to be judged. This algorithm would then take the original unmodified document as its auxiliary input so that any sanitized version of it would instantly exhibit the sought collision in the hash. The judging algorithm then merely verifies that the obtained collision refers to the key of the sanitizer and if the sanitization has been correct. If so, then it classifies the document as coming from the sanitizer, otherwise it is from the signer.

Security

Common to both redactable and sanitizable signature schemes are the following security requirements:

Unforgeability: No one should be able to compute a valid signature on behalf of the signer or the sanitizer (if one exists) without knowledge of the respective secret keys. This will remain infeasible even if the attacker can request signatures for arbitrary documents.

Privacy: No one should be able to gain any knowledge about redacted message blocks from their signature without having access to the original message blocks. This property is sometimes called *hiding*.

Transparency: No one should be able to decide whether a given digitally signed document is original or has been sanitized (this property is usually not demanded for redactable signatures).

Notice that the requirement of transparency is not in conflict with the judging algorithm for a sanitizable signature, since transparency only requires that no one except the signer and the sanitizer should be able to distinguish the original from the sanitized document. The sanitizable signature sketched above is an example of a scheme that is private but not transparent. However, the converse implication is indeed true, as privacy does follow from transparency (see Figure 3.8) [97].

Specifically for sanitizable signatures, additional security requirements are imposed:

Immutability: The sanitizer must not be able to modify any part of the document that has not been designated for sanitizing by the signer (in the above sketched construction, such modifications are prevented since the immutable parts of the document are cryptographically, but not chameleon hashed).

(In-)Visibility: The verifier may be allowed to or prevented from seeing which parts of the document are mutable. This property is only meaningful for sanitizable signatures, since redactable signatures allow every part of the document to be removed.

Accountability: This means that it can be decided who was the last to update the document and signature – the signer or the sanitizer. This property is achieved by the Judge algorithm (and its auxiliary Proof algorithm). For example, it may help prevent situations in which the sanitizer tries to publish unauthorized information on the apparent behalf of the signer. The resulting dispute between them can be settled by the Judge algorithm.

Accountability can be refined: *Sanitizer accountability* means that a malicious sanitizer should be unable to convince the judge that the document is still original, even though it has been sanitized. *Signer accountability* refers to the reverse attack, demanding that a malicious signer cannot convince the judge to mistakenly accuse the sanitizer of having done modifications.

A variation is *(noninteractive) public accountability*, in which a third party can correctly determine the document's origin (signer/sanitizer), possibly without interacting with either one in the noninteractive version. Transparency is logically incompatible with public accountability, but a nontransparent scheme is not automatically publicly accountable [98].

Restrict-to-Values: This restricts the sanitizer's ability for replacements to a fixed set of substitutes that the signer defines [99].

Security is defined as resilience against the following attacks, all of which involve the adversary engaging in a number of previous algorithm executions (signing, sanitizations, etc.) and collecting data from these executions to run the attack. In all cases, the adversary knows the public signing and public sanitizing key and can ask for a number of signatures, sanitizations, and proofs for chosen inputs. This is a learning phase for the adversary to facilitate his or her subsequent attack.

Attack 3.3 (Forgery). The attack succeeds if the adversary manages to use his or her learned knowledge to output a forged document that verifies under the signer's and sanitizer's public key for which no original signature has been requested.

Attack 3.4 (Unauthorized sanitizing). Using the learned knowledge, the attack succeeds if the adversary either produces a forged sanitizer key and document that verifies under the signer's public key and the forged sanitizer key, or if he or she outputs a document with at least one block that was originally not admissible for sanitization.

Attack 3.5 (Disclosure of sanitized parts). The attacker chooses two messages m_0, m_1 and submits them for sanitization. The honest sanitizer secretly chooses one document and returns its sanitized version. The attack succeeds if the adversary correctly guesses which of the two documents has been sanitized.

Notice that the modifications must be the same for both documents, for otherwise the task of discovering which document has been used would be trivial (recognizable using the different modifications). The above way of discovering modifications by distinguishing documents is equivalent to *semantic security*, and in fact is inspired by this notion from public key encryption.

Attack 3.6 (Recognizing a sanitization). The attacker wins if he or she can correctly recognize a (signed) document as either being original (i.e., unchanged, or having been sanitized). This choice is based on a document that is presented to the attacker that has secretly been sanitized or left original.

Attack 3.7 (Accusing a signer). The attack succeeds if the adversary manages to use the learned data to output a forged document, forged sanitization key, and forged proof data such that the Judge algorithm on these inputs falsely indicates the honest signer as being the creator of the forged signed document. Of course, the forged signature has to verify under the forged sanitization key and the signature key of the honest signer.

Attack 3.8 (Accusing a sanitizer). This attack runs exactly as Attack 3.7, except that the final goal is to convince the judge to falsely indicate the sanitizer to be the creator of the forged document and signature.

Definition 3.5 (Security of sanitizable signatures). A sanitizable signature scheme is called

- *unforgeable*, if Attack 3.3 succeeds with negligible probability.

- *immutable*, if Attack 3.4 succeeds with negligible probability.
- *private*, if Attack 3.5 succeeds with a chance negligibly close to $1/2$.
- *transparent*, if Attack 3.6 succeeds with a chance negligibly close to $1/2$.
- *signer-accountable*, if Attack 3.7 succeeds with negligible probability.
- *sanitizer-accountable*, if Attack 3.8 succeeds with negligible probability.

Given a sanitizable signature scheme that is immutable, transparent, sanitizer- and signer-accountable, several implications among these security properties exist. Figure 3.8 gives an illustration in which an arrow represents a logical implication, where it is important to notice that properties with no incoming arrows are *not* implied by any other property or combinations thereof (i.e., there are schemes that have one property, but not the other).

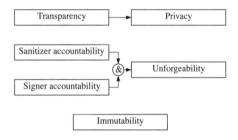

Figure 3.8 Relations and implications among security properties [96].

We refer the reader to [96] for a complete description of a sanitizable signature scheme that satisfies the requirements, which demonstrates that schemes having these security properties indeed exist.

Remarks on Redactable and Sanitizable Signatures

Coming back to redactable signatures for a moment, sanitizable signatures can be used as redactable signatures that permit only certain parts of the document to be modified. Since the designation of the sanitizer is established by knowledge of his or her secret key, one can equally well include the public and secret key for the sanitization process in the document signature to give anyone the ability to compute collisions for the mutable parts in the document. Hence, this creates a signature scheme somewhere in the middle between redactable and sanitizable signatures. The difference in a redactable signature is the restriction to predefined mutable parts of a document, whereas in a redactable signature scheme, any part could be replaced. A *hybrid* scheme can be constructed by extending the hash construction of the described redactable signature scheme by applying a chameleon hash in the first place to the sanitizable parts of the document (i.e., a mixture of the two constructions). If the security proof of the underlying sanitizable signature scheme makes no reference to the inner structure of the hash, then it applies to the modified scheme, too.

An extension toward *multiple sanitizers* is equally straightforward by using different public keys for each sanitizer and its designated mutable document parts. See also [100] for a detailed treatment of multiple signers and sanitizers.

Using the same trick, one can as well restrict the ability to redact the document any further. Any sanitizable signature scheme can be turned into a redactable signature scheme by including the sanitization secret key in the document or signature. Removing this information turns the chameleon hash into a normal hash and prohibits future manipulations for any party that has not yet seen the document's sanitization key in the past.

The degree to which redactable or sanitizable signatures provide a proof of authenticity according to the law depends on country-specific legal requirements. Digital signatures normally indicate *unauthorized* modifications that happened *after* the document was signed. For redactable and sanitizable signatures, modifications are possible without notifying the signer. His or her agreement to this is thus *implicit*. Legal regulations, however, may require the signer's *explicit* consent to every change. Therefore, neither redactable nor sanitizable signatures are equally strong as conventional digital signatures when settling arguments in front of a court (see [101] for a comprehensive treatment), especially if transparency prohibits figuring out the origin of a signature. To achieve better law compliance, the notion of public accountability [98] has been introduced.

Homomorphic and Malleable Signatures

We note that redactable and sanitizable signatures are just one class of homomorphic or malleable signature schemes that allow computations on authenticated data. Another somewhat related recent variant are blank digital signatures [102], which allow a designated proxy to compute a signature for a message from a signature of a template issued by an originator, such that the message signature will only verify if it is compliant with the template (while verification hides the template). Other computations of interest are arithmetics. For instance, homomorphic signatures for polynomial functions [103] (generalized as linearly homomorphic signatures [104]) allow, when given a set of vectors with corresponding signatures, to compute a signature for some vector in the span of the aforementioned set without having access to the private signing key. This allows us to compute authenticated linear operations such as computing an authenticated weighted sum of signed data and an authenticated Fourier transform. A general framework for such signature schemes has been proposed in [105] (called P-homomorphic signatures) and has been further extended in [106] to cover logical formulas on predicates P_i corresponding to different (classes of) P_i-homomorphic signatures. This field of research is very young and many interesting results can be expected in the future.

3.4 PRIVACY PRESERVING ACCESS TO RESOURCES

Contents in Brief

What is this? Methods to hide access patterns and client identities.

What can it do? Prevent a service provider from learning which data items have been accessed in which order by which client.

How can it be used in cloud computing? Assurance for the client that the service provider cannot record behavior profiles nor identities of any of his or her clients.

Occasionally, a client may seek to hide his or her identity when accessing a server. We have already discussed various methods for anonymous authentication (see Section 3.1) in this context. However, as a prerequisite for all these techniques one requires *anonymous communication* technologies, discussed in Section 3.4.1. Such technologies can be used to anonymously send information back and forth between a client and a provider, while the latter learns nothing but the existence of a connection and the data that is transmitted. *Private information retrieval* (PIR), which we meet in Section 3.4.2, is a technique to access data items at a server, while preventing the server from learning *which* particular data items have been accessed. *Oblivious RAM* (ORAM) visited in Section 3.4.3 also attempts to hide access patterns but in contrast to PIR also supports oblivious write operations.

3.4.1 Anonymous Communication

Contents in Brief

What is this? Protocols to anonymously communicate with a service provider.

What can it do? Establish a channel between the client and the service provider, such that neither any intermediate relay nor the addressee of the communication learns the sender's identity.

How can it be used in cloud computing? Client can access a cloud resource without exposing his or her identity through the protocol information (IP-addresses or similar).

Anonymous communication attempts to send a message from an initiator to a receiver such that the receiver cannot discover the sender's identity, and no relay node along the channel gets to know the initiator's or receiver's identity. As the origin of the message plays an exceptional role by initiating the channel construction, we distinguish this *initiator* from a normal relay that we call a *sender* in the following. In most cases, senders are simple proxies, and a protocol can employ many of them. However, there is usually only a single initiator. All schemes presented in the following rely on the assumption that the network's logical connections form a complete graph. Practically, anonymous communication is often implemented via overlay networks.

Different protocols come with different degrees of anonymity. Let the attacker have sniffed the data D from the network. He or she uses the information D to decide whether a given node X is the initiator I or not. Abbreviate the event "X is the initiator" as $X = I$. We call the initiator *exposed* if the conditional likelihood $\Pr[X = I|D] = 1$. We say that X is *probably innocent*, if $\Pr[X = I|D] \leq \frac{1}{2}$, i.e., if X is no more likely to be the initiator than not to be the initiator. Likewise, we say that anonymity is *beyond suspicion* if $\Pr[X|D] \leq \frac{1}{N}$ when there are N nodes in the network. That is, X is no more likely to be the initiator than any other node in the network. Finally, we speak of *absolute privacy* if not even the existence of the anonymous channel can be ascertained by the attacker. These anonymity notions are common, but not the only existing ones (see, e.g., [107] for a k-anonymous communication scheme).

Mixnets and Onion Routing

Mix networks consist of several routers whose purpose is to hide the relations between incoming and outgoing packets so as to make the channel hard to trace. This concealing is achieved by *random reordering*, *encryption*, and *random delays* applied to incoming packets. A channel is thus established over multiple mixes acting as proxies, so that each relaying device gets nothing to know besides where to forward the packet next. In this fashion, only the first relay along the path knows the initiator, and only the last relay knows the final receiver. Figure 3.9 illustrates this *telescoping process* using a simple example with four hops until the receiver R. It is assumed that the initiator I knows the entire network topology as well as the authentic public keys of each mix. The protocol therefore inherits its security from the security of the underlying public key primitives. An incoming packet in the mix M_i is decrypted into the pair (M_{i+1}, c_{i+1}), where M_{i+1} is the next mix along the chosen path and c_{i+1} is the encrypted packet for the next hop. This layered encryption led to the name *onion routing* for this technique. Sending replies is done by the initiator attaching a *reply block* to his message for R. This reply block contains the layered encryption information of the backward channel, and the receiver can just attach the reply block to his or her response, which causes telescoping back to the initiator.

Prominent anonymity services of this kind are type I, II, or III remailers [108–112], which can be used to send e-mails anonymously. Onion routing has been implemented in the Tor system (*the onion router*) [113] and is used for low-latency communication such as transmission control protocol (TCP) connections.

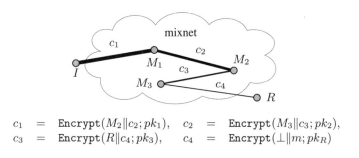

$$c_1 = \texttt{Encrypt}(M_2\|c_2; pk_1), \quad c_2 = \texttt{Encrypt}(M_3\|c_3; pk_2),$$
$$c_3 = \texttt{Encrypt}(R\|c_4; pk_3), \quad c_4 = \texttt{Encrypt}(\bot\|m; pk_R)$$

Figure 3.9 Transmission in the mixnet.

The telescoping achieves sender and receiver anonymity, conditional on the security of the underlying public key encryption. The initiator and receiver are only known to the first and last relay mixes along the path, so in order to avoid one mix discovering both the initiator and receiver, one ought to use at least two mixes on the path. The system remains secure if there is only one mixing proxy; however, this shifts all responsibility to this particular trusted mix. More importantly, to escape traffic flow analysis for discovering the sender and receiver, the anonymity of the mixnet rests on two more assumptions:

1. At least one mix along the transmission path is honest.
2. The users and servers in the network send and receive approximately equal amounts of data.

The Crowds System

Crowds [114] achieves (only) sender anonymity by randomized forwarding: each packet is of the form (R, m), where R is the receiver's address and m is the payload. A forwarding relay, called a *jondo* (referring to the unknown person "John Doe") in the Crowds system, flips a biased coin to decide whether to send the packet directly to R with probability $p_f > \frac{1}{2}$ (*forwarding parameter*), or to otherwise forward it to another randomly chosen jondo. Note that the initiator, after starting the transmission, acts exactly as every other jondo, and hence cannot be recognized as the initiator by any other jondo. Figure 3.10 sketches this process as a state-machine.

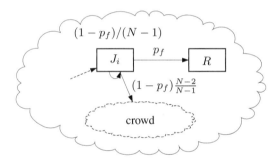

Figure 3.10 Random walk in the crowd toward the receiver R.

The average length of the random path is $\frac{p_f}{1-p_f} + 2$ hops. As every jondo knows the receiver, only the initiator is anonymous. For the receiver, I is *anonymous beyond suspicion*. Otherwise, the degree of anonymity depends on the number N of jondos in the crowd, the capabilities of the adversary, and p_f. If the attacker can observe all traffic from and into an arbitrary node and the jondos are all honest, then the initiator is *exposed* as being the first to transmit. If links cannot be observed, but c malicious jondos collaborate and pool their information to discover I's identity, then Crowds requires at least $N \geq \frac{p_f}{p_f - \frac{1}{2}}(c+1)$ jondos in total to maintain *probable innocence* against any coalition of c attackers.

Responding to a Crowds transmission is done by tracking all jondos along the path and using the same path to convey the response back to the initiator. It is important to notice that this reply path should be *static* for all transmissions, in order to avoid collaborating jondos to narrow down the initiator candidate set by intersecting sets of nodes that have been active (the initiator would be the only node showing up in all these sets).

The Hordes System

Hordes [115] replaces the backward channel by a multicast in which the reply is sent to a set of k nodes (see Figure 3.11), including the initiator, who chooses this group to enjoy k-anonymity. Let there be N nodes in the network. If c among them, including a potentially malicious receiver, collaborate to discover I, then their success-probability p is bounded as $\frac{c}{N} < p < \frac{c}{N} + \frac{1}{k}$ (see [116] for an exact formula for p). This gives a practical guideline on how large k should be chosen.

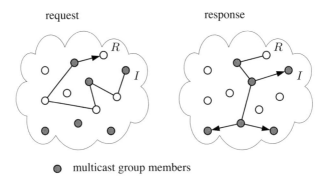

Figure 3.11 Transmission in the Hordes system.

Dining Cryptographer Nets

Given shared secrets between all N participants in an anonymous communication system, Chaum's *dining cryptographer's network* (DC net) [117] provides perfect anonymity via broadcasting only. That is, an external observer sees only broadcasts among the nodes, but cannot tell who spoke to whom exactly in the network.

However, for its high communication overhead ($\mathcal{O}(N^2)$ packets for N nodes) and the need for preshared secrets for symmetric encryption, it appears rather unattractive for client-server communication in a practical application.

Attacks on Anonymous Communication Services

No anonymous communication channel is perfect, and traffic flow analysis is the usual attack to prevent (see [118] for a respective report on the Tor system). Perhaps the most generic attack on such channels is based on repeated establishment of sessions between the same initiator I and receiver R. If such sessions are observed and can be related to each other, then the initiator is eventually discovered as appearing more frequently in the session than any other node. Sessions can be correlated in various ways; for example, by intersecting sets of nodes that were observed as being active (*intersection attack*) or by tracking packet timings (a "too much immediate" response is likely to come from the receiver) or packet counts. This *predecessor attack* due to [119] applies to a large class of anonymous communication schemes, especially the aforementioned ones. Specifically, the following results have been found [119] where N is the number of nodes in the system, c of which collaborate to discover the initiator. For mixnets/onion routing, no more than $\mathcal{O}\left(\left(\frac{N}{c}\right)^{\ell}\log N\right)$ rounds, where $\ell \geq 2$ is the path length are sufficient to discover I based on the frequency of show-ups in sessions, and c collaborating attackers among N. For Crowds, the same bound but with $\ell = 1$ applies. While these somewhat inexplicit bounds due to the Landau asymptotic notation are rather opaque in practice, the crux about this is the following:

1. Sessions should exhibit no correlations insofar as this is possible.
2. If sessions can be correlated, then the initiator must take care that not too many such sessions are established, so as to remain hidden within the regular background traffic.

It is important to notice that one *cannot* safely integrate an anonymous communication scheme (e.g., Crowds) into a larger protocol as a communication primitive, since anonymity may deteriorate in compositions of such anonymous channels [116]. This rather counterintuitive effect has first been reported in [120], so it is advisable to run simulations, especially regarding predecessor attacks, before putting a self-made anonymous communication scheme into practice.

Provable resilience against traffic flow analysis is defined in terms of the observed activity pattern on the links leaking no information about the specific communication relations ("who talks to whom"). Technically, the observed communication pattern should be the same between any two (different) settings when

N nodes talk to each other in pairs of two. A simple modification of mixnets given by [121] achieves this kind of provable unlinkability within $\mathcal{O}(\log N)$ steps (hops), as shown in [122]. The same reference proves this path length to be optimal (i.e., not improvable). The scheme hinges on *synchronized* forwarding – all nodes need to send their packets roughly at the same time, which may be an obstacle for a practical implementation.

For readers who want to dig deeper into this field, we recommend the anonymity bibliography [123] for an up-to-date overview of relevant papers.

3.4.2   Private Information Retrieval

Contents in Brief

What is this? A method to access a set of data items without exposing any access pattern.

What can it do? Retrieve data from a provider while preventing the provider from learning which data items have been accessed, so that no behavior profiles can be built.

How can it be used in cloud computing? Prevents the cloud provider from inference toward sensitive information by using access patterns.

PIR [124] allows clients to query data items from a server without revealing to the server which item is retrieved. Consequently, PIR schemes are interactive two-party protocols between a client and a server trying to perform the following task: Let x be a bitstring of length n held by some server(s). A user wants to query the ith bit x_i, for $1 \leq i \leq n$, from the server(s), without disclosing any information about i to the server(s). In this traditional setting, the database is modeled as string of bits, where the generalization to a real DB is simple. Augmenting queries to larger strings can be trivially obtained by running many PIR instances in parallel, but this will rapidly become expensive. Thus, for a practical setting, it is interesting to design protocols that allow us to efficiently query larger strings. In a setting where one wants to obliviously retrieve (blocks of) files in a block-oriented storage setting, such a generalized approach seems more suitable. A PIR scheme has to be:

Correct: In every invocation of the PIR protocol, the client retrieves the value of the bit (block) he or she is interested in (i.e., x_i).

Private: In every invocation of the PIR protocol the server does not gain any information about the index of the retrieved bit (block) (i.e., i).

When PIR techniques are used in a setting where clients access resources, such as when outsourcing data to the cloud, the storage providers do not obtain information on access patterns for the stored items. For example, such information can be confidential business information in the cloud computing setting [125]. Cloud providers may use these side channels to learn the access history, which reveals user's habits and privileges. The fact that there exist reads to the same file from different users may indicate common interest or a collaborative relationship, and the access frequency of files may also reveal individual and enterprise related interests, respectively.

A naive PIR construction (trivial PIR) that satisfies the required properties is to download all the data from the server(s) and then locally access the data item of interest. Although this provides perfect privacy guarantees to the client, as soon as the amount of data stored at the server(s) increases, this approach is entirely impractical. Hence, it is of interest to find more efficient approaches from the point of view of communication complexity. Consequently, when the database provided by the server(s) has n bits, then a PIR scheme should have communication complexity sublinear in n to outperform the naive approach.

Classification

PIR approaches can be generally classified according to the privacy guarantees for the clients:

Computational PIR (cPIR): These schemes provide computational privacy guarantees to the users (i.e., privacy against computationally bounded server(s)). In this case the privacy of the user depends on computational intractability assumptions.

Information-theoretic PIR (itPIR): These schemes provide information-theoretic privacy guarantees to the users (i.e., privacy against computationally unbounded server(s)).

Furthermore, one can classify PIR schemes according to whether the data is hosted by a single server or multiple independent (noncollaborating) servers, each of which hosts an identical copy of the entire data:

Single-server PIR: The entire database x is hosted by a single server and all queries are issued to this single server.

Multiserver PIR: The entire database x is replicated to ℓ servers, and every server hosts an identical copy of the database x and the queries are issued to $k \leq \ell$ of these servers simultaneously.

In the latter case, the requirement for identical replicas can be relaxed, which results in so-called *r-independent PIR* schemes (i.e., not every server holds a replicated copy of the data and no coalition of up to r servers can determine the contents of the entire database (information-theoretically) [126]). However, this is rather of theoretical interest, since servers are obliged to hold static random content and it needs to be reinitialized on every change of the database.

Efficiency of PIR

It is not very surprising that single-server PIR with information-theoretic privacy and sublinear communication overhead cannot exist. It can also be shown that server-side computation is always in $\Omega(n)$, because each response to a query must necessarily involve all bits of the database of size n. Otherwise, the server(s) would learn that the remaining bits are not of interest to the user.

Besides communication, the computation complexity is also of interest for practical application of PIR. Many single-server PIRs, besides linear algebra based ones [127,128], usually involve costly modular arithmetic. In their paper, [129] Sion and Carbunar conclude that single-server PIRs applying such costly operations are rather of theoretical interest. Consequently, their conclusion is that it would be more efficient to apply the trivial PIR scheme since the server requires much more time to compute a response to a query than it would take to transmit the entire database. Hence, computational complexity is of particular interest for a practical setting.

A more recent work by Olumofin and Goldberg [130] provides a rigorous performance evaluation and demonstrates that linear algebra based single-server PIR and in particular recent multiserver PIR [131] are indeed practical from both perspectives. In the cloud setting, where storage space is quite cheap, the multiserver PIR approach appears interesting.

Below, we present selected candidates of single-server as well as multiserver PIR schemes. For brevity, we will spare detailed discussions of correctness and privacy of the schemes and refer the interested readers to the literature. However, in most of the discussed schemes, their properties and correctness are easily verified. Our presentation is not meant to be an exhaustive survey of all published work on PIR and we do not focus on PIRs providing the lowest asymptotic upper bounds, since this does not mean that they can be meaningfully applied in a practical setting. Nevertheless, we provide pointers to literature where the omitted details can be found.

3.4.2.1 Single-Server PIR

Kushilevitz and Ostrovsky came up with a single-server PIR, whose privacy rests on common computational intractability assumptions [132]. Their initial construction relied on algebraic properties and in particular the homomorphic property of the Goldwasser-Micali public key encryption scheme. Over the years, lots of other (more efficient) schemes have been proposed, and we refer the reader to [133] for a comprehensive and sound survey of single-server PIR.

Below, we present a general, but rather inefficient construction from homomorphic encryption schemes (see Section 4.2.1) covering many existing single-server PIR constructions. See [127, 128] for more efficient constructions based on linear algebra relying on lattice assumptions.

Group Homomoprhic Encryption Based PIR

Let $(\texttt{KeyGen}, \texttt{Encrypt}, \texttt{Decrypt})$ be an IND-CPA secure public key encryption scheme working over Abelian groups G, G', where the plaintext is from $(\mathsf{G}, \circ)$, and the ciphertext is in $(\mathsf{G}', *)$. Furthermore, let G be cyclic of order N and with a generator g. The chosen cryptosystem needs to be homomorphic in the sense that

$$\texttt{Decrypt}(\texttt{Encrypt}(a; pk) \circ \texttt{Encrypt}(b; pk); sk) = a * b$$

for all $a, b \in \mathsf{G}$ and all honestly generated key pairs (sk, pk).

We define the database to be stored at the server as $X = (x_1, \ldots, x_n)$, where x_i, $1 \leq i \leq n$, is either a bit or an integer in $\{0, \ldots, N-1\}$. In the latter case we require that discrete logarithms in G are efficiently computable, which holds if we let G and G' be additive groups and we require $g \in \mathsf{G}$ to be an element of order greater than 1. Let (sk, pk) be a key pair of the respective cryptosystem, where sk is solely known to the client. A client who wants to obliviously query x_i computes n queries $(q_1, \ldots, q_n)$ for the server, such that $\texttt{Decrypt}(q_j; sk) = 0$ for all $j \neq i$ and $\texttt{Decrypt}(q_j; sk) = g$ for $j = i$. Then the user sends $(q_1, \ldots, q_n)$ to the server, who responds with

$$r = \sum_{j=1}^{n} x_j * q_j,$$

where $*$ is the group operation in G'. The client receives r and computes $x' = \texttt{Decrypt}(r; sk)$. If the single elements of the database are bits, then the client sets $x_i = 1$ if $x' = g$ and 0 otherwise. If elements of the database are from the set $\mathbb{Z}_N$, the client computes x_i as the discrete logarithm of x' to the base g.

The above presented protocol is inefficient in terms of communication over-head, since it takes the same effort as the trivial scheme. However, by organizing the data in a $\sqrt{n} \times \sqrt{n}$ matrix $\mathbf{X}$ or a higher dimensional cube and applying some additional tricks for optimization, the communication complexity can be reduced enormously. For further refinements and improvements, we refer the interested reader to [133].

3.4.2.2   Multiserver PIR

In multiserver PIR schemes the database x is replicated to $\ell > 1$ servers. Usually, one assumes in this setting that all servers are honest but curious, meaning that these servers are not communicating, not colluding, and always follow the protocol specification when answering queries. This among others means that they will never manipulate responses and will always respond to queries. Since these assumptions are very optimistic, over the years several improvements to this simple ℓ-server PIR setting have been proposed:

t-private ℓ-server PIR: PIR schemes in which the privacy of the query is information-theoretically protected, even if up to t of the ℓ servers ($t < \ell$) collude.

t-private ℓ-computationally private ℓ-server PIR: PIR schemes, in which the query is information-theoretically protected, even if up to t of the ℓ servers ($t < \ell$) collude. Here, one still has computational protection of the query even if up to all ℓ servers collude.

t-private k-out-of ℓ PIR: PIR schemes in which the client can retrieve the answer to a query if at least k of the ℓ servers respond. As above, no coalition of up to t servers can learn any information about the query.

t-private v-Byzantine-robust k-out-of ℓ PIR: In addition to the above properties, the client should be able to reconstruct the correct query result even if v out of the k servers who are required to respond to a query are Byzantine (i.e., send malformed or incorrect answers).

Below, we present an improvement on the initial work of Chor et al. [124] as described by Goldberg [131]. This is a t-private v-Byzantine-robust k-out-of-ℓ itPIR.

Goldberg's PIR

Goldberg [131] presents an approach that yields a t-private v-Byzantine-robust k-out-of ℓ itPIR. This means that the scheme involves ℓ replicated versions of the database, provides query privacy if up to t servers collude, and for reconstructing the query result it is sufficient that at least k servers respond, from which at most v are allowed to respond Byzantine.

Goldberg's PIR scheme employs Shamir's polynomial secret-sharing to improve the robustness. The database x is treated as a $r \times s$ matrix $\mathbf{X}$ holding r data items of size b and the database is fully replicated to ℓ servers. Every data item is divided into words of size w and every data item consists of $s = b/w$ words, whereas every word x_{ij} represents an element of a suitable finite field F. Consequently, the database can be considered to be the matrix

$$\mathbf{X} = \begin{pmatrix} x_{11} & x_{12} & \cdots & x_{1s} \\ x_{21} & x_{22} & \cdots & x_{2s} \\ \vdots & \vdots & \ddots & \vdots \\ x_{r1} & x_{r2} & \cdots & x_{rs} \end{pmatrix}$$

Assume a client wants to obliviously query the qth data item in $\mathbf{X}$; that is, the qth row vector $\mathbf{x}_q = (x_{q1}, \ldots, x_{qs})$. To this end, he or she takes the respective standard basis vector $\mathbf{e}_q$ (i.e., the vector having the qth element set to 1 and all remaining elements to 0). To conceal the desired index q to the servers, $\mathbf{e}_q$ is split into k vectors of shares $s_1, \ldots, s_k$ (for the ease of presentation, let us assume that we send the query to servers with index $1, \ldots, k$ and we do not send it to a larger number of servers as it would be the case when we assume that servers might fail responding). Each of these k share vectors contains r elements. In order to compute these share vectors, the client chooses r random polynomials $p_1, \ldots, p_r$ over F of degree t, with the constant term $p_i(0) = 1$ if $i = q$, and $p_i(0) = 0$ otherwise. Then the shares are computed as $\mathbf{s}_j = (p_1(j), \ldots, p_r(j))$ and the query for server j is $\mathbf{s}_j$. Every server computes the response vector containing s elements as the matrix-vector product $\mathbf{r}_j = \mathbf{s}_j \cdot \mathbf{X}$. Finally, the client computes the desired data item x_q from all his or her response vectors by using s instances of Lagrange interpolation on inputs $(r_{1,i}, \ldots, r_{k,i})$ for $1 \leq i \leq s$. (Note that only $t+1$ values are necessary per Lagrange interpolation. However, for the ease of presentation we take all k values.)

In this protocol, the client sends $r = n/b$ elements of F to each of the ℓ servers and receives as response $s = b/w$ elements of F of every responding server (note that at least k servers need to respond and we assume that k respond). Let us assume that it takes u bits to encode an element of the finite field F. For efficiency, it is recommended to take a field of the type F_{2^n} for some suitable n. In this case we will have $u = w$ when setting the field to be F_{2^w}. If we set $b = \sqrt{nw}$ we have $r = s = \sqrt{n/w}$. Then the cost to retrieve one row of $\mathbf{X}$ (which amounts to retrieving $\sqrt{nw}$ bits) gives $2\ell u\sqrt{n/w}$ and in our binary field setting we have $u = w$ and thus $2\ell\sqrt{nw}$ which is in $\mathcal{O}(\sqrt{nw})$.

The v-Byzantine-robust feature of this PIR scheme is achieved via list-decoding (which we will not discuss here) and can be dropped for non-Byzantine servers. The Byzantine robustness for Goldberg's PIR scheme was recently further improved in [134], and ℓ-computationally privacy can be added by using homomorphic encryption [131].

3.4.2.3   Hardware-Assisted PIR

The basic idea behind hardware-assisted PIR is to use trusted hardware between the client and the server, which acts as a trusted computing component and a cache [135]. For instance, one may use a secure coprocessor K at the server, which is assumed to be tamper-resistant. Clients then send queries encrypted under K's key to K, K decrypts the query, scans the entire database of the server for the required index and sends the encrypted query result back to the client. As a drawback however, K has $\mathcal{O}(n)$ communication complexity, since K has to read the entire database on every query. In [136] this approach is made more efficient by using off-line precomputations and some amount of temporal storage in K. Essentially, their approach uses the oblivious RAM square-root approach (see Section 3.4.3) of [137]. Here, K requires $\mathcal{O}(\sqrt{n})$ internal working memory and the data items of the server are encrypted and need to be reencrypted (shuffled) from time to time. More recent approaches reduce the complexity of reshuffling from $\mathcal{O}(n)$ down to $\mathcal{O}(\sqrt{n})$ [138, 139].

3.4.2.4   Symmetric PIR

SPIR schemes [140] have the additional property that the client querying data item x_i only learns x_i but no information about the remaining blocks in x. Note that this is not required by the definition of PIR. Consequently, besides giving the client privacy guarantees SPIR gives the server additional privacy guarantees.

Imagine a scenario where users need to pay for the number of accesses to some remote subscription services while their access privacy is still maintained. Since in the symmetric PIR setting all the items in the database are equally priced, one may be interested in a database with items having different prices. Henry et al. have recently proposed an extension to Golberg's multiserver PIR supporting item-based pricing and they additionally support access control lists [141, 142].

3.4.2.5 (Priced) Oblivious Transfer

OT schemes and in particular 1-out-of-n OT schemes evolved from the notion of 1-out-of-2 OT schemes. Thereby, one may think of a magic machine that lets a sender input an ordered pair of bits (b_0, b_1) and a receiver send an index $i \in \{0, 1\}$ and receive b_i from the machine while learning nothing about b_{1-i}. 1-out-of-n OT is a generalization to n inputs and typically one is interested in larger strings instead of bits [143, 144] and to implement OT without any TTP (magic machine) in between sender and receiver.

We briefly present an instantiation of 1-out-of-n OT from [144], which we already mentioned in the context of anonymous password authentication in Section 3.1.1.

Suppose that a server S (the sender) holds n bitstrings $(x_1, \ldots, x_n)$ of size ℓ bits each and allows a client C (receiver) to retrieve exactly 1 bitstring (at index $1 \leq i \leq n$) from this n strings without learning anything about the remaining $n - 1$ bitstrings. Therefore, let $H : \{0, 1\} \mapsto \{0, 1\}^\ell$ be a cryptographic hash function and G be a cyclic group of prime order p with generators g and h. Then the protocol works as follows:

- C wants to receive the bitstring at index i and therefore chooses $r \in_R \mathbb{Z}_p$ and sends the query $Q_i = g^r h^i$ (an unconditionally hiding Pedersen commitment) to S.
- For every $1 \leq j \leq n$, S chooses $k_j \in_R \mathbb{Z}_p$ and computes $\beta_j = H((Q_i(h^j)^{-1})^{k_j} \| j) \oplus x_j$ and sends the answers $A = ((\beta_i, g^{k_1}), \ldots, (\beta_n, g^{k_n}))$ to C.
- C takes (β_i, g^{k_i}) from A and computes $x_i = \beta_i \oplus H((g^{k_i})^r \| i)$.

As already noted above, OT generally has no requirement for sublinear communication complexity (i.e., transmitting fewer data than all n bitstrings). Indeed, in many OT schemes the focus is in reducing the computation cost while allowing a larger bandwidth consumption (i.e., more than all n bitstrings). This clearly renders the OT approaches rather impractical in the cloud storage setting when working with large amounts of data.

The idea of different pricing, as discussed above in the context of SPIR, is not new and can be realized using OT [145]. Within the last few years several OT-based solutions to the aforementioned problem have been proposed [146–148].

3.4.3   Oblivious RAM

Contents in Brief

What is this? A method to read and write a set of data items without exposing any access pattern.

What can it do? Retrieve data from and write data to a provider, while preventing the provider from learning which data items have been accessed and what operation has been performed.

How can it be used in cloud computing? Prevents the cloud provider from inference toward sensitive information by using access patterns.

PIR is designed for allowing oblivious read access to data but does not consider oblivious write operations (besides hardware-assisted PIR, which, however, strictly spoken is an application of ORAM). To realize fully oblivious storage [149] (i.e., supporting private read and write operations on outsourced data), the concept of ORAM [137] can be used. Initially it was intended as a means for software protection, but the ideas became increasingly attractive with the popularity of outsourced data storage. ORAM is a a highly dynamic field today and thus we will only describe the basic approaches here and provide pointers to more advanced methods throughout the section.

3.4.3.1   The Square-Root Approach

A very intuitive approach is the so-called square-root algorithm of [137]. Here, to provide oblivious access to n items stored at a server, one reserves additional $2\sqrt{n}$ memory units containing $\sqrt{n}$ dummy items and a buffer of size $\sqrt{n}$ at the server. The n items along with the $\sqrt{n}$ dummy items are inserted in a permuted order by applying a random permutation and need to be continuously reshuffled after $\sqrt{n}$ operations (we discuss this below).

Upon every access, the client scans the buffer of size $\sqrt{n}$ and checks if the desired item is contained in this buffer. Note that the entire buffer has to be scanned in a predetermined order in order not to reveal if an item was found or not. If the item is found in the buffer, a randomly chosen dummy item from the server is fetched to conceal the fact that the item is in the buffer and the dummy item is placed in the buffer. Otherwise, the client retrieves the item from the server and places the retrieved item in the buffer.

When the buffer gets full, the client obliviously reorganizes (shuffles) the items at the server. Therefore, [137] propose to use a Batcher network [150] (a type of sorting network), and the random permutation is done by sorting the items according to item tags. By applying Batcher's sorting network, one needs to perform $\mathcal{O}(n(\log n)^2)$ comparisons, where the two items to compare are always downloaded from the server, compared, and written back to the server in the resulting order. The sorting network is required because the sequence of accesses is fixed and independent of the input. The shuffling can be made more efficient for the square-root approach and also for the hierarchical approach of [137], as for instance discussed in [151, 152] by using an oblivious version of merge sort. Note that write operations require reencryption of the buffer on every operation, and also note that oblivious sorting requires reencryption of the items, so as to prevent simple matching of read and written items.

3.4.3.2 The Hierarchical Approach and Other Directions

The hierarchical solution of [137] organizes the data in levels, where each level is twice the size of the former level. In each level, items stored at the server are mapped into locations based on random hash functions only known to the client. When a client wants to read an item, he or she scans level by level, and like before, even if the item is found at some level, the client continues to scan all levels to not reveal information about the found item to the server. To write back a data item to the server, it is always inserted in the top levels and when the top level gets full, reshuffling is done to move items to the next level and reorder them. Consequently, after 2^i accesses level i needs to be reshuffled with level $i+1$. This reorganization of data is a quite complex task, and there are different approaches to do this. Goldreich and Ostrovsky originally proposed the use of different types of sorting networks (AKS or Batcher networks); Williams et al. [152] use an oblivious merge sort, and by assuming that a client can store $\mathcal{O}(\sqrt{n})$ items temporarily, obtain a better shuffling performance as in the original approach. Pinkas and Reinman [151] further improve this result by using a randomized shell sort and [153] use partitioning and show that their construction achieves much better efficiency in practice.

3.4.3.3 Recent Developments and Remarks

Quite recently, in [154] the most efficient ORAM construction with small client storage has been proposed, which has already been applied to the cloud storage setting [155]. We refer the interested reader also to [151, 153, 154] for an in-depth discussion and overview of current ORAM approaches.

Generally, ORAM is not designed for use with multiple users. In [156], who apply the square-root approach in the cloud computing setting, in order to overcome the problem of sharing too much state between the clients, the authors use $c\sqrt{n}$ dummy items, $\sqrt{n}$ for every one of the c potential users (which needs to be known before setting up the ORAM). Hence, reducing the shared state comes at the cost of additional storage at the cloud storage provider. Furthermore, we note that cloud storage has boosted efforts in integrating ORAM into practical implementations, e.g., [155, 157, 158].

References

[1] D. Boneh and M. K. Franklin, "Anonymous Authentication with Subset Queries (extended abstract)," in *CCS*, pp. 113–119, ACM, 1999.

[2] S. M. Bellovin and M. Merritt, "Encrypted Key Exchange: Password-Based Protocols Secure against Dictionary Attacks," in *IEEE Symposium on Security and Privacy*, pp. 72–84, IEEE, 1992.

[3] M. Bellare, D. Pointcheval, and P. Rogaway, "Authenticated Key Exchange Secure against Dictionary Attacks," in *EUROCRYPT*, vol. 1807 of *LNCS*, pp. 139–155, Springer, 2000.

[4] D. Viet, A. Yamamura, and H. Tanaka, "Anonymous Password-Based Authenticated Key Exchange," in *INDOCRYPT*, vol. 3797 of *LNCS*, pp. 244–257, Springer, 2005.

[5] M. Abdalla and D. Pointcheval, "Interactive Diffie-Hellman Assumptions with Applications to Password-Based Authentication," in *FC*, vol. 3570 of *LNCS*, pp. 341–356, Springer, 2005.

[6] J. Yang and Z. Zhang, "A New Anonymous Password-Based Authenticated Key Exchange Protocol," in *INDOCRYPT*, vol. 5365 of *LNCS*, pp. 200–212, Springer, 2008.

[7] S. Shin, K. Kobara, and H. Imai, "Very-Efficient Anonymous Password-Authenticated Key Exchange and Its Extensions," in *AAECC*, vol. 5527 of *LNCS*, pp. 149–158, Springer, 2009.

[8] A. Boldyreva, "Threshold Signatures, Multisignatures and Blind Signatures Based on the Gap-Diffie-Hellman-Group Signature Scheme," in *PKC*, vol. 2567 of *LNCS*, pp. 31–46, Springer, 2003.

[9] M. Abdalla, M. Izabachène, and D. Pointcheval, "Anonymous and Transparent Gateway-Based Password-Authenticated Key Exchange," in *CANS*, vol. 5339 of *LNCS*, pp. 133–148, Springer, 2008.

[10] M. Abdalla, O. Chevassut, P.-A. Fouque, and D. Pointcheval, "A Simple Threshold Authenticated Key Exchange from Short Secrets," in *ASIACRYPT*, vol. 3788 of *LNCS*, pp. 566–584, Springer, 2005.

[11] Y. Yang, J. Zhou, J. Weng, and F. Bao, "A New Approach for Anonymous Password Authentication," in *ACSAC*, pp. 199–208, ACM, 2009.

[12] Y. Yang, J. Zhou, J. W. Wong, and F. Bao, "Towards Practical Anonymous Password Authentication," in *ACSAC*, pp. 59–68, ACM, 2010.

[13] S. Shin, K. Kobara, and H. Imai, "A Secure Construction for Threshold Anonymous Password-Authenticated Key Exchange," *IEICE Transactions*, vol. 91-A, no. 11, pp. 3312–3324, 2008.

[14] A. Menezes, P. C. van Oorschot, and S. A. Vanstone, *Handbook of Applied Cryptography*. CRC Press, 1996.

[15] T. P. Pedersen, "Non-Interactive and Information-Theoretic Secure Verifiable Secret Sharing," in *CRYPTO*, vol. 576 of *LNCS*, pp. 129–140, Springer, 1992.

[16] J. Camenisch and A. Lysyanskaya, "A Signature Scheme with Efficient Protocols," in *SCN' 02*, vol. 2576 of *LNCS*, pp. 268–289, Springer, 2002.

[17] J. Camenisch and A. Lysyanskaya, "Signature Schemes and Anonymous Credentials from Bilinear Maps," in *CRYPTO*, vol. 3152 of *LNCS*, pp. 56–72, Springer, 2004.

[18] D. Boneh, X. Boyen, and H. Shacham, "Short Group Signatures," in *CRYPTO*, vol. 3152 of *LNCS*, pp. 41–55, Springer, 2004.

[19] J. Camenisch and A. Lysyanskaya, "Dynamic Accumulators and Application to Efficient Revocation of Anonymous Credentials," in *CRYPTO*, vol. 2442 of *LNCS*, pp. 61–76, Springer, 2002.

[20] S. Schechter, T. Parnell, and A. Hartemink, "Anonymous Authentication of Membership in Dynamic Groups," in *FC*, vol. 1648 of *LNCS*, pp. 184–195, Springer, 1999.

[21] Y. Lindell, "Anonymous Authentication," *Journal of Privacy and Confidentiality*, vol. 2, no. 4, 2011.

[22] D. Slamanig, P. Schartner, and C. Stingl, "Practical Traceable Anonymous Identification," in *SECRYPT*, pp. 225–232, INSTICC Press, 2009.

[23] D. Slamanig, "Anonymous Authentication from Public-Key Encryption Revisited - (Extended Abstract)," in *CMS*, vol. 7025 of *LNCS*, pp. 247–249, Springer, 2011.

[24] M. Bellare, A. Boldyreva, and S. Micali, "Public-Key Encryption in a Multi-user Setting: Security Proofs and Improvements," in *EUROCRYPT*, vol. 1807 of *LNCS*, pp. 259–274, Springer, 2000.

[25] J. Håstad, "Solving Simultaneous Modular Equations of Low Degree," *SIAM Journal on Computing*, vol. 17, no. 2, pp. 336–341, 1988.

[26] D. Slamanig and S. Rass, "Anonymous But Authorized Transactions Supporting Selective Traceability," in *SECRYPT*, pp. 132–141, SciTePress & IEEE, 2010.

[27] M. Bellare, A. Boldyreva, and A. O'Neill, "Deterministic and Efficiently Searchable Encryption," in *CRYPTO*, vol. 4622 of *LNCS*, pp. 535–552, Springer, 2007.

[28] R. Cramer, I. Damgård, and B. Schoenmakers, "Proofs of Partial Knowledge and Simplified Design of Witness Hiding Protocols," in *CRYPTO*, vol. 839 of *LNCS*, pp. 174–187, Springer, 1994.

[29] R. L. Rivest, A. Shamir, and Y. Tauman, "How to Leak a Secret," in *ASIACRYPT*, vol. 2248 of *LNCS*, pp. 552–565, Springer, 2001.

[30] P. Persiano and I. Visconti, "A Secure and Private System for Subscription-Based Remote Services," *ACM Trans. Inf. Syst. Secur.*, vol. 6, no. 4, pp. 472–500, 2003.

[31] Y. Dodis, A. Kiayias, A. Nicolosi, and V. Shoup, "Anonymous Identification in Ad Hoc Groups," in *EUROCRYPT*, vol. 3027 of *LNCS*, pp. 609–626, Springer, 2004.

[32] G. Ateniese, J. Camenisch, M. Joye, and G. Tsudik, "A Practical and Provably Secure Coalition-Resistant Group Signature Scheme," in *CRYPTO*, vol. 1880 of *LNCS*, pp. 255–270, Springer, 2000.

[33] J. Kilian and E. Petrank, "Identity Escrow," in *CRYPTO*, vol. 1462 of *LNCS*, pp. 169–185, Springer, 1998.

[34] M. F. Lee, N. P. Smart, and B. Warinschi, "The Fiat-Shamir Transform for Group and Ring Signature Schemes," in *SCN*, vol. 6280 of *LNCS*, pp. 363–380, Springer, 2010.

[35] M. Abe, M. Ohkubo, and K. Suzuki, "1-out-of-n Signatures from a Variety of Keys," in *ASIACRYPT*, vol. 2501 of *LNCS*, pp. 415–432, Springer, 2002.

[36] E. Bresson, J. Stern, and M. Szydlo, "Threshold Ring Signatures and Applications to Ad-hoc Groups," in *CRYPTO*, vol. 2442 of *LNCS*, pp. 465–480, Springer, 2002.

[37] J. Herranz and G. Sáez, "Forking Lemmas for Ring Signature Schemes," in *INDOCRYPT*, vol. 2904 of *LNCS*, pp. 266–279, Springer, 2003.

[38] F. Zhang and K. Kim, "ID-Based Blind Signature and Ring Signature from Pairings," in *ASIACRYPT*, vol. 2501 of *LNCS*, pp. 533–547, Springer, 2002.

[39] M. H. Au, J. K. Liu, P. P. Tsang, and D. S. Wong, "A Suite of ID-Based Threshold Ring Signature Schemes with Different Levels of Anonymity." Cryptology ePrint Archive, Report 2005/326, 2005. http://eprint.iacr.org/.

[40] A. Bender, J. Katz, and R. Morselli, "Ring Signatures: Stronger Definitions, and Constructions Without Random Oracles.," in *TCC*, vol. 3876 of *LNCS*, pp. 60–79, Springer, 2006.

[41] L. Wang, G. Zhang, and C. Ma, "A Survey of Ring Signatures," *Frontiers of Electrical and Electronic Engineering in China*, vol. 3, no. 1, pp. 10–19, 2008.

[42] D. Chaum and E. van Heyst, "Group Signatures," in *EUROCRYPT*, vol. 547 of *LNCS*, pp. 257–265, 1991.

[43] A. Kiayias, Y. Tsiounis, and M. Yung, "Traceable Signatures," in *EUROCRYPT*, vol. 3027 of *LNCS*, pp. 571–589, Springer, 2004.

[44] B. Libert and M. Yung, "Efficient Traceable Signatures in the Standard Model," in *Pairing*, vol. 5671 of *LNCS*, pp. 187–205, Springer, 2009.

[45] G. Ateniese, D. X. Song, and G. Tsudik, "Quasi-Efficient Revocation in Group Signatures," in *FC*, vol. 2357 of *LNCS*, pp. 183–197, Springer, 2002.

[46] J. Camenisch, M. Kohlweiss, and C. Soriente, "An Accumulator Based on Bilinear Maps and Efficient Revocation for Anonymous Credentials," in *PKC*, vol. 5443 of *LNCS*, pp. 481–500, Springer, 2009.

[47] D. Boneh and H. Shacham, "Group Signatures with Verifier-Local Revocation," in *CCS*, pp. 168–177, ACM, 2004.

[48] S. Xu and M. Yung, "Accountable Ring Signatures: A Smart Card Approach," in *CARDIS*, pp. 271–286, Kluwer, 2004.

[49] V. Benjumea, S. G. Choi, J. Lopez, and M. Yung, "Anonymity 2.0 - X.509 Extensions Supporting Privacy-Friendly Authentication," in *CANS*, vol. 4856 of *LNCS*, pp. 265–281, Springer, 2007.

[50] A. Abed and S. Canard, "One Time Anonymous Certificate: X.509 Supporting Anonymity," in *CANS*, vol. 6467 of *LNCS*, pp. 334–353, Springer, 2010.

[51] L. von Ahn, A. Bortz, N. J. Hopper, and K. O'Neill, "Selectively Traceable Anonymity," in *PETS*, vol. 4258 of *LNCS*, pp. 208–222, Springer, 2006.

[52] J. Camenisch and V. Shoup, "Practical Verifiable Encryption and Decryption of Discrete Logarithms," in *CRYPTO*, vol. 2729 of *LNCS*, pp. 126–144, Springer-Verlag, 2003.

[53] S. Canard and M. Girault, "Implementing Group Signature Schemes with Smart Cards," in *CARDIS*, pp. 1–10, USENIX, 2002.

[54] L. Chen, M. Enzmann, A.-R. Sadeghi, M. Schneider, and M. Steiner, "A Privacy-Protecting Coupon System," in *FC*, vol. 3570 of *LNCS*, pp. 93–108, Springer, 2005.

[55] L. Nguyen, "Privacy-Protecting Coupon System Revisited," in *FC*, vol. 4107 of *LNCS*, pp. 266–280, Springer, 2006.

[56] S. Canard, A. Gouget, and E. Hufschmitt, "A Handy Multi-coupon System," in *ACNS*, vol. 3989 of *LNCS*, pp. 66–81, Springer, 2006.

[57] L. Chen, A. N. Escalante, H. Löhr, M. Manulis, and A.-R. Sadeghi, "A Privacy-Protecting Multi-Coupon Scheme with Stronger Protection Against Splitting," in *FC*, vol. 4886 of *LNCS*, pp. 29–44, Springer, 2007.

[58] A. N. Escalante, H. Löhr, and A.-R. Sadeghi, "A Non-Sequential Unsplittable Privacy-Protecting Multi-Coupon Scheme," in *INFORMATIK 2007*, vol. 110 of *LNI*, pp. 184–188, Springer, 2007.

[59] D. Chaum, "Security without Identification: Transaction Systems to Make Big Brother Obsolete," *Communications of the ACM*, vol. 28, no. 10, pp. 1030–1044, 1985.

[60] D. Chaum, "Blind Signatures for Untraceable Payments," in *CRYPTO*, pp. 199–203, Plemum Press, 1982.

[61] M. Abe and E. Fujisaki, "How to Date Blind Signatures," in *ASIACRYPT*, vol. 1163 of *LNCS*, pp. 244–251, Springer, 1996.

[62] M. Abe and T. Okamoto, "Provably Secure Partially Blind Signatures," in *CRYPTO*, vol. 1880 of *LNCS*, pp. 271–286, Springer, 2000.

[63] S. G. Stubblebine, P. F. Syverson, and D. M. Goldschlag, "Unlinkable Serial Transactions: Protocols and Applications," *ACM Trans. Inf. Syst. Secur.*, vol. 2, pp. 354–389, Nov. 1999.

[64] D. Slamanig and S. Rass, "Selectively Traceable Anonymous and Unlinkable Token-Based Transactions," in *e-Business and Telecommunications*, vol. 222 of *CCIS*, pp. 289–303, Springer, 2012.

[65] A. Lysyanskaya, R. L. Rivest, A. Sahai, and S. Wolf, "Pseudonym Systems," in *SAC*, vol. 1758 of *LNCS*, pp. 184–199, Springer, 2000.

[66] S. Brands, *Rethinking Public-Key Infrastructures and Digital Certificates: Building in Privacy.* MIT Press, 2000.

[67] J. Camenisch and A. Lysyanskaya, "An Efficient System for Non-transferable Anonymous Credentials with Optional Anonymity Revocation," in *EUROCRYPT*, vol. 2045 of *LNCS*, pp. 93–118, 2001.

[68] E. R. Verheul, "Self-Blindable Credential Certificates from the Weil Pairing," in *ASIACRYPT*, vol. 2248 of *LNCS*, pp. 533–551, Springer, 2001.

[69] P. Persiano and I. Visconti, "An Anonymous Credential System and a Privacy-Aware PKI," in *ACISP*, vol. 2727 of *LNCS*, pp. 27–38, Springer, 2003.

[70] M. Belenkiy, J. Camenisch, M. Chase, M. Kohlweiss, A. Lysyanskaya, and H. Shacham, "Randomizable Proofs and Delegatable Anonymous Credentials," in *CRYPTO*, vol. 5677 of *LNCS*, pp. 108–125, Springer, 2009.

[71] IBM Research - Zurich, "The Identity Mixer (idemix)." http://www.zurich.ibm.com/security/idemix/, 2010.

[72] Microsoft Research, "U-Prove." http://research.microsoft.com/en-us/projects/u-prove/, 2012.

[73] S. Brands, "Restrictive Blinding of Secret-Key Certificates," in *EUROCRYPT*, vol. 921 of *LNCS*, pp. 231–247, Springer, 1995.

[74] G. Bleumer, "Biometric Yet Privacy Protecting Person Authentication," in *IH*, vol. 1525 of *LNCS*, pp. 99–110, 1998.

[75] J. Lapon, M. Kohlweiss, B. D. Decker, and V. Naessens, "Analysis of Revocation Strategies for Anonymous Idemix Credentials," in *CMS*, vol. 7025 of *LNCS*, pp. 3–17, 2011.

[76] L. Sweeney, "k-Anonymity: A Model for Protecting Privacy," *International Journal of Uncertainty, Fuzziness and Knowledge-Based Systems*, vol. 10, pp. 557–570, Oct. 2002.

[77] P. Golle, "Revisiting the Uniqueness of Simple Demographics in the US Population," in *WPES*, pp. 77–80, ACM, 2006.

[78] K. Wang, Y. Xu, A. W. C. Fu, and R. C. W. Wong, "FF-Anonymity: When Quasi-Identifiers Are Missing," in *ICDE*, pp. 1136–1139, IEEE, 2009.

[79] R. Motwani and Y. Xu, "Efficient Algorithms for Masking and Finding Quasi-Identifiers," in *SDM* (K. Liu and R. Wolff, eds.), pp. 11–20, SIAM, 2008.

[80] K. E. Emam, "Heuristics for De-identifying Health Data," *IEEE Security & Privacy*, vol. 6, no. 4, pp. 58–61, 2008.

[81] M. Koot, M. Mandjes, G. van 't Noordende, and C. de Laat, "Efficient Probabilistic Estimation of Quasi-Identifier Uniqueness," in *NWO ICT.Open 2011*, pp. 119–126, 2011.

[82] K. LeFevre, D. J. DeWitt, and R. Ramakrishnan, "Incognito: Efficient Full-Domain K-Anonymity," in *SIGMOD*, pp. 49–60, ACM, 2005.

[83] A. Machanavajjhala, D. Kifer, J. Gehrke, and M. Venkitasubramaniam, "ℓ-Diversity: Privacy Beyond k-Anonymity," *ACM Transactions on Knowledge Discovery from Data*, vol. 1, March 2007.

[84] N. Li and T. Li, "t-Closeness: Privacy Beyond k-Anonymity and ℓ-Diversity," in *ICDE*, IEEE, 2007.

[85] X. Xiao and Y. Tao, "Anatomy: Simple and Effective Privacy Preservation," in *VLDB*, pp. 139–150, VLDB Endowment, 2006.

[86] S. Chawla, C. Dwork, F. McSherry, A. Smith, and H. Wee, "Toward Privacy In Public Databases," in *TCC*, vol. 3378 of *LNCS*, pp. 363–385, Springer, 2005.

[87] Q. Zhang, N. Koudas, D. Srivastava, and T. Yu, "Aggregate Query Answering on Anonymized Tables," in *ICDE*, pp. 116–125, IEEE, april 2007.

[88] B. C. M. Fung, K. Wang, R. Chen, and P. S. Yu, "Privacy-Preserving Data Publishing: A Survey of Recent Developments," *ACM Comput. Surv.*, vol. 42, pp. 14:1–14:53, June 2010.

[89] R. Johnson, D. Molnar, D. X. Song, and D. Wagner, "Homomorphic Signature Schemes," in *CT-RSA*, vol. 2271 of *LNCS*, pp. 244–262, Springer, 2002.

[90] D. Slamanig and S. Rass, "Generalizations and Extensions of Redactable Signatures with Applications to Electronic Healthcare," in *CMS*, vol. 6109 of *LNCS*, pp. 201–213, Springer, 2010.

[91] H. C. Pöhls, K. Samelin, H. de Meer, and J. Posegga, "Flexible Redactable Signature Schemes for Trees – Extended Security Model and Construction," in *SECRYPT*, pp. 113–125, SciTePress, 2012.

[92] J. Benaloh and M. de Mare, "One-Way Accumulators: A Decentralized Alternative to Digital Signatures," in *EUROCRYPT*, vol. 765 of *LNCS*, pp. 274–285, Springer, 1994.

[93] B. H. Bloom, "Space/Time Trade-Offs in Hash Coding with Allowable Errors," *Communications of the ACM*, vol. 13, no. 7, pp. 422–426, 1970.

[94] D. Slamanig and C. Stingl, "k-Anonymity in Context of Digitally Signed CDA Documents," in *HEALTHINF*, pp. 62–69, INSTICC Press, 1 2010.

[95] G. Ateniese, D. H. Chou, B. de Medeiros, and G. Tsudik, "Sanitizable Signatures," in *ESORICS*, vol. 3679 of *LNCS*, pp. 159–177, Springer, 2005.

[96] C. Brzuska, M. Fischlin, T. Freudenreich, A. Lehmann, M. Page, J. Schelbert, D. Schröder, and F. Volk, "Security of Sanitizable Signatures Revisited," in *PKC*, vol. 5443 of *LNCS*, pp. 317–336, Springer, 2009.

[97] C. Brzuska, H. Busch, O. Dagdelen, M. Fischlin, M. Franz, S. Katzenbeisser, M. Manulis, C. Onete, A. Peter, B. Poettering, and D. Schröder, "Redactable Signatures for Tree-Structured Data: Definitions and Constructions," in *ACNS*, vol. 6123 of *LNCS*, pp. 87–104, Springer, 2010.

[98] C. Brzuska, H. C. Pöhls, and K. Samelin, "Non-Interactive Public Accountability for Sanitizable Signatures," in *EuroPKI*, LNCS, Springer, 2012.

[99] S. Canard and A. Jambert, "On Extended Sanitizable Signature Schemes," in *CT-RSA*, vol. 5985 of *LNCS*, pp. 179–194, Springer, 2010.

[100] S. Canard, A. Jambert, and R. Lescuyer, "Sanitizable Signatures with Several Signers and Sanitizers," in *AFRICACRYPT*, vol. 7374 of *LNCS*, pp. 35–52, Springer, 2012.

[101] H. C. Pöhls and F. Höhne, "The Role of Data Integrity in EU Digital Signature Legislation – Achieving Statutory Trust for Sanitizable Signature Schemes," in *STM*, vol. 7170 of *LNCS*, pp. 175–192, Springer, June 2012.

[102] C. Hanser and D. Slamanig, "Blank Digital Signatures," in *ASIACCS*, pp. 95–106, ACM, 2013. http://eprint.iacr.org/2013/130.

[103] D. Boneh and D. M. Freeman, "Homomorphic Signatures for Polynomial Functions," in *EUROCRYPT*, vol. 6632 of *LNCS*, pp. 149–168, 2011.

[104] D. M. Freeman, "Improved Security for Linearly Homomorphic Signatures: A Generic Framework," in *PKC*, vol. 7293 of *LNCS*, pp. 697–714, Springer, 2012.

[105] J. H. Ahn, D. Boneh, J. Camenisch, S. Hohenberger, A. Shelat, and B. Waters, "Computing on Authenticated Data," in *TCC*, vol. 7194 of *LNCS*, pp. 1–20, Springer, 2012.

[106] B. Deiseroth, V. Fehr, M. Fischlin, M. Maasz, N. F. Reimers, and R. Stein, "Computing on Authenticated Data for Adjustable Predicates," in *ACNS*, LNCS, Springer, 2013.

[107] P. Wang, P. Ning, and D. S. Reeves, "A k-Anonymous Communication Protocol for Overlay Networks," in *ASIACCS*, pp. 45–56, ACM, 2007.

[108] O. Berthold, H. Federrath, and S. Köpsell, "Web MIXes: A System for Anonymous and Unobservable Internet Access," in *International Workshop on Anonymity and Unobservability*, vol. 2009 of *LNCS*, pp. 115–129, Springer, 2001.

[109] E. Hughes, "A Cypherpunk's Manifesto," 1993. http://www.activism.net/cypherpunk/manifesto.html.

[110] L. Sassaman, U. Möller, C. Tuckley, E. Arneson, A. Kirk, P. Palfrader, and L. M. Cottrell, "Mixmaster," 2008. http://mixmaster.sourceforge.net/.

[111] C. Gülcü and G. Tsudik, "Mixing Email with Babel," in *NDSS*, pp. 2–16, IEEE, 1996.

[112] G. Danezis, R. Dingledine, and N. Mathewson, "Mixminion: Design of a Type III Anonymous Remailer Protocol," in *IEEE Symposium on Security and Privacy*, pp. 2–15, IEEE, 2003.

[113] R. Dingledine, N. Mathewson, and P. Syverson, "Tor: The Second-Generation Onion Router," in *USENIX Security Symposium*, pp. 303–320, USENIX Association, 2004.

[114] M. K. Reiter and A. D. Rubin, "Crowds: Anonymity for Web Transactions," *ACM Transactions on Information and System Security*, vol. 1, pp. 66–92, 1998.

[115] B. N. Levine and C. Shields, "Hordes: A Multicast Based Protocol for Anonymity," *Journal of Computer Security*, vol. 10, pp. 213–240, 2002.

[116] G. Danezis and E. Käsper, "The Dangers of Composing Anonymous Channels," in *IH*, vol. 7692 of *LNCS*, Springer, 2012.

[117] D. Chaum, "The Dining Cryptographers Problem: Unconditional Sender and Recipient Untraceability," *J. Cryptol.*, vol. 1, pp. 65–75, Mar. 1988.

[118] S. J. Murdoch and G. Danezis, "Low-Cost Traffic Analysis of Tor," in *IEEE Symposium on Security and Privacy*, pp. 183–195, IEEE, 2005.

[119] M. K. Wright, M. Adler, B. N. Levine, and C. Shields, "The Predecessor Attack: An Analysis of a Threat to Anonymous Communications Systems," *ACM Transactions on Information System Security*, vol. 7, no. 4, pp. 489–522, 2004.

[120] V. Shmatikov, "Probabilistic Analysis of Anonymity," in *CSFW*, pp. 119–128, IEEE, 2002.

[121] R. Berman, A. Fiat, and A. Ta-Shma, "Provable Unlinkability against Traffic Analysis," in *FC*, vol. 3110 of *LNCS*, pp. 266–280, Springer, 2004.

[122] M. Gomulkiewicz, M. Klonowski, and M. Kutylowski, "Provable Unlinkability against Traffic Analysis Already after $O(\log(n))$ Steps!," in *ISC*, vol. 3225 of *LNCS*, pp. 354–366, Springer, 2004.

[123] Freehaven Project, "Selected Papers in Anonymity." http://www.freehaven.net/anonbib/, 2013.

[124] B. Chor, O. Goldreich, E. Kushilevitz, and M. Sudan, "Private Information Retrieval," in *FOCS*, pp. 41–50, IEEE, 1995.

[125] Y. Chen, V. Paxson, and R. H. Katz, "What's New About Cloud Computing Security?," Tech. Rep. UCB/EECS-2010-5, University of California, Berkeley, 2010.

[126] Y. Gertner, S. Goldwasser, and T. Malkin, "A Random Server Model for Private Information Retrieval or How to Achieve Information Theoretic PIR Avoiding Database Replication," in *RANDOM*, vol. 1518 of *LNCS*, pp. 200–217, Springer, 1998.

[127] C. Aguilar-Melchor and P. Gaborit, "Lattice-Based Computationally-Efficient Private Information Retrieval Protocol," in *WEWoRC 2007*, vol. 4945 of *LNCS*, pp. 183–199, Springer, 2007.

[128] C. A. Melchor and P. Gaborit, "A Fast Private Information Retrieval Protocol," in *ISIT*, pp. 1848–1852, IEEE, 2008.

[129] R. Sion and B. Carbunar, "On the Practicality of Private Information Retrieval," in *NDSS*, 2007.

[130] F. G. Olumofin and I. Goldberg, "Revisiting the Computational Practicality of Private Information Retrieval," in *FC*, vol. 7035 of *LNCS*, pp. 158–172, Springer, 2011.

[131] I. Goldberg, "Improving the Robustness of Private Information Retrieval," in *IEEE Symposium on Security and Privacy*, pp. 131–148, IEEE, 2007.

[132] E. Kushilevitz and R. Ostrovsky, "Replication is NOT Needed: SINGLE Database, Computationally-Private Information Retrieval," in *FOCS*, pp. 364–373, IEEE, 1997.

[133] R. Ostrovsky and W. E. S. III, "A Survey of Single-Database Private Information Retrieval: Techniques and Applications," in *PKC*, vol. 4450 of *LNCS*, pp. 393–411, Springer, 2007.

[134] C. Devet, I. Goldberg, and N. Heninger, "Optimally Robust Private Information Retrieval," in *USENIX Security Symposium*, USENIX Association, 2012.

[135] S. W. Smith and D. Safford, "Practical Server Privacy with Secure Coprocessors," *IBM Systems Journal*, vol. 40, no. 3, pp. 683–695, 2001.

[136] D. Asonov and J. C. Freytag, "Almost Optimal Private Information Retrieval," in *PETS*, vol. 2482 of *LNCS*, pp. 209–223, Springer, 2002.

[137] O. Goldreich and R. Ostrovsky, "Software Protection and Simulation on Oblivious RAMs," *Journal of the ACM*, vol. 43, no. 3, pp. 431–473, 1996.

[138] Y. Yang, X. Ding, R. H. Deng, and F. Bao, "An Efficient PIR Construction Using Trusted Hardware," in *ISC*, vol. 5222 of *LNCS*, pp. 64–79, Springer, 2008.

[139] L. Krzywiecki, M. Kutylowski, H. Misztela, and T. Struminski, "Private Information Retrieval with a Trusted Hardware Unit – Revisited," in *Inscrypt*, vol. 6584 of *LNCS*, pp. 373–386, Springer, 2010.

[140] Y. Gertner, Y. Ishai, E. Kushilevitz, and T. Malkin, "Protecting Data Privacy in Private Information Retrieval Schemes," in *STOC*, pp. 151–160, ACM, 1998.

[141] R. Henry, F. G. Olumofin, and I. Goldberg, "Practical PIR for Electronic Commerce," in *CCS*, pp. 677–690, ACM, 2011.

[142] R. Henry, Y. Huang, and I. Goldberg, "Poster: (Symmetric) PIR over Arbitrary Sized Records," in *IEEE Symposium on Security and Privacy*, 2012.

[143] M. Naor and B. Pinkas, "Efficient Oblivious Transfer Protocols," in *SODA*, pp. 448–457, ACM/SIAM, 2001.

[144] W.-G. Tzeng, "Efficient 1-Out-n Oblivious Transfer Schemes," in *PKC*, vol. 2274 of *LNCS*, pp. 159–171, Springer, 2002.

[145] W. Aiello, Y. Ishai, and O. Reingold, "Priced Oblivious Transfer: How to Sell Digital Goods," in *EUROCRYPT*, vol. 2045 of *LNCS*, pp. 119–135, Springer, 2001.

[146] J. Camenisch, M. Dubovitskaya, and G. Neven, "Oblivious Transfer with Access Control," in *CCS*, pp. 131–140, ACM, 2009.

[147] J. Camenisch, M. Dubovitskaya, and G. Neven, "Unlinkable Priced Oblivious Transfer with Rechargeable Wallets," in *FC*, vol. 6052 of *LNCS*, pp. 66–81, 2010.

[148] J. Camenisch, M. Dubovitskaya, G. Neven, and G. M. Zaverucha, "Oblivious Transfer with Hidden Access Control Policies," in *PKC*, vol. 6571 of *LNCS*, pp. 192–209, Springer, 2011.

[149] D. Boneh, D. Mazières, and R. A. Popa, "Remote Oblivious Storage: Making Oblivious RAM Practical," Tech. Rep. MIT-CSAIL-TR-2011-018, MIT, 2011.

[150] K. E. Batcher, "Sorting Networks and Their Applications," in *AFIPS Spring Joint Computing Conference*, pp. 307–314, 1968.

[151] B. Pinkas and T. Reinman, "Oblivious RAM Revisited," in *CRYPTO*, vol. 6223 of *LNCS*, pp. 502–519, Springer, 2010.

[152] P. Williams, R. Sion, and M. Sotáková, "Practical Oblivious Outsourced Storage," *ACM Trans. Inf. Syst. Secur.*, vol. 14, no. 2, p. 20, 2011.

[153] E. Stefanov, E. Shi, and D. Song, "Towards Practical Oblivious RAM," in *NDSS*, 2012.

[154] E. Stefanovy, M. van Dijk, E. Shi, C. Fletcher, L. Ren, X. Yu, and S. Devadas, "Path O-RAM: An Extremely Simple Oblivious RAM Protocol," *CoRR*, vol. abs/1202.5150, 2012.

[155] E. Stefanov and E. Shi, "ObliviStore: High Performance Oblivious Cloud Storage," in *IEEE Symposium on Security and Privacy*, IEEE, 2013.

[156] M. Franz, P. Williams, B. Carbunar, S. Katzenbeisser, A. Peter, R. Sion, and M. Sotáková, "Oblivious Outsourced Storage with Delegation," in *FC*, vol. 7035 of *LNCS*, pp. 127–140, Springer, 2011.

[157] P. Williams, R. Sion, and A. Tomescu, "PrivateFS: A Parallel Oblivious File System," in *CCS*, pp. 977–988, ACM, 2012.

[158] J. R. Lorch, B. Parno, J. Mickens, M. Raykova, and J. Schiffman, "Toward Practical Private Access to Data Centers via Parallel ORAM," in *USENIX FAST*, 2013.

Chapter 4

Privacy-Enhancing Encryption

4.1 ACCESS CONTROL THROUGH ENCRYPTION

Encryption and access control are often technically separated system components and the latter is typically realized by means of application logic. In this section, we review some recent research directions and results aiming at a combined solution that controls access to encrypted data by restricting decryption capabilities. While conventional encryption is an all-or-nothing operation in the sense of either giving the full plaintext or nothing at all, attribute-based, predicate, and functional encryption realize fine-grained access control directly via the decryption process. Consequently, access control no longer rests on application logic, but is enforced by cryptographic means.

4.1.1 Attribute-Based Encryption

Contents in Brief

What is this? Encryption schemes that allow us to realize fine-grained access control to data directly via the decryption process.

What can it do? Encrypt data not only for a specific person, but allow decryption for anyone carrying a chosen set of attributes satisfying policies defined over attributes.

How can it be used in cloud computing? Supports access policies that prescribe a data processor to have certain attributes, so that the data remains inaccessible unless the provider's or user's role or privileges adhere to the policy.

Attribute-based encryption (ABE) is introduced in [1] as a generalization of identity-based encryption (IBE) [2]. Whereas IBE uses any (user-defined) string as a public key, ABE can use any combination of attributes chosen from a fixed universe as the public encryption key. For cloud storage, plain encryption may severely limit the data owner's ability to selectively grant access to the data. Using an example in [3], suppose a user wishes to grant access to an encrypted log of his or her internet traffic, but is restricted to a particular range of dates and subnet IP addresses. Conventional encryption would inevitably reveal the whole traffic (plaintext) if the secret decryption key is released for that matter. Likewise, suppose a user has medical records stored remotely. Granting access to the most recent medications but keeping irrelevant information secret is another scenario in which conventional encryption would reveal too much. Both examples closely relate to cloud storage, and legal pressure and requirements on related storage and processing services have given rise to the concept of ABE. The idea of ABE is to restrict decryption privileges not to a particular identity but to entities with a defined set of attributes such as biometric features or roles.

More formally, let Ω denote a universe of attributes, possibly strings or any other kind of information, and suppose that an arbitrary user U is characterized by a subset $U \subseteq \Omega$ of attributes. Note that these do not necessarily uniquely define U's identity, since we could for instance use ABE to encrypt some information for all department heads in a company, but prevent their employees from getting the message since they lack the "department leader" attribute. The idea of ABE is to let anyone encrypt a payload under an identity U' such that everyone having at least $d \geq 1$ attributes in common with U' will be able to decrypt. Formally, $U' \subseteq \Omega$ and $|U \cap U'| \geq d$ should be sufficient to decrypt. Here, we review one of the original constructions in [1] due to their simplicity and sufficiency to convey the idea of subsequent generalizations such as [3]. The basics are as follows: we encrypt the payload m by multiplying it with a value g^y so that the exponent y can be reconstructed from at least d values in the recipient's possession (secret-sharing). The decryption will then work by reconstructing the secret y within the exponent (so to hide y throughout the lifetime of the system), and later dividing out the factor g^y to recover the message m. We put this idea to work now but define the general structure of ABE first, which also captures more general constructions than reviewed in the following.

Definition 4.1. Let Ω be a set of entities. An *access structure* $\mathcal{A}$ is a collection of nonempty subsets of P. We call this structure *monotone*, if $A \in \mathcal{A}$ implies $B \in \mathcal{A}$ for all supersets $B \supseteq A$.

Speaking of attributes that are required to decrypt, Ω could be the set of all attributes, and $\mathcal{A}$ tells which attribute combinations are granted the right to decrypt (in case of ABE). Likewise, for secret-sharing, $\mathcal{A}$ would collect all member coalitions that should be able to reconstruct the secret. Monotony then just asserts that having more than the required attributes is not prohibitive. Correspondingly, the complement set $2^\Omega \setminus \mathcal{A}$ is the family of all attribute or player combinations that should *not* be granted access (to the secret or the ciphertext). This is called an *adversary structure*.

The above definition is more general than required to state the exemplary attribute-based encryption below; however, it as well suits more general constructions that are based on the scheme given here. For example, the access policy could be composed from a Boolean expression involving AND/OR combinations of several attributes. We discuss ways to implement such restrictions below. In its simplest form of granting access if at least d attributes are present, the respective access structure is monotone and given by $\mathcal{A} = \{U \subseteq \Omega : |U| \geq d\} \subseteq 2^\Omega$.

Setup: This probabilistic algorithm takes a number n of attributes and an access structure $\mathcal{A}$. It outputs the public and secret master key as well as the public system parameters. The system parameters are an input to all other algorithms and hence not further mentioned explicitly.

KeyGen: This is a randomized algorithm that takes a set of attributes U as input and outputs a secret decryption key for U.

Encrypt: This is a probabilistic algorithm that takes a message and a set of n attributes $U \subseteq \Omega$ as input and outputs a ciphertext.

Decrypt: This algorithm takes a ciphertext as input, along with a set of attributes U and outputs the plaintext if U has the necessary attributes.

We stress that as in identity-based cryptography, a user gets his or her secret key from a trusted authority (*secret key generator*). To avoid this authority knowing all secret keys, multiauthority ABE [4, 5] has been proposed as a remedy. Furthermore, it is important that ABE schemes are *collusion-resistant*. That is, different users should not be able to pool their keys such that a collection of keys from different users satisfy a policy, whereas none of the single users would satisfy the policy on his or her own.

To illustrate the general idea that ABE can be based on, let us give a concrete scheme. In the context of our presentation we assume (as in the original paper) that U defines the set of attributes making up an identity and we require that at least d of the elements in U match during decryption to successfully decrypt a message. Subsequent improvements and more sophisticated schemes can easily be constructed using the general principle sketched now. Let p be a prime so that the discrete logarithm problem in $\mathbb{Z}_p$ is intractable. Moreover, call G a group of prime order p that is generated by some value g. Additionally, let $e : \text{G} \times \text{G} \to \text{G}_T$ be a bilinear pairing, mapping into another group G_T whose order is as well p. Define the Lagrange coefficient $\Delta_{i,S}$ for $i \in \mathbb{Z}_p$ and a set $S \subseteq \mathbb{Z}_p$ in the usual way as

$$\Delta_{i,S}(x) \equiv \prod_{\substack{j \in S \\ j \neq i}} (x - j)(i - j)^{-1} \quad (\text{mod } p)$$

and recall that for a polynomial secret-sharing scheme using a d-degree polynomial $q(x)$, the secret is $q(0)$ and is recovered by a weighted sum of points $q(i)$, with the weights given by the Lagrange coefficient above. An identity is composed from a set of n elements (attributes) in $\Omega = \mathbb{Z}_p$, and will be associated with a random polynomial q with $q(0)$ being the secret master key. For generality, since we aim at using strings for our attributes, let $H : \{0,1\}^* \to \mathbb{Z}_p$ be a collision-resistant hash function mapping into $\mathbb{Z}_p$.

Setup: This takes integers n, d as input, where d is the minimal number of "matching" attributes for decryption, and n counts the number of attributes making up an identity. We compute $g_1 := g^y$ for a randomly chosen $y \in \mathbb{Z}_p$ and let $g_2 \in_R \text{G}$. Next, choose uniformly random elements $t_1, \ldots, t_{n+1} \in \text{G}$ and let $N = \{1, 2, \ldots, n + 1\}$. Define a function T as

$$T(x) = g_2^{(x^n)} \prod_{i=1}^{n+1} t_i^{\Delta_{i,N}(x)} \text{ MOD } p.$$

Observe that $T(x) = g_2^{x^n} g^{h(x)}$ for some polynomial h. The public key is $(g_1, g_2, t_1, \ldots, t_{n+1})$, and the secret master key is y.

KeyGen: To generate a secret decryption key for an identity U, we choose a $d - 1$ degree polynomial q with $q(0) = y$ and random coefficients. The decryption key consists of a set $\{D_i\}_{i \in U}$ and another set $\{d_i\}_{i \in U}$. To construct the ith elements D_i and d_i, choose a random number $r_i \in_R \mathbb{Z}_p$ and compute

$$D_i = g_2^{q(i)} T(i)^{r_i} \text{ MOD } p, \quad \text{and} \quad d_i = g^{r_i} \text{ MOD } p.$$

Encrypt: To encrypt a message $m \in G_T$ under an identity U' (public key), choose a random value $s \in_R \mathbb{Z}_p$, and compute the ciphertext

$$\texttt{Encrypt}(m) = (U', E' = m \cdot e(g_1, g_2)^s, E'' = g^s, \{E_i = T(i)^s\}_{i \in U'}).$$

Decrypt: Given a ciphertext E, any person U with at least d attributes overlapping with U' can recover the plaintext as follows: choose an arbitrary d-element subset $S \subseteq U \cap U'$ and compute

$$m \equiv E' \cdot \prod_{i \in U} \left[\frac{e(d_i, E_i)}{e(D_i, E'')} \right]^{\Delta_{i,S}(0)}$$

$$\equiv m \cdot e(g_1, g_2)^s \cdot \prod_{i \in U} \left[\frac{e(d_i, T(i)^s)}{e(g_2^{q(i)} T(i)^{r_i}, g^s)} \right]^{\Delta_{i,S}(0)}$$

$$\equiv m \cdot e(g_1, g_2)^s \cdot \prod_{i \in U} \left[\frac{e(g^{r_i}, T(i)^s)}{e(g_2^{q(i)}, g^s) \cdot e(T(i)^{r_i}, g^s)} \right]^{\Delta_{i,S}(0)}$$

$$\equiv m \cdot e(g_1, g_2)^s \cdot \prod_{i \in U} \frac{1}{e(g, g_2)^{s q(i) \Delta_{i,S}(0)}} \equiv m \pmod{p},$$

by the properties of bilinear pairings (note that the terms $e(g^{r_i}, T(i)^s)$ and $e(T(i)^{r_i}, g^s)$ are identical and thus cancel out) and the fact that the last product produces the expression $\sum_{i \in U} q(i) \Delta_{i,S}(0) = q(0) = y$, thus effectively resembles the secret-sharing's $\texttt{Reconstruct}$ algorithm in the exponent. Hence, the factor $e(g_1, g_2)^s = e(g^y, g_2)^s = e(g, g_2)^{ys}$ is divided out and m is recovered.

Notice that the size of the public key and thus the size of the ciphertext grow linearly with the number n of attributes that constitute an identity. Consequently, the usability of the scheme is to be reconsidered if the number of attributes becomes large. Its efficiency is dominated by $2d$ evaluations of the pairing, and its security is based on resilience against the following attack.

Attack 4.1 (Fuzzy selective ID). The adversary sets up the cryptosystem with parameters n and d and declares an identity $A \subset \Omega (= \mathbb{Z}_p)$. He or she is then allowed to obtain secret keys from the key generation center for many identities $A_1, A_2, \ldots$ with the constraint that $|A_i \cap A| < d$. Then he or she submits two distinct equal-length plaintexts m_0 and m_1, and the challenger secretly encrypts one of them, say m_b for $b \in_R \{0, 1\}$ under the attacker's identity A. After receiving the ciphertext, the adversary may again ask for more secret decryption keys in the same way as before. The attack succeeds, if he or she can use this knowledge to tell which one of m_0, m_1 has been encrypted, with a nonnegligibly better chance than by a fair coin-flip.

Notice that it would not make sense to allow the adversary to query encryption keys A_i having $|A_i \cap A| \geq d$, since this would render the attack trivial. Moreover, notice that this attack is rather similar to the notion of ciphertext indistinguishability (equivalently semantic security) under chosen plaintexts of conventional encryption.

Fact 4.1. If the decisional bilinear Diffie-Hellman assumption holds, then Attack 4.1 fails with overwhelming probability.

The above fact is in the selective model, where the adversary before seeing the system parameters needs to fix the identity A before being challenged. This model is considered as too weak and only seems suitable as an intermediate step toward proving full security. We refer the interestd reader to [6] for recent results on security of ABE.

Working with General Access Policies

Now, suppose that our access policy is such that decryption should be granted if an (arbitrary) Boolean expression is satisfied by the attributes of the addressee. For example, a person should be of age ≥ 18 years OR [be at least 16 years old AND have a written permission by his or her parents] to access (decrypt) some encrypted data. Access structures encapsulating Boolean formulae of this kind can easily be represented by a tree; see Figure 4.1. A leaf node is associated with an attribute. An inner node x is associated with a polynomial q_x of degree d_x, so that $d_x + 1$ of its children must be "satisfied" in order to reconstruct the secret $q_x(0)$ associated with x. Recursively, the secrets for the inner nodes are then points to reconstruct polynomials associated with higher-level inner nodes in the tree.

Now, to enforce an attribute combination that satisfies the logical structure, let us work our way bottom-up, starting at the leaf nodes. At a leaf node ℓ with parent node x, we check if the attribute associated with ℓ is held by (contained in) the identity U. If so, we compute *one* point $e^{q_x(i)}$ (for some index i that is uniquely associated with the parent node x) on the polynomial q_x associated with the parent x of the leaf ℓ. Here, e is a shorthand for some pairing on the system parameters (for the concrete scheme above, this was $e = e(g_1, g_2)$). Now, distinguish two cases:

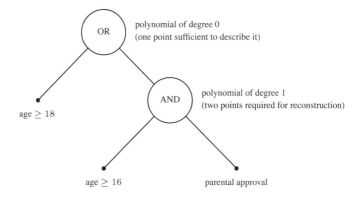

Figure 4.1 Example of a simple access tree.

- If the parent x is an AND node, we must be able to decrypt all its children into points $q_x(i_1), \ldots, q_x(i_{d_x+1})$ so as to get enough points to decrypt one point on the polynomial associated with x's parent node.

- If the parent x is an OR node, then only one child node's decryption suffices to give the sought point on q_x.

- Nodes with thresholds other than 1 (OR) or the full number n of children (AND) can be constructed by choosing the polynomial with the degree $d = t - 1$ whenever the threshold should be t. In the following, we call such nodes (t, n)-*threshold nodes* (OR and AND nodes are obviously included in this class).

In this way, we can continue level by level up until the root of the tree, which has a polynomial associated with it that encodes the secret master key to be divided out of the ciphertext in order to discover the message. Consequently, the decryption algorithm is recursive and applied to the root of the access tree in the first place. The scheme in full detail is given in [3]. Its security is the same as for the scheme above (see Fact 4.1). Figure 4.2 illustrates this using the example tree in Figure 4.1.

Delegating Keys

The generalized construction of [3] (sketched in the previous paragraph) allows users to act as key-generation centers for other users. That is, a user U can modify his or her own secret key to generate a new one for a delegate V that has restricted

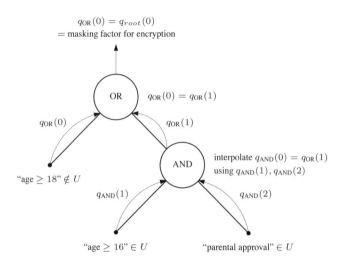

Figure 4.2 Illustration of an example access structure and ABE.

access rights. Such modifications concern altering the access tree toward a more restrictive version of it. In the following, let (t, n) denote a node that has threshold t and n children. The modifications are as follows:

1. Add a trivial $(1, 1)$ threshold node to the tree: this does nothing else than add a new parent above some other node, so no change to the private decryption key is required.

2. Convert existing (t, n)-threshold node x by increasing t to $t+1$ and modifying n into $n-1$ or $n+1$: in either case, we would reassign the chosen polynomial for x from q_x toward increasing the polynomial's degree by 1 (so as to achieve a one larger threshold), and optionally add a new subtree below x in order to increase n. To decrease n, we can simply delete the decryption keys corresponding to the no-longer-existing subtree. A matter of simple calculations shows that the respective decryption keys can be updated by a mere multiplication with appropriate constants derived from the existing tree (see [3] for details).

3. Rerandomization of the keys: in order to make the restricted access tree independent of its origin, all polynomials are rerandomized by adding another randomization polynomial Q to q_x. As with the other modifications, [3] provides direct formulae to update the respective decryption keys.

Fact 4.2. Every access tree T' being more restrictive than the original tree T can be constructed using the above modifications.

The derivation of a decryption key for a restricted version T' of the access structure T is easily accomplished in three steps:

1. Add a trivial $(1, 1)$-threshold node as parent of the root node in T and modify it into a $(2, 2)$-threshold node by increasing the polynomial's degree by one and adding T' as a new child node.

2. Update the decryption keys within the (now subtree) T and derive the decryption keys in T' (details in [3]).

3. Rerandomize all keys.

Since the $(2, 2)$-threshold on top of the new tree is an AND between T and its restricted version T', the derived decryption keys are valid for T' itself.

The plain ABE scheme presented here builds the access policy into the user's identity. Alternatively, ABE can be set up to implement the access policy in the ciphertext (*ciphertext policy attribute based encryption* [7]). This adds further security, since the data can be kept confidential even if the storage server is corrupted. Schemes that assemble user-specific data into the decryption policy in an attempt to prevent this have been proposed in [8]. For further pointers on various constructions of ABE we refer the interested reader to [6] and the references therein.

4.1.2 Predicate Encryption

Contents in Brief

What is this? Encryption schemes whose ciphertexts permit the evaluation of predicates on the hidden plaintext.

What can it do? Encrypt a plaintext so that the message itself remains hidden, but a (set of) predefined predicate(s) can be evaluated to check the hidden plaintext for certain properties (access permissions) prior to a decryption.

How can it be used in cloud computing? Supports access control at a very fine-grained level. That is, the same ciphertext can be given to multiple processing instances, with each of them receiving permission to decrypt and process different parts of the data. The access policy can be specified within the plaintext directly.

Predicate encryption (PE) generalizes attribute-based encryption and identity-based encryption towards allowing plaintext hidden inside some ciphertext to be tested for certain properties. An entity seeking to decrypt the ciphertext would request a decryption key for the predicate f, so that the plaintext m can be recovered if and only if f evaluates to 1 for m. Unlike conventional encryption, the ciphertext thus releases a strictly defined piece of information in the form of the predicate, and decryption can be tied to the validity or absence of certain predicates of the plaintext and the decrypting party (built-in access control). As conventional encryption, predicate encryption is available in two flavors:

Asymmetric: A public key is associated with a predicate f, and the ciphertext encryption process takes the plaintext and some attribute I, so that decryption of a "tagged" ciphertext c_I is possible if and only if $f(I) = 1$.

Symmetric: Here, the encryption processes the plaintext m only, and the requested encryption/decryption key sk_f (specific for the attribute f) will recover m if and only if $f(m) = 1$.

Both variants can themselves be either *predicate-only* or *full-fledged*. The above description refers to a full-fledged implementation, where the decryption is dependent on the predicate. On the contrary, a predicate-only scheme would only allow us to use the ciphertext to evaluate the predicate f on the hidden plaintext but not to learn the plaintext.

The structure and interplay of algorithms and parameters is sketched in Figure 4.3, where the security parameter κ is generally chosen to render the underlying computational infeasibility assumptions reasonable. Those vary between different cryptosystems, and are briefly summarized later.

Giving the full details of recent predicate encryption would go far beyond our scope here, but the basic idea and construction is simple and will be sketched briefly, especially as the constructions of asymmetric and symmetric schemes are very similar. Moreover, we confine ourselves to predicate-only schemes, deferring the general technique to construct a full-fledged scheme to a later paragraph.

Predicates

Predicates are understood as general functions that evaluate on strings into the set $\{0, 1\}$. It has been shown [9] that inner products are a very expressive tool that allow to construct logical expressions or polynomial equations. Formally, let N be a large integer and consider attributes as being vectors in $\mathbb{Z}_N^{\ell}$ for some (fixed) integer ℓ. A

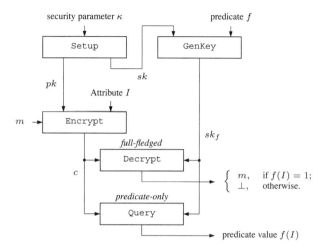

(a) Asymmetric predicate encryption

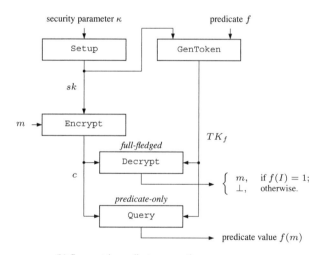

(b) Symmetric predicate encryption

Figure 4.3 General structure of predicate encryption.

predicate is a function from the set $\mathcal{F} = \left\{ f_\mathbf{x} \mid \mathbf{x} \in \mathbb{Z}_N^\ell \right\}$, where

$$f_\mathbf{x}(\mathbf{y}) = 1 \iff \langle \mathbf{x}, \mathbf{y} \rangle = \sum_{i=1}^{N} x_i \cdot y_i \equiv 0 \pmod{N},$$

where x_i, y_i refer to the ith component of $\mathbf{x}$ or $\mathbf{y}$ respectively. Many general predicates can be written as inner products:

Equality tests: Let the predicate be $f(x) = 1 \iff x = J$ for some fixed value $J \in \mathbb{Z}_N$. Then simply set $\mathbf{p} = (1, J)$ and encrypt a plaintext carrying the attribute $I \in \mathbb{Z}_N$ by using a vector $\mathbf{w} = (-I, 1)$. It follows that $\langle \mathbf{p}, \mathbf{w} \rangle = (1, J) \cdot \binom{-I}{1} = -I + J = 0 \iff I = J$. This can be used to construct anonymous IBE from predicate encryption, for example. In anonymous IBE, the identity under which the message has been encrypted is hidden, which would here correspond to the identity I being part of the plaintext, and thus be concealed via the encryption.

Polynomials: Let a polynomial $p(x) = a_0 + a_1 x + a_2 x^2 + \cdots + a_d x^d$ with $a_i \in \mathbb{Z}_N$ be given, so that the predicate f is defined as $f(x) = 1 \iff p(x) = 0$ for $x \in \mathbb{Z}_N$. Using an inner product, we can easily recreate $p(x)$ from an inner product via setting $\mathbf{p} = (a_0, a_1, \ldots, a_d)$ and $\mathbf{w} = (x^0 \text{ MOD } N, x^1 \text{ MOD } n, \ldots, x^d \text{ MOD } N)$, where $x = I$ is the attribute of the plaintext that the encryption incorporates (see Figure 4.3a). Taking the inner product $\langle \mathbf{p}, \mathbf{w} \rangle$ then instantly recovers $p(x)$. Multivariate polynomials are straightforwardly constructed by considering mixed power terms in $\mathbf{w}$ (e.g., $x_1^i x_2^j$ in the bivariate case, where $i + j \leq d$ for all these terms).

Logical OR/AND: Logical disjunctions and conjunctions are easily constructed via polynomials. For example, for $f_{\text{OR}}(x_1, x_2) = 1 \iff [x_1 = I_1 \vee x_2 = I_2]$, the polynomial $p(x) = (x_1 - I_1) \cdot (x_2 - I_2)$ evaluates to zero on I exactly under the sought condition. Similarly, $f_{\text{AND}}(x_1, x_2) = 1 \iff [x_1 = I_1 \wedge x_2 = I_2]$ is modeled by the polynomial $p(x_1, x_2) = r \cdot (x_1 - I_1) + (x_2 - I_2)$ for random $r \in_R \mathbb{Z}_N$. It is easy to see that $[x_1 = I_1 \wedge x_2 = I_2]$ implies $p(x_1, x_2) = 0$, whereas $[x_1 \neq I_1 \vee x_2 \neq I_2]$ with high probability yields $p(x_1, x_2) \neq 0$. There is a slight catch with this construction, since the secret key may leak information about r so that an adversary could possibly construct values x_1, x_2 so that the conjunction fails but still $p(x_1, x_2) = 0$. So, security is occasionally proved in scenarios in which the adversary commits to the test messages x_1, x_2 at the beginning of the attack [9].

Exact thresholds: Recall that attribute-based cryptography allowed decryption if at least t attributes between the identity U' and the legitimate recipient identity U overlap. Inner products allow exact thresholds; that is, $f(U') = 1 \iff |U \cap U'| = t$. Define a vector $\mathbf{p} \in \mathbb{Z}_N^{\ell+1}$ with components $p_i = 1 \iff i \in U$ for $1 \leq i \leq \ell$ and $p_{\ell+1} = 1$. The attribute $\mathbf{w}$ is set with components

$w_i = 1 \iff i \in U'$ for $1 \le i \le \ell$ and $w_{\ell+1} = -t \, \mathrm{MOD} \, N$. It follows that $|U \cap U'| = t$ if and only if $\langle \mathbf{p}, \mathbf{w} \rangle = 0$.

Security Model

The two example schemes [9, 10] cited here are secure under certain indistinguishability assumptions. Since the technical formulation of these is rather cumbersome and of no particular use to understand the concept of predicate encryption, we refer the reader to the given references for details and confine ourselves to stating that the validity of the assumptions in place implies the hardness of factoring the integer N.

Security must be redefined for predicate encryption, since semantic security no longer holds for obvious reasons (the ciphertext at least leaks the information conveyed by the predicate's value). Security in terms of *attribute hiding* is defined as resilience against the following attack:

Attack 4.2. The attacker commits itself to two attributes I_0, I_1 and sets up the system, after which it is allowed to request keys for as (polynomially) many attributes $f_1, f_2, \ldots$ as he or she likes, subject to the restriction that $f_i(I_0) = f_i(I_1)$. The attacker then outputs two equal-length messages m_0, m_1. If keys have been issued for some f_i with $f_i(I_0) = f_i(I_1)$ then $m_0 = m_1$ is prescribed. Next, the attacker is presented with a ciphertext $c = \mathtt{Encrypt}(I_b, m_b)$ for a randomly chosen $b \in \{0, 1\}$. The attack succeeds if, after having requested another set of keys as before, the adversary can successfully tell which message and attribute have been encrypted.

Notice that the seemingly cumbersome condition of $f_i(I_0) = f_i(I_1)$ that may imply $m_0 = m_1$ is only there to prevent an evaluation of both predicates on the ciphertext to uniquely indicate which predicate and plaintext has been chosen.

Definition 4.2. A predicate encryption scheme is called *attribute hiding* (or simply *secure*) if the chance for Attack 4.2 to succeed is negligible.

A different notion is *predicate privacy*, which seeks to hide even the predicate itself from the evaluating entity. For example, if a cloud provider ought to classify emails based on subjects, then the owner may want to hide the classification rules from the cloud provider. These rules are then predicates to be evaluated over encrypted emails to correctly classify (and process) them. Hiding the predicates is, however, difficult in a public key setting. For the email subject classification example, a malicious provider may encrypt an email with a chosen subject and test for the token at hand whether nor not it correctly decrypts the ciphertext, thus gaining information about the underlying predicate by trial and error. This has been one motivation to construct symmetric key predicate encryption schemes, as sketched in Figure 4.3b.

The Basic Construction Idea

Let the plaintext or attribute be represented by a vector $\mathbf{w} \in \mathbb{Z}_N^n$, and let the predicate f be represented by a vector $\mathbf{p} \in \mathbb{Z}_N^n$, so that $f(\mathbf{x}) = 1 \iff \langle \mathbf{x}, \mathbf{p} \rangle \equiv 0 \pmod{N}$. For simplicity, we just sketch the basic construction idea and refer to the literature for the particular details of concrete schemes. Here, we will just look at the common denominator in terms of structure.

The trick is to encode the scalar product evaluation within the exponent, like for a discrete logarithm commitment, and to evaluate the inner product entirely within the exponent. More precisely, let $g, h \in \mathsf{G}$ be generators of some cyclic group G of composite order N, then take the commitment c encapsulating $\mathbf{w} = (w_1, \ldots, w_n) \in \mathbb{Z}_N^n$ to be

$$c = (g^{w_1}, g^{w_2}, \ldots, g^{w_n}). \tag{4.1}$$

Likewise, a decryption key sk_f or a token TK_f to evaluate the predicate $\mathbf{p} = (p_1, \ldots, p_n) \in \mathbb{Z}_N^n$ can be taken as

$$TK_f = (h^{p_1}, h^{p_2}, \ldots, h^{p_n}). \tag{4.2}$$

Now, look what happens if we apply a bilinear pairing $e : \mathsf{G} \times \mathsf{G} \to \mathsf{G}_T$ (where G_T is some target group of order N) to c and TK_f per component, and use the usual rules for bilinear pairings:

$$e(g^{w_1}, h^{p_1}) \cdot e(g^{w_2}, h^{p_2}) \cdots e(g^{w_n}, h^{p_n})$$
$$= e(g, h)^{w_1 p_1 + w_2 p_2 + \cdots + w_n p_n} = e(g, h)^{\langle \mathbf{w}, \mathbf{p} \rangle},$$

where the last term is

$$e(g, h)^{\langle \mathbf{w}, \mathbf{p} \rangle} = 1 \iff \langle \mathbf{w}, \mathbf{p} \rangle = 0. \tag{4.3}$$

The terms g^{w_i}, h^{p_i} hide the plaintext's attributes *and* predicate in the same way as a standard discrete logarithm commitment does. Moreover, the pairing allows us to evaluate the inner product most elegantly completely inside the exponent. While this is already the basic functionality, practical schemes add additional multiplicative factors to guard against simple manipulations:

1. Pairing parts of the ciphertext, decryption key, or token with each other. For example, $e(g^{w_i}, g^{w_j})e(g^{w_k}, g^{w_\ell}) = e(g, g)^{w_i w_k + w_j w_\ell}$ would let us calculate inner products among elements of the plaintext (attribute).

2. Reordering the components or partial evaluations of the predicate.

Both of these issues can be resolved by adding appropriate masking factors to the DL-commitments (4.1) and (4.2), so that pairing parts of the same data element or leaving out certain parts will yield an incorrect result or no result at all. To put this to work, practical schemes [9, 10] take the integer N as a product of at least three primes $N = pqr$, and write G_p, G_q, G_r for the order p, q, r subgroups of the larger group of order N. The masking can be done in the following way:

- For the ciphertext, replace g^{w_i} by $g^{w_i} \cdot Q_i$, where $Q_i \in_R G_q$. Likewise, replace the token element h^{p_i} by $h^{p_i} \cdot R_i$, where $R_i \in_R G_r$. Notice that $g^{w_i} \in G_p$ so the element is from a different subgroup whose order is p and thus coprime to the primes q and r. Pairing parts of the ciphertext (or token) then retains a blinding factor $e(Q_i, Q_j)$,

$$e(g^{w_i} Q_i, g^{w_j} Q_j) = e(g, h)^{w_i w_j} e(Q_i, Q_j),$$

whereas factors from different subgroups will cancel out; that is,

$$e(g^{w_i} Q_i, g^{p_i} R_i) = e(g, h)^{w_i p_i} \underbrace{e(Q_i, R_i)}_{=1} = e(g, h)^{w_i p_i}.$$

- To prevent partial or out-of-order processing of the ciphertext, the same subgroup trick can be used to encode a second check equation in the exponent that evaluates to the identity element if and only if all components are used in order. Technically, a similar trick as with the above masking factors is applied that modifies equation (4.3) into

$$e(g, h)^{(\alpha f_1 + \beta f_2) \cdot \langle \mathbf{w}, \mathbf{p} \rangle},$$

for random values f_1, f_2, α, β that are assembled into the components of the attribute, predicate, and/or ciphertext. The expression $\alpha f_1 + \beta f_2$ is constructed to equate 1 if and only if all components appear in the correct ordering or processing.

Note that the above scheme is predicate-only in the sense that the ciphertext ("attribute commitment") allows only for testing the predicate's validity (what we have sketched here is thus part of the `Query` algorithm in Figure 4.3). To get a full-fledged predicate encryption scheme, we can use the same masking as for plain ElGamal encryption (see Section 4.2.1.2 for full details): basically, the message m is masked as $m \cdot c$, where c is a commitment to a shared secret key. A full-fledged predicate encryption does the same masking, but uses an expression like (4.3) for the masking, so that the decryption is essentially a predicate evaluation, and hence

$$\texttt{Decrypt}(\textit{ciphertext}) \text{ yields } m \cdot e(g,h)^{\langle \mathbf{w}, \mathbf{p} \rangle} = m \iff \langle \mathbf{w}, \mathbf{p} \rangle = 0,$$

whereas the message m otherwise remains hidden behind a random masking $e(g,h)^{\text{some value}}$ if the predicate does not hold true.

4.1.3 Functional Encryption

Contents in Brief

What is this? Encryption schemes that generalize attribute-based and predicate encryption.

What can it do? Evaluation of a priori specified functions on a plaintext, given only the ciphertext and keys as input to the function.

How can it be used in cloud computing? For example in cloud storage, this allows us to search ciphertexts for keywords without decrypting them.

In the way in which predicate encryption generalizes attribute-based encryption, both notions (and others) are subsumed by the more general notion of functional encryption. Informally, one can specify a set of functions F so that given a ciphertext c for some unknown plaintext m, one can evaluate the function $f(m)$ using an algorithm that takes the ciphertext c and a key derived for $f \in F$ as input, but *not* the plaintext. If the function is a predicate, then this boils down to predicate encryption or even attribute-based or identity-based encryption if f is chosen from a restricted family of predicates. More formally, the cryptosystem's key generation algorithm takes a description of the function f and outputs a decryption key sk_f that can be used to evaluate $f(m)$ based on the ciphertext c and sk_f as the sole inputs.

This recent subarea of cryptography is still in its infancy, and presents a variety of interesting theoretical but also practical challenges (see [11]). For conventional public key cryptography, security is normally defined as *semantic security*, which roughly requires that everything that can be computed from the ciphertext can be approximately computed without this information as well, or *ciphertext indistinguishability*, which demands that a ciphertext must not leak any distinguishing properties of a particular plaintext. For functional encryption, one could intuitively go on by rephrasing semantic security as saying that the possible function evaluations do not help to compute anything beyond what could have been computed from the ciphertext alone [12]. Likewise, *ciphertext indistinguishability* can be understood as the adversary's inability to distinguish two distinct plaintexts based only on a given ciphertext and decryption keys requested for it (subject to the constraint that all functions agree on the two candidate plaintexts in order to avoid trivial recognitions of one of them based on a unique pattern of function values). Unfortunately, it turns out that these two notions, known to be equivalent for conventional public key encryption, are no longer equivalent for functional encryption in general [12,13]. Even worse, it can be shown that classical approaches to define and prove security fail under the general setting of functional encryption, and that some proposed security definitions are provably impossible to satisfy [13].

For the sake of completeness, let us give the so-far agreed upon structure of functional encryption, which subsumes the notions presented in foregoing sections. A *functionality* $f : K \times M \to \{0, 1\}^*$ is a deterministic algorithm taking an element k from the keyspace K (including a designated special "empty" key for technical reasons) and a plaintext m from the plaintext space M. Functional encryption is defined by the following algorithms:

Setup: On input of a security parameter, this (probabilistic) algorithm outputs a public key pk and secret (master) key sk.

KeyGen: On input of a description of a functionality f and the secret (master) key sk, this algorithm outputs an *evaluation token* sk_f.

Encrypt: On input of the public key pk and a message m the algorithm outputs a ciphertext c. The algorithm Decrypt inverts this process using the secret key sk.

Evaluate: On input of an evaluation token sk_f and the ciphertext c (for the plaintext m), this algorithm outputs $f(m)$ (with probability 1).

Despite research still being in the process of looking for sound security definitions, we will sketch a simple functional encryption scheme here that is particularly suitable for cloud storage applications. It is known as *searchable encryption* (see Section 5.3), and achieves the following: given encrypted data stored at an untrusted (cloud) provider, a client can query a database of ciphertexts for particular entries without the (cloud) provider learning the queries or the content of matched items. Moreover, this search is equally fast as a conventional database search.

As an example instantiation of the above framework, consider the proposal of [14] for searchable encryption: let $AE = (\texttt{KeyGen}, \texttt{Encrypt}, \texttt{Decrypt})$ be a public key encryption scheme whose setup algorithm $\texttt{KeyGen}$ takes a security parameter κ. We say that AE is a δ-*efficiently searchable encryption* if a function $\delta(\cdot) < 1$ and deterministic algorithms $\texttt{F}, \texttt{G}$ with the following properties exist:

Perfect Consistency: For every κ, every plaintext m and corresponding ciphertext $c = \texttt{Encrypt}(m; pk)$, we have $\texttt{F}(pk, m) = \texttt{G}(pk, c)$ with probability 1. So, if the function $\texttt{F}(m)$ returns either true or false, depending on whether the sought string is found in the plaintext m, we can do this search equivalently by executing $\texttt{G}$ on the respective pieces of ciphertext without having to decrypt.

Computational Soundness: For every κ, any two plaintexts m_0, m_1 and $c_1 = \texttt{Encrypt}(m_1; pk)$, we have

$$\Pr[\texttt{F}(pk, m_0) = \texttt{G}(pk, c_1)] \leq \delta(\kappa),$$

that is, the chance for a false-positive finding is at most δ, where this bound depends on the security parameter.

To fit this into the general structure given before, one may think of $\texttt{F}$ as being the *functionality* provided by the cryptosystem, and $\texttt{G}$ corresponds to the $\texttt{Evaluate}$ algorithm.

We omit presenting the searchable encryption scheme from [14] here for the sake of a more detailed discussion of various improved schemes in Section 5.3.

4.1.4 Summary

Access control via encryption can be done in several ways. We briefly list them in Table 4.1, along with references to various schemes and a short discussion of possible application scenarios.

Note that functional encryption [12, 13, 15] takes an exceptional role here, as it technically unifies all of the above approaches, yet it has no typical example implementation. Like PBE, it creates keys that are not necessarily for decryption (only), but let the key-holder evaluate some function on the inner plaintext (preferably without decrypting the plaintext or releasing any other information about it besides the function's value). Doing a key-word search over encrypted data items (via searchable encryption) is a typical example application from this area.

Table 4.1

Overview of Different Encryption-Based Access Control Techniques

System	Main feature: *decryption is possible if and only if...*	Example Application
Fuzzy IBE [1]	...a certain minimal number of decryption attributes are known.	Error-tolerant decryption (e.g., binding the decryption ability to biometric attributes).
Key-policy attribute-based encryption (ABE) [3]	...a prespecified Boolean expression is satisfied by the user's attributes. The user's decryption keys are computed by the data owner separately for each user and access rights restrictions.	Cloud stores an encrypted file. File owner can allow different users to access different parts of the file by computing individual decryption keys for specific access rights.
Ciphertext-policy ABE [7]	...the person trying to decrypt carries a set of attributes that satisfy a prespecified Boolean condition. Set of admissible users does not need to be known in advance.	Same setting as above. File owner can grant access to the file to any (yet unknown) person with particular attributes.
Predicate encryption (PBE) [9, 10]	...the underlying plaintext carries a set of attributes such that a prespecified predicate is true. If needed, decryption can be prevented even in that case, so that only the predicate value may be obtained.	Same setting as above. File owner releases decryption keys for different attributes. Hence a specific decryption key is only good for ciphertexts encapsulating plaintexts with specific properties.

4.2 COMPUTING ON ENCRYPTED DATA

Until quite recently no satisfactory general usable method as a solution to the problem of processing encrypted data has been available. It is well-known that adding interaction and the use of secure hardware can help to compute on encrypted data [16]. However, it would be desirable to achieve computations on encrypted data without requiring interaction or relying on secure hardware (appended to remote infrastructure). As early as 1978, Rivest et al. [17] introduced the notion of a *privacy homomorphism*, asking the question whether it is possible to perform simple computations on encrypted data. Although all but the RSA example in [17] have been shown to be insecure [18], this is the first known discussion of homomorphic encryption, a concept which we will discuss in more detail subsequently. Later in Section 4.2.4, we will briefly come back to alternative approaches built on interaction.

In the following, we are interested in homomorphic encryption schemes, which are public key encryption schemes for which algebraic manipulations on ciphertexts (addition and multiplication) propagate through the encryption and take effects on the inner plaintext (the encryption function is a homomorphism). Intuitively, this means that a third party who is given two ciphertexts $\mathtt{Encrypt}(m_1; pk)$ and $\mathtt{Encrypt}(m_2; pk)$, being elements of some group $(\mathsf{G}_2, *)$, can compute

$$\mathtt{Encrypt}(m_1 \circ m_2; pk) = \mathtt{Encrypt}(m_1; pk) * \mathtt{Encrypt}(m_2; pk),$$

without the secret key and without gaining knowledge about the plaintexts $m_1, m_2 \in (\mathsf{G}_1, \circ)$ or the result $m_1 \circ m_2$. The concrete operations $\circ, *$, as well as the number of supported operations depend on the choice of the encryption scheme. In the case of only a single operation, we speak of group homomorphic encryption schemes, whereas schemes supporting two operations $(+, \cdot)$ on the plaintexts (respectively $(\oplus, \otimes)$ on the ciphertexts) are called *ring homomorphic* or *fully homomorphic* encryption schemes (the cryptosystem then works on a ring or field). These can compute arbitrary functions on encrypted data. *Somewhat homomorphic* encryption schemes only allow a specific class of functions to be computed on ciphertexts and usually support an arbitrary number of one operation, but only a limited (bounded) number of the second operation. Since addition and multiplication are common operations provided by homomorphic cryptosystems, we will use the operations $+, \cdot$ for operations on the plaintexts and $\oplus, \otimes$ for their counterpart operations on the ciphertext, whenever the ciphertext space is different from the plaintext space.

4.2.1 Group Homomorphic Encryption

Contents in Brief

What is this? Group homomorphic encryption schemes are public key encryption schemes that allow us to compute an operation on ciphertexts being equivalent to some binary operation on the corresponding plaintexts.

What can it do? Compute an operation on plaintexts while only having access to ciphertexts, no knowledge of the secret key, and no knowledge of the resulting plaintext.

How can it be used in cloud computing? When the cloud is given ciphertexts it can compute the corresponding operations on the plaintexts without learning the result and having access to the secret key.

A group homomorphic encryption scheme is an encryption scheme where the encryption function forms a group homomorphism. More formally, if $M \in (\mathsf{M}, \cdot)$ is the set of plaintexts to be encrypted under a public key pk into a ciphertext space $(\mathsf{C}, \otimes)$, it holds that $\forall m_1, m_2 \in \mathsf{M}$:

$$\mathtt{Encrypt}(m_1 \cdot m_2; pk) = \mathtt{Encrypt}(m_1; pk) \otimes \mathtt{Encrypt}(m_2; pk) = c_1 \otimes c_2.$$

Consequently, for any pairs of ciphertexts $c_1 = \mathtt{Encrypt}(m_1; pk)$ and $c_2 = \mathtt{Encrypt}(m_2; pk)$ and secret key sk for the public key pk, we have

$$\mathtt{Decrypt}(c_1 \otimes c_2; sk) = m_1 \cdot m_2.$$

This means that (1) we can repeatedly perform the operation $\otimes$ on ciphertexts always resulting in another valid ciphertext, and (2) if we finally perform a decryption of the final ciphertext, we obtain a plaintext representing the result as if we would have performed all respective $\cdot$ operations on the corresponding plaintexts. Note that, however, doing numerics with this requires some care, as we are computing in finite groups. If we run too many multiplications within a, say modulo group $\mathbb{Z}_n$, then eventually the result will exceed n and hence be reduced MOD n. But since n is typically large (e.g., 10^{350} for 1024-bit RSA) this may not be problematic for most practical applications.

The plaintext operation can be an addition (additively homomorphic encryption) or a multiplication (multiplicatively homomorphic encryption), whereas the corresponding operations on the ciphertexts may be quite different and perhaps complex.

Figure 4.4 illustrates an example scenario where some party A continuously sends values m_i encrypted under party B's public key to some cloud provider, which stores the ciphertext. Then, at some point in time, party B wants to receive the sum of n values hidden in the ciphertext. The cloud computes this sum on the ciphertexts and sends the resulting ciphertexts to party B, which in turn needs a single decryption operation using its secret key and may then for example compute the arithmetic mean of the values.

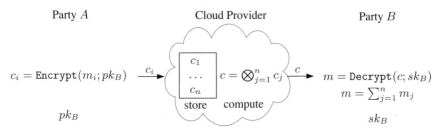

Figure 4.4 Simple computation (adding up ciphertexts) in the cloud.

Subsequently, we examine some public key encryption schemes providing a group homomorphism.

4.2.1.1   RSA Cryptosystem

As our first example, we briefly present the multiplicatively homomorphic property of the well-known RSA encryption scheme. Recall the RSA setting where p and q are two large primes, $n = pq$ the RSA modulus, and e, d two integers satisfying $ed \equiv 1 \pmod{\varphi(n)}$. Let $pk = (n, e)$ be the public key and $sk = (d, n)$ the secret key. Encryption of a message $m \in \mathbb{Z}_n$ amounts to computing the ciphertext $c = m^e \text{ MOD } n$ and decryption of a ciphertext amounts to computing $m = c^d \text{ MOD } n$. Now let us denote the ciphertexts corresponding to messages m_1 and m_2 encrypted under pk as c_1 and c_2 respectively, as

$$\text{Encrypt}(m_1 \cdot m_2; pk) \equiv (m_1 \cdot m_2)^e \equiv m_1^e \cdot m_2^e$$
$$\equiv \text{Encrypt}(m_1; pk) \cdot \text{Encrypt}(m_2; pk) \pmod{n},$$

where $\cdot$ being the multiplication in $\mathbb{Z}_n$. Although this allows us to perform multiplication of messages in the encrypted domain, since the textbook version of the RSA encryption scheme is not IND-CPA secure, it is advisable not to use it in practice. More precisely, the RSA encryption scheme is deterministic and thus allows us to test for the message hidden in a ciphertext by simply encrypting candidate messages under the public key and testing whether the resulting ciphertext matches the target ciphertext. Since in practical applications the set of potential messages will be typically polynomially bounded, this testing becomes entirely practical.

In general, it is not advisable to use homomorphic encryption schemes that are not IND-CPA secure. On the other hand, it is quite obvious and easy to show (although we omit this here) that encryption schemes providing homomorphic properties cannot be IND-CCA2 secure. Fortunately, there are IND-CCA1 secure public key encryption schemes (quasi "in the middle"), like an IND-CCA1 variant of ElGamal encryption [19], which provide homomorphic properties.

4.2.1.2 ElGamal Cryptosystem

The ElGamal public key encryption scheme is a prominent example for a homomorphic encryption scheme used in several applications. Before discussing homomorphic properties we present its IND-CPA secure version [20] (IND-CCA1 secure variants are found in [19], and an IND-CCA2 secure version *without* homomorphic properties is given in [21]).

KeyGen: This probabilistic algorithm takes a security parameter and generates a prime q and computes a safe prime $p = 2q+1$ of a size indicated by the security parameter. It chooses an element $g \in \mathbb{Z}_p^*$ that generates the q order subgroup of $\mathbb{Z}_p^*$, a random element $x \in \mathbb{Z}_q^*$, computes $y = g^x \bmod p$ and outputs $sk = x$ as the secret key, and $pk = (g, p, y)$ as the public key.

Encrypt: This probabilistic algorithm takes a message $m \in \mathbb{Z}_p^*$ and the public key, chooses a random element $k \in \mathbb{Z}_q^*$ (a randomizer), and outputs the ciphertext $(c_1, c_2) = (g^k \bmod p, m \cdot y^k \bmod p)$.

Decrypt: This deterministic algorithm takes a ciphertext (c_1, c_2) and the secret key, and outputs the message $m = c_2 \cdot (c_1^x)^{-1} \bmod p$.

The correctness is readily checked, since

$$c_2 \cdot (c_1^x)^{-1} \equiv m \cdot y^k (g^{xk})^{-1} \equiv m \cdot g^{xk} (g^{xk})^{-1} \equiv m \pmod{p}.$$

When multiple receivers shall receive the same message m, the encryption algorithm can effectively and without security losses reuse its random coins as follows: instead of transmitting n pairs $(g^{k_1}, m \cdot y_1^{k_1}), \ldots, (g^{k_n}, m \cdot y_n^{k_n})$, we can instead multicast $(g^k, m \cdot y_1^k, \ldots, m \cdot y_n^k)$, (re)using the same k for all recipients. This cuts the bandwidth requirements by about 50%. Such *randomness reuse* is fully treated in [22], where conditions are given under which IND-CPA and IND-CCA, security is retained in light of randomness reuse in general encryption schemes (not restricted to ElGamal encryption only), respectively.

Multiplicative Homomorphisms

The ElGamal encryption scheme as presented above provides a multiplicative homomorphism. In particular, the operation $\cdot$ is the multiplication in $\mathbb{Z}_p^*$ and the operation $\otimes$ is defined as the componentwise multiplication of ciphertexts in $\mathbb{Z}_p^*$. To see that this is actually correct, observe that

$$
\begin{aligned}
&\texttt{Encrypt}(m_1; pk) \otimes \texttt{Encrypt}(m_2; pk) \\
&= \;(g^{k_1}, m_1 \cdot y^{k_1}) \otimes (g^{k_2}, m_2 \cdot y^{k_2}) \\
&= \;(g^{k_1} \cdot g^{k_2}, m_1 \cdot m_2 \cdot y^{k_1} \cdot y^{k_2}) \\
&= \;(g^{k_1+k_2}, m_1 \cdot m_2 \cdot y^{k_1+k_2}) = \texttt{Encrypt}(m_1 \cdot m_2; pk).
\end{aligned}
$$

Let $k' = (k_1 + k_2) \operatorname{MOD} q$, then we see that the tuple resulting from componentwise multiplication of the ciphertext components is a valid ciphertext under pk using randomizer k' and indeed represents an encryption of $(m_1 \cdot m_2) \operatorname{MOD} p$.

This line of arguments works for any messages in $\mathbb{Z}_p^*$ and can be performed when dropping the requirement for IND-CPA security. However in order to still provide IND-CPA security, the message space is limited to the subgroup consisting of quadratic residues modulo p, which is by our construction the order q cyclic subgroup of $\mathbb{Z}_p^*$. Unfortunately, this requires encoding messages into elements of this order q subgroup, which destroys a meaningful homomorphic property. The latter fact also holds for standard ElGamal on elliptic curves, since messages are mapped to points and adding points does not yield a meaningful sum when interpreted as a message. Notice also that encoding-free variants of ElGamal [23] (that are popular in the elliptic curve setting) do *not* enjoy homomorphic properties at all. Here, the actual encryption happens by XORing the plaintext m with the hash of a group element.

Nevertheless, using the trick below applied to standard ElGamal on elliptic curves provides additive homomorphic properties for restricted message spaces.

Additive Homomorphisms

By using a restriction on the size of the message space, the ElGamal encryption scheme as defined above can be made additively homomorphic while preserving IND-CPA security. This rests on the following theorem:

Fact 4.3. Any finite cyclic group G of order n is isomorphic to $(\mathbb{Z}_n, +)$. Let g be a generator of G, then the mapping $f_g : \mathbb{Z}_n \to$ G as $f_g(i) = g^i$ is a bijection and $f_g(i) \cdot f_g(j) = f_g((i+j) \operatorname{MOD} n)$.

Looking at our setting from before, we can look at messages to be encrypted no longer as elements of $\mathbb{Z}_p^*$, but can represent them as powers of the generator element g of a prime order q subgroup. Consequently, we work with messages in $(\mathbb{Z}_q, +)$, a subgroup of $\mathbb{Z}_p$, which we discuss subsequently (actually, this would even give us a prime field, but we do only need the multiplicative group thereof). Consequently, the ciphertext corresponding to a message $m \in \mathbb{Z}_q$ will be $(c_1, c_2) = (g^k, g^m \cdot y^k)$. Now taking two ciphertexts for messages m_1 and m_2 one can see that

$$
\begin{aligned}
& \texttt{Encrypt}(g^{m_1}; pk) \otimes \texttt{Encrypt}(g^{m_2}; pk) \\
= \ & (g^{k_1}, g^{m_1} \cdot y^{k_1}) \otimes (g^{k_2}, g^{m_2} \cdot y^{k_2}) \\
= \ & (g^{k_1} \cdot g^{k_2}, g^{m_1} \cdot g^{m_2} \cdot y^{k_1} \cdot y^{k_2}) \\
= \ & (g^{k_1 + k_2}, g^{m_1 + m_2} \cdot y^{k_1 + k_2}) = \texttt{Encrypt}(g^{m_1 + m_2}; pk).
\end{aligned}
$$

However, since we now encrypt messages of the form g^m, in order to obtain m from a decrypted ciphertext, we need to efficiently compute the discrete logarithm $m = \log_g g^m$. This is intractable, unless we shrink the message space to a size that is polynomial in the security parameter so that known algorithms to compute discrete logarithms can be applied. After all, many practical applications work well in a restricted message space (e.g., adding up a few hundred integers).

4.2.1.3 Paillier Cryptosystem and Variants

Another class of encryption schemes with additive homomorphic properties overcomes the limitations discussed before. Starting in chronological order of development, the Goldwasser-Micali cryptosystem [24], allowing additions modulo 2 (XOR), was later generalized into the Benaloh-Fischer [25] as well as Naccache-Stern [26] cryptosystems. Subsequent improvements are the Okamoto-Uchiyama scheme [27], unfortunately being insecure against chosen ciphertext attacks, and the Paillier cryptosystem [28] being discussed now. This last one represents the state-of-the-art of this class of encryption schemes, and the best known scheme providing an additive homomorphic property so far.

All these schemes can be considered as trapdoor discrete logarithm-based schemes that arise from the algebraic setting of (high degree) residuosity classes. In these schemes, the message space is a ring R of modulo residues, and ciphertexts are elements of a group G of invertible elements of some particular ring of integers modulo a number hard to factor. The ciphertext of a message m is always a group element $\texttt{Encrypt}(m; pk) = g^m \cdot r^e$ of group G where e is some public integer,

g some fixed group element being part of the public key pk, and r is chosen at random in some particular subgroup H of the group G. Due to choosing r from some subgroup, these schemes have the additive homomorphic property as we will see soon.

First, and for the sake of simplicity, we look at the Goldwasser-Micali scheme [24] where we have R $= \mathbb{Z}_2$, G $=$ H $= (\mathbb{Z}_n^*, +, \cdot)$ with $n = p \cdot q$ being an RSA modulus, $e = 2$ and g being a pseudosquare modulo n. Here, we have $pk = (g, n)$ and $sk = (p, q)$ the factorization of n. The basic idea is to use the fact that deciding quadratic residuosity is hard without knowledge of the factorization of n, but easy if the factors p and q are known (using the Legendre symbol). To encrypt $m \in \{0, 1\}$, one chooses r at random from $\mathbb{Z}_n^*$ and computes the ciphertext c as $\mathtt{Encrypt}(m; pk) = (g^m \cdot r^2) \, \mathrm{MOD} \, n$. Note that by construction, $r^2 \, \mathrm{MOD} \, n$ is a quadratic residue, and g is by construction a nonresidue. So, the ciphertext c is a quadratic nonresidue, unless $m = 0$ in which case $g^0 \equiv 1 \pmod{n}$ yields $c = r^2$. The additive homomorphic property follows from the fact that given two ciphertexts $c_1 = \mathtt{Encrypt}(m_1; pk) = g^{m_1} \cdot r_1^2 \, \mathrm{MOD} \, n$ and $c_2 = \mathtt{Encrypt}(m_2; pk) = g^{m_2} \cdot r_2^2 \, \mathrm{MOD} \, n$, we have

$$c_1 \cdot c_2 = g^{m_1} \cdot r_1^2 \cdot g^{m_2} \cdot r_2^2 \equiv g^{m_1 + m_2} \cdot (r_1 r_2)^2 \pmod{n}$$

and as above by construction $(r_1 r_2)^2 \, \mathrm{MOD} \, n$ is a quadratic residue. Consequently, decrypting the product $c_1 \cdot c_2$ gives 0 exactly if either $m_1 = m_2 = 0$ or $m_1 = m_2 = 1$, which represents the addition modulo 2, or equivalently, an XOR operation.

The Paillier scheme [28] overcomes the restriction of the message space to be $\mathbb{Z}_2$ (which makes the Goldwasser-Micali scheme impractical), and augments the message space to R $= (\mathbb{Z}_n, +, \cdot)$ where $n = p \cdot q$ is an RSA modulus. Here, the setting is G $= \mathbb{Z}_{n^2}^*$, H $= \mathbb{Z}_n^*$, $e = n$ and g is an element of order divisible by n. In contrast to relying on the quadratic residuosity assumption, this scheme relies on the *decisional composite residuosity assumption*; that is, given $n = p \cdot q$, it is hard to decide whether an element in $\mathbb{Z}_{n^2}^*$ is an nth power of an element in $\mathbb{Z}_{n^2}^*$. In the Paillier scheme, we have $pk = (g, n)$ and the secret key $sk = \mathrm{lcm}(p - 1, q - 1)$. Encrypting a message $m \in \mathbb{Z}_n$ works analogously to the Goldwasser-Micali scheme; that is, $\mathtt{Encrypt}(m; pk) = g^m \cdot r^n \, \mathrm{MOD} \, n^2$, where r is randomly sampled from $\mathbb{Z}_n^*$. The additive homomorphic property follows from the fact that given two ciphertexts $c_1 = \mathtt{Encrypt}(m_1; pk) = g^{m_1} \cdot r_1^n \, \mathrm{MOD} \, n^2$ and $c_2 = \mathtt{Encrypt}(m_2; pk) = g^{m_2} \cdot r_2^n \, \mathrm{MOD} \, n^2$, we have

$$c_1 \cdot c_2 = g^{m_1} \cdot r_1^n \cdot g^{m_2} \cdot r_2^n \equiv g^{m_1 + m_2} \cdot (r_1 r_2)^n \pmod{n^2},$$

which is a valid Paillier ciphertext again. We will not discuss the theory behind Paillier encryption since it requires some theory of nth residuosity classes and related problems and, for this reason we also omit the decryption procedure here.

4.2.2 Somewhat Homomorphic Encryption

Contents in Brief

What is this? Encryption that allows the computation of a certain (limited) class of functions on an encrypted plaintext.

What can it do? Evaluate a function on an unknown plaintext via the ciphertext only and without knowledge of the secret key.

How can it be used in cloud computing? When the cloud is given a ciphertext, it can evaluate a specific class of functions without learning the result and having access to the secret key.

Somewhat homomorphic encryption (SHE) schemes are more sophisticated than pure group homomorphic schemes and allow a specific class of functions to be evaluated on ciphertexts. Usually they support an arbitrary number of one operation but only a limited (bounded) number of the second operation. Before the invention of fully homomorphic encryption schemes, the only (efficient) SHE scheme was the Boneh-Goh-Nissim (BGN) scheme [29]. By then, it was the first construction capable of additions and multiplications, while their scheme is able to handle an arbitrary number of additions but just one multiplication (followed by arbitrary additions). It is based on bilinear pairings, but later on Gentry et al. [30] showed that a similar cryptosystem can also be realized in a different setting.

We note that Sander et al. [31] constructed an SHE scheme that allows us to evaluate circuits corresponding to Boolean functions that are in NC^1, which is the set of functions computable by circuits of fan-in two that have depth $O(\log n)$ for inputs of size n. This restriction is due to the fact that the ciphertext length in their system grows exponentially in the depth of the circuits. Recently, Aguilar-Melchor et al. [32] proposed a scheme that allows us to homomorphically evaluate (multivariate) polynomials on ciphertexts, whereas their scheme has the drawback that the ciphertext grows exponentially in the degree of the polynomial.

We will present the BGN scheme subsequently and postpone a further discussion until the next section. This is due to the fact that fully homomorphic encryption schemes can be obtained from "bootstrappable encryption" schemes, which in turn can be constructed from specific SHE schemes (see Section 4.2.3).

4.2.2.1   The BGN Cryptosystem

Basically, the idea behind the BGN cryptosystem is related to the Paillier encryption scheme sketched in Section 4.2.1.3. However, it works on an elliptic curve group G over F_p of composite order $n = q_1 \cdot q_2$ for primes q_1 and q_2, employing a symmetric pairing $e : G \times G \rightarrow G_T$, whereas G_T is a group of order n. For convenience, we will write the elliptic curve group G multiplicatively. Similar to the tweaked additively homomorphic ElGamal encryption, the BGN cryptosystem also requires the message space M to be polynomially bounded in the security parameter.

KeyGen: On input a security parameter this probabilistic algorithm chooses primes q_1 and p_2, two groups G, G_T of order $n = q_1 \cdot q_2$ and a pairing $e : G \times G \rightarrow G_T$. It chooses $g, u \in_R G$, computes $h = u^{q_2}$ being a generator of the order q_1 subgroup of G, and outputs the public key $pk = (n, G, G_T, e, g, h)$ and the secret key $sk = q_1$.

Encrypt: Given a public key pk and a message $m \in M$, choose $r \in_R \mathbb{Z}_n$, compute, and return the ciphertext

$$c = g^m h^r.$$

Decrypt: Given a secret key $sk = q_1$ and a ciphertext c, compute

$$c^{q_1} = (g^m h^r)^{q_1} = (g^m u^{q_2^r})^{q_1} = (g^{q_1})^m (u^n)^r = (g^{q_1})^m$$

and since the message space is polynomially bounded, compute the message as $m = \log_{g^{q_1}} c^{q_1}$ and output m.

As being somewhat homomorphic, this scheme allows an arbitrary number of additions but just one multiplication (followed any number of additions again). *Additions before the multiplication:* Given two ciphertexts c_1 and c_2 for messages m_1, m_2 and randomizers r_1, r_2, respectively, choose a fresh randomizer $r \in \mathbb{Z}_n$ and compute

$$c_1 \cdot c_2 \cdot h^r = g^{m_1} h^{r_1} \cdot g^{m_2} h^{r_2} \cdot h^r = g^{m_1+m_2} h^{r_1+r_2+r} = g^{m_1+m_2} h^{r'},$$

which is indeed a valid BGN ciphertext for the message $(m_1 + m_2) \text{ MOD } n$, where $r' = (r_1 + r_2 + r') \text{ MOD } n$ is a random integer. We note that the multiplication by h^r may be omitted and it still results in a valid ciphertext. Then, this homomorphic addition operation is deterministic; that is, the new randomizer is $r' = (r_1 + r_2) \text{ MOD } n$.

Multiplication: To homomorphically multiply encrypted messages, we need some additional observations. Let $e(g, g) = g_1$ be a generator of the order n group G_T and let $e(g, h) = h_1$ be another element of G_T. Note that $e(g, h) = e(g, u^{q_2}) = e(g, u)^{q_2} = h'^{q_2} = h_1$. Since G_T is of order $n = q_1 \cdot q_2$, the element h_1 needs to be of order q_1. Additionally, we write $h = g^{aq_2}$ for some $a \in \mathbb{Z}$. Now, let the setting be as above (i.e., we have two ciphertexts c_1 and c_2). Then, choose a random $r \in \mathbb{Z}_n$, and compute $c = e(c_1, c_2) \cdot e(g, h)^r$, which by using bilinearity, is

$$
\begin{aligned}
c = e(c_1, c_2) \cdot e(g, h)^r &= e(g^{m_1} h^{r_1}, g^{m_2} h^{r_2}) \cdot h_1^r \\
&= e(g^{m_1}, g^{m_2} h^{r_2}) \cdot e(h^{r_1}, g^{m_2} h^{r_2}) \cdot h_1^r \\
&= e(g^{m_1}, g^{m_2}) \cdot e(g^{m_1}, h^{r_2}) \cdot e(h^{r_1}, g^{m_2}) \cdot e(h^{r_1}, h^{r_2}) \cdot h_1^r \\
&= g_1^{m_1 m_2} h_1^{m_1 r_2} h_1^{m_2 r_1} h_1^{a q_2 r_1 r_2} h_1^r = g_1^{m_1 m_2} h_1^{m_1 r_2 + m_2 r_1 + q_2 r_1 r_2 + r} \\
&= g_1^{m_1 m_2} h_1^{r'}
\end{aligned}
$$

The element c represents a valid ciphertext for $(m_1 \cdot m_2) \text{ MOD } n$, since $r' = (m_1 r_2 + m_2 r_1 + q_2 r_1 r_2 + r) \text{ MOD } n$ is a random element in $\mathbb{Z}_n$, and decryption still works since h_1 is an element of order q_1 and thus $(h_1^{r'})^{q_1} = (h_1^{q_1})^{r'} = 1 \in \mathsf{G}_T$ when performing decryption. The plaintext is then found by computing the discrete logarithm of c^{q_1} to the base $g_1^{q_1}$ in G_T. Observe that the ciphertext resulting from a homomorphic multiplication is an element of $\mathsf{G}_T \neq \mathsf{G}$, so we are stuck in the target group on which the pairing function no longer works. Consequently, we are limited to a single multiplication.

Addition after Multiplication: Nevertheless, we still can homomorphically add ciphertexts when they are elements in G_T. If we want to obtain ciphertexts in G_T, we can produce a ciphertext by directly producing an encryption of a message m^* in G_T by computing $c^* = g_1^{m^*} h_1^{r^*}$. If we are already given a ciphertext c^* in G, then we can transform this ciphertext into G_T by pairing it with an encryption of 1; that is, computing $\hat{c} = e(c^*, gh^{r'})$ for some random $r' \in \mathbb{Z}_n$. Adding two ciphertexts c_1 and c_2 in G_T simply amounts to choosing a fresh $r \in_R \mathbb{Z}_n$, and computing (in G_T)

$$
c_1 \cdot c_2 \cdot h_1^r = g_1^{m_1} h_1^{r_1} g_1^{m_2} h_1^{r_2} h_1^r = g_1^{m_1 + m_2} h_1^{r_1 + r_2 + r} = g_1^{m_1 + m_2} h_1^{r'},
$$

which is a valid ciphertext for $(m_1 + m_2) \, \text{MOD} \, n$ and $r' = (r_1 + r_2 + r) \, \text{MOD} \, n$ is a random integer. As with the addition in G the multiplication with h_1^r can be omitted, but the operation is then deterministic.

4.2.3 Fully Homomorphic Encryption

Contents in Brief

What is this? Encryption that allows us to compute arbitrary functions on an encrypted plaintext.

What can it do? Evaluate any function on a ciphertext by only having access to a ciphertext without knowledge of the secret key.

How can it be used in cloud computing? When the cloud is given encrypted data it can evaluate any function without learning the result and having access to the secret key.

Fully homomorphic encryption (FHE) schemes are the most sophisticated class of homomorphic encryption schemes and allow arbitrary functions to be evaluated on ciphertexts. It had been an open question until 2009 whether such schemes exist, but Gentry [33–35] provided the first construction along with a general blueprint to construct such schemes from less powerful schemes. Since then, research in FHE can be considered as one of the main research topics in modern cryptography and lots of improvements and approaches from alternate assumptions have been proposed [36–43]. Vaikuntanathan provides an interesting survey of recent advances in FHE [44].

Before we go into more details, we present an abstract discussion. A homomorphic (public key) encryption scheme is defined by the following efficient algorithms.

KeyGen: This probabilistic algorithm takes a security parameter and produces and outputs a public key pk, a public evaluation key evk, and a secret key sk.

Encrypt: This probabilistic algorithm takes a message $m \in \{0, 1\}$ and a public key pk and outputs a ciphertext $c = \text{Encrypt}(m; pk)$.

Decrypt: This deterministic algorithm takes a ciphertext c and a secret key sk and outputs $m = \text{Decrypt}(c; sk)$.

Eval: This algorithm takes an evaluation key evk, a function $f : \{0,1\}^k \to \{0,1\}$ and k ciphertexts and outputs a ciphertext $c_f = \texttt{Eval}(f, c_1, \ldots, c_k; evk)$.

Above, messages are defined to be bits, as it is common in the context of FHE, but this can be generalized to larger message spaces. Furthermore, IND-CPA security for FHE schemes is defined analogously to public key encryption schemes, whereas here the adversary has additionally access to the public evaluation key.

Let $\mathcal{C} : \{0,1\}^{\ell(\cdot)} \mapsto \{0,1\}$ be a class of functions for some polynomial function ℓ (typically in the security parameter κ of the encryption scheme). A homomorphic encryption scheme as defined above is *somewhat homomorphic with respect to $\mathcal{C}$* (or *$\mathcal{C}$-homomorphic*) if the probability that

$$\texttt{Decrypt}(\texttt{Eval}(f, \texttt{Encrypt}(m_1; pk), \ldots, \texttt{Encrypt}(m_k; pk); evk); sk)$$
$$\neq f(m_1, \ldots, m_k)$$

is negligible for all honestly generated keys (sk, pk, evk). Consequently, for all functions in $\mathcal{C}$ (related to the respective security parameter), we want a homomorphic evaluation followed be a decryption to provide the same result (with overwhelming probability) as if we would have evaluated f on the plaintext. In order to exclude classes of uninteresting functions (like trivial disclosures by evaluating the identity function, giving back the plaintext), FHE schemes need to be *compact*. This means that the output length of the homomorphic evaluation algorithm is bounded by some polynomial (in the security parameter); that is, neither depends on the number of inputs to f nor the function f itself.

Definition 4.3 (Fully homomorphic encryption scheme). A homomorphic encryption scheme $(\texttt{KeyGen}, \texttt{Encrypt}, \texttt{Eval}, \texttt{Decrypt})$ is called *fully homomorphic* if it is compact and homomorphic with respect to the class of functions representing all arithmetic circuits over F_2.

Basically, this means that the scheme is capable of computing addition as well as multiplication modulo 2; that is, any operation in the field F_2 and thus evaluating any function over the ciphertext, which is represented as an arithmetic circuit (gate by gate). One can make an additional restriction related to SHE by limiting the depth of the arithmetic circuits to a value L. Then, $\texttt{KeyGen}$ is given the additional parameter L (typically influencing only the key evk) and the resulting scheme is capable of homomorphically evaluating any binary arithmetic circuit of at most depth L, where the compactness definition remains independent of L. Such schemes are denoted as *leveled FHE* schemes. Below, we present other important features:

i hop/multihop: FHE schemes do not explicitly require that ciphertexts resulting from an execution of $\texttt{Eval}$ are structurally identical to those resulting from

Encrypt. Consequently, it is not guaranteed that those ciphertexts are legal inputs for another instance of the Eval algorithm. In [45], Gentry et al. therefore introduce the notion of i hop or multihop FHE. The former means that Eval can be called on its own output up to i times while still being able to decrypt the result. If this works for any such i, then the FHE scheme is called multihop. The authors in [45] discuss a bootstrapping technique that can be used to convert any FHE scheme into an i hop scheme for any i.

Circuit privacy: In the FHE setting so far, the input to f is hidden within the ciphertext(s) from the party running the Eval algorithm. However, it is not clear whether the input f to the Eval algorithm is also hidden from the party performing the decryption. *Circuit privacy* demands that f remains secret and will not be learned by the decrypting party.

4.2.3.1   Gentry's Blueprint

Along with the first construction of an FHE scheme, Gentry also provided a blueprint to construct FHE schemes. The idea is as follows:

- Take an SHE scheme that is capable of evaluating ℓ-variate polynomials homomorphically. Thereby, ℓ is a parameter that is typically a polynomial in the security parameter of the encryption scheme and the monomials have bounded degree.

- To obtain FHE by Gentry's *bootstrapping theorem*, when given an SHE scheme that can evaluate its own decryption function plus an additional operation, one can transform it into a *leveled FHE* scheme. Such an SHE scheme is called a *bootstrappable encryption scheme*.

- Unfortunately, the SHE schemes available to Gentry when coming up with this blueprint were incapable of evaluating their own decryption function and thus were not bootstrappable. However, Gentry introduced a way to *squash the decryption circuit* (i.e., to transform the scheme into one with the same homomorphic capacity, but a decryption circuit that is simple enough to allow bootstrapping).

- Furthermore, if it is secure to encrypt the secret key of the bootstrappable encryption scheme under it's own public key, a notion known as *circular security*, then Gentry's transformation yields an FHE scheme.

4.2.3.2 A Simple Scheme from Secret Key FHE

Now we sketch the construction of an FHE scheme from [40] whose security is based on the LWE assumption (see Section 2.4.4). We only discuss a symmetric version of the FHE scheme here since Rothblum has shown [46] that any such scheme can be turned into a public key FHE scheme using his generic compiler. Furthermore, we restrict ourselves to a high-level (semiformal) description to capture the intuition of the scheme. We start with the SHE scheme and then sketch how to create an FHE scheme.

Encrypt: Let q be a prime and n be an integer. The secret key in the scheme is a vector $s \in \mathbb{Z}_q^n$, and to encrypt a message $m \in \{0, 1\}$, one chooses a random vector $\mathbf{a} \in \mathbb{Z}_q^n$ and a *noise* e and computes the ciphertext c as

$$c = (\mathbf{a}, b) \in \mathbb{Z}_q^n \times \mathbb{Z}_q, \quad \text{where} \quad b = \langle \mathbf{a}, s \rangle + 2e + m$$

with $\langle \mathbf{a}, s \rangle$ being the inner product of $\mathbf{a}$ and s modulo q.

Decrypt: The important observation for a working decryption is that the mask $\langle \mathbf{a}, s \rangle$ and the even mask $2e$ do not interfere with each other. Consequently, one can decrypt this ciphertext by removing the two masks one after the other. The decryption algorithm recomputes the mask $\langle \mathbf{a}, s \rangle$ and subtracts it from b, resulting in $(2e + m) \bmod q$. Since $e \ll q$, we have that $(2e + m) \bmod q = 2e + m$. Removing the second mask and recovering the message m now simply amounts to reducing the last result modulo 2.

In order to make the discussion of the homomorphic properties more compact, it is convenient to introduce a function $f_{\mathbf{a},b} : \mathbb{Z}_q^n \mapsto \mathbb{Z}_q$ defined as

$$f_{\mathbf{a},b}(\mathbf{x}) = b - \langle \mathbf{a}, \mathbf{x} \rangle$$

where $\mathbf{x}$ is a vector of variables. Decrypting a ciphertext $c = (\mathbf{a}, b)$ thus amounts to computing $m = f_{\mathbf{a},b}(c) \bmod 2$.

Addition: Given two ciphertexts $c = (\mathbf{a}, b)$ and $c' = (\mathbf{a}', b')$, the addition of ciphertexts corresponds to the addition of two linear functions, which is again a linear function. In particular, $f_{\mathbf{a}+\mathbf{a}',b+b'}(\mathbf{x}) = f_{\mathbf{a},b}(\mathbf{x}) + f_{\mathbf{a}',b'}(\mathbf{x})$ is the linear function corresponding to the ciphertext $c'' = (\mathbf{a} + \mathbf{a}', b + b')$. Note that the second component of c'' is equal to

$$\langle \mathbf{a}, s \rangle + 2e + m + \langle \mathbf{a}', s \rangle + 2e' + m' = \langle \mathbf{a} + \mathbf{a}', s \rangle + 2(e + e') + (m + m')$$

where the noise is twice as large as within a single ciphertext and decryption works as above.

Multiplication: As above, given two ciphertexts $c = (\mathbf{a}, b)$ and $c' = (\mathbf{a}', b')$, the multiplication can be described by means of the corresponding linear functions; that is, by computing $f_{\mathbf{a},b}(\mathbf{x}) \cdot f_{\mathbf{a}',b'}(\mathbf{x})$. However, observe that this results in

$$f_{\mathbf{a},b}(\mathbf{x}) \cdot f_{\mathbf{a}',b'}(\mathbf{x}) = \left(b - \sum_{i=1}^{n} a_i \cdot x_i \right) \cdot \left(b' - \sum_{i=1}^{n} a'_i \cdot x_i \right)$$

and when multiplying those terms, this results in a degree-2 polynomial in the variables in $\mathbf{x}$, which we can write as the product of the linear functions by sorting out linear and quadratic terms with (new) coefficients h_i for terms linear in x_i and h_{ij} for quadratic terms $x_i x_j$,

$$h_0 + \sum_{i=1}^{n} h_i \cdot x_i + \sum_{i,j=1}^{n} h_{ij} \cdot x_i \cdot x_j. \qquad (4.4)$$

Decryption requires evaluating this quadratic expression on the secret key s and then reducing modulo 2. However, there is a problem, since the decryption algorithm would have to know all the coefficients of this quadratic polynomial and thus the size of the ciphertext increases from $n + 1$ elements to (roughly) $n^2/2$. In order to fix this, [40] introduce a *relinearization* technique to reduce the ciphertext size back to $n + 1$ elements. Basically, the idea is to publish encryptions of all the linear and quadratic terms in the secret key s (i.e., all the entries s_i as well as $s_i \cdot s_j$, under a new secret key t). Those encryptions $b_{i,j}$ for all the quadratic terms, when ignoring the error terms are approximately $b_{i,j} = \langle a_{ij}, \mathbf{t} \rangle + s_i \cdot s_j$, and we can rewrite (4.4) as

$$h_0 + \sum_{i=1}^{n} h_i(b_i - \langle \mathbf{a}_i, \mathbf{t} \rangle) + \sum_{i,j} h_{i,j}(b_{i,j} - \langle \mathbf{a}_{i,j}, \mathbf{t} \rangle)$$

which is again a linear function, but in t. Consequently, multiplication and relinearization results in a linear function (again with $n + 1$ coefficients), whose evaluation on the new secret key t results in the product of the two original messages when reduced modulo 2.

The description is somewhat incomplete, since one has to take care that the h coefficients do not become too large. We refer the reader to [40] for details on how to handle this problem. Essentially, this is achieved by increasing the number of pairs $(\mathbf{a}_{i,j}, b_{i,j})$ by a logarithmic factor in q.

Due to this process required for homomorphic multiplication, the error term increases by a factor of $\mathcal{O}(n^3)$, which makes the scheme only somewhat homomorphic. By a suitable choice of the parameters, however, one can enable evaluation of depth L circuits and then one can use Gentry's bootstrapping technique to turn the scheme into an FHE scheme.

4.2.3.3 Implementations

At present, FHE is still considered as being impractical. However, since the introduction of the first FHE scheme of Gentry [34], there has been much progress in finding alternative and more efficient realizations of FHE schemes.

A first working implementation of Gentry's scheme [47] should, however, not be taken as a benchmark for state-of-the-art schemes. Quite recently, Gentry et al. [48] provided a full implementation of a much more recent FHE scheme (a modified version of the LWE-based scheme presented above) that allows us to evaluate the AES block cipher with time required per block of roughly 40 minutes on a machine with 24 cores of Intel Xeon CPUs running at 2.0 GHz with 18 MB cache and 256 GB of RAM. Besides implementations of FHE, Naehrig et al. [49] recently argued that for many practical purposes it is sufficient to rely on "sufficiently powerful" SHE schemes that allow evaluation of common functions like arithmetic mean, standard deviation, or logistic regression.

4.2.4 Alternative Approaches

A perhaps cheap and easy-to-implement alternative to FHE is offered by relying on interaction and trusted server-side hardware. The former field comprises secure two-party as well as multiparty computation and is a well-established field with lots of results. The latter field (initiated by Goldreich and Ostrovsky [50]) on secure hardware is also quite well-established and has been touched on in Section 3.4.3. We refer the reader to [16] for a more comprehensive discussion on the use of secure hardware. However, we generally note that relying on secure hardware in the field of cloud computing clearly limits the power of outsourcing computations due to the required availability of this hardware and since this trusted hardware is typically very resource constrained.

We will only briefly discuss Yao's garbled circuits [51] to realize secure two-party computation here, since this approach has recently attracted attention in the cloud computing field. At the end of this section, we provide some pointers to literature.

Yao's Garbled Circuits

The concept of garbled circuits (GCs) was introduced by Yao in [51] as a means to realize secure computation of arbitrary functions (more precisely, he focused on secure two-party computation). While this was considered as a purely theoretical approach for a long time, various optimizations have made the concept practical [52]. The setting is that we are given a function f and two inputs x_1 and x_2, and want to obtain the output $y = f(x_1, x_2)$. Typically, input x_1 is provided by one party and input x_2 by another party (only knowing their parts of the input), and the result y should be jointly computed without a participating party learning anything about the other input. Now, one can ask how this can be used in the cloud setting. Basically, assume the client knows the entire inputs x_1 and x_2 (more generally, n inputs) and provides them encrypted along with some "garbled" version of f to the cloud. The cloud then evaluates the unknown function, the output of the client is nothing, whereas the output of the cloud contains the encrypted output of f, which is then sent back to the client.

Basically, the function f to be computed is represented as a Boolean circuit C and the client (the garbled circuit generator) generates an encrypted version of C including the inputs, whereas this is called a garbled circuit C'. The cloud (the garbled circuit evaluator) then obliviously computes the output of the circuit without learning either any intermediate values or the output itself. More precisely, the user takes each input wire w_i of C and assigns two randomly chosen symmetric keys w_i^0 and w_i^1 that correspond to the respective values 0 and 1. Note that w_i^0 and w_i^1 do not reveal any information about the plain values as both keys look random. Then, for each binary gate $g : \{0,1\} \times \{0,1\} \to \{0,1\}$ (e.g., an AND) of C with input wires i and j and output wire k, the generator creates helper information in the form of a garbled table entry. This information is four ciphertexts of the form $\text{Encrypt}(w_k^{g(b_i, b_j)}; w_i^{b_i} \| w_j^{b_j})$ for all choice of $b_i, b_j \in \{0,1\}$ and is stored in a random order. For all gates, this helper information together forms the garbled circuit C'. The evaluator must then obtain the appropriate keys for the input wires that allow him or her to decrypt only the output key from the gate's input keys revealing nothing about the actual value(s) of the gate(s). The garbled gates are evaluated one-by-one by the evaluator using the entries in the garbled table. Consequently, the evaluator obtains finally the corresponding garbled output values which he or she sends back to the generator. This allows the generators to decrypt output values into the corresponding plain output value y representing the evaluation of the function f on the secret input. Note that without knowledge of the random permutation applied to the entries in the garbled circuit the evaluator learns nothing about the corresponding values.

At present, [53] seems to offer the most efficient application of GCs up to now, employing all known optimizations that were proposed since Yao's initial publication. For instance, they realize AES encryption of a single 128-bit block with respect to a 128-bit key such that solely the cloud knows the secret key and solely the user knows the input in about 0.2 seconds without and 0.06 seconds with precomputation. In contrast to the results from [52], which requires about 3 seconds per message block for AES evaluation via GCs, [53] identifies the minimal subset of the computation that needs to be performed in a privacy-preserving manner, and only uses garbled circuits for that portion of the computation, which results in this enormous speedup.

A severe drawback of garbled circuits is that they need to be built by the client and have to be rebuilt for different inputs to the function f. By using FHE as a black box, Gennaro et al. [54], however, show how garbled circuits can be safely reused for different inputs. Furthermore, they show how to realize verifiably outsourcing computation based on GCs (i.e., users can check whether the computation in the encrypted domain has been performed correctly without reexecuting the entire computation by themselves). As another solution to eliminate this bottleneck, Bugiel et al. [55] recently proposed the so-called *twin clouds* approach that combines cheap trusted clouds, as for example private clouds, and public untrusted clouds, to achieve better performance in practice. A similar idea employing additional secure hardware denoted as *token-based cloud computing* has also recently been proposed by Sadeghi et al. [56]. We refer the interested reader to these two aforementioned works since they also investigate alternative approaches (combinations of secure hardware, FHE, and GCs) to efficiently realize arbitrary computation while achieving confidentiality, integrity, and verifiability.

4.2.5 Summary

Homomorphic encryption is currently receiving much research attention, and many refinements to the basic schemes presented here are being developed. To briefly summarize the possibilities of homomorphic encryption as a decision support for an implementation, Table 4.2 may be helpful. Notice that homomorphic encryption is by definition malleable. Restricting the manipulations to the ciphertext is an issue that requires measures beyond what the cryptosystem can do alone. Nevertheless, recent results in the context of FHE show that one can achieve *targeted malleability* [57] (i.e., to restrict the homomorphic computations can be performed on encrypted data). Furthermore, it must be emphasized that homomorphy is a theoretical achievement that merely lets us *arithmetically* add and multiply plaintexts encapsulated inside a ciphertext. In theory, this allows the execution of any algorithm complex manipulations like text replacements or similar, but putting this to practice requires the design (compilation) of a specific circuit representation for the algorithm at hand. This may be a nontrivial task.

Table 4.2

Homomorphic Encryption: Overview

Type	Example System	Plaintext operations	
		Additions	**Multiplications**
Homomorphic [20, 24, 58] [26, 28]	Unpadded RSA, ElGamal	None	Unlimited
	Paillier, ElGamal (variant)	Unlimited	None
Somewhat homomorphic [29]	BGN	Unlimited	Limited (to 1 for BGN)
Fully homomorphic [36–43]	Gentry [33–35]	Unlimited	Unlimited

References

[1] A. Sahai and B. Waters, "Fuzzy Identity-Based Encryption," in *EUROCRYPT*, vol. 3494 of *LNCS*, pp. 457–473, Springer, 2005.

[2] L. Martin, *Introduction to Identity-Based Encryption*. Artech House, 2008.

[3] V. Goyal, O. Pandey, A. Sahai, and B. Waters, "Attribute-Based Encryption for Fine-Grained Access Control of Encrypted Data," in *CCS*, pp. 89–98, ACM, 2006.

[4] M. Chase and S. S. M. Chow, "Improving Privacy and Security in Multi-Authority Attribute-Based Encryption," in *CCS*, pp. 121–130, ACM, 2009.

[5] A. B. Lewko and B. Waters, "Decentralizing Attribute-Based Encryption," in *EUROCRYPT*, vol. 6632 of *LNCS*, pp. 568–588, Springer, 2011.

[6] A. B. Lewko and B. Waters, "New Proof Methods for Attribute-Based Encryption: Achieving Full Security through Selective Techniques," in *CRYPTO*, vol. 7417 of *LNCS*, pp. 180–198, Springer, 2012.

[7] J. Bethencourt, A. Sahai, and B. Waters, "Ciphertext-Policy Attribute-Based Encryption," in *IEEE Symposium on Security and Privacy*, pp. 321–334, IEEE, 2007.

[8] J. Li, K. Ren, B. Zhu, and Z. Wan, "Privacy-Aware Attribute-Based Encryption with User Accountability," in *ISC*, vol. 5735 of *LNCS*, pp. 347–362, Springer, 2009.

[9] J. Katz, A. Sahai, and B. Waters, "Predicate Encryption Supporting Disjunctions, Polynomial Equations, and Inner Products," in *EUROCRYPT*, vol. 4965 of *LNCS*, pp. 146–162, Springer, 2008.

[10] E. Shen, E. Shi, and B. Waters, "Predicate Privacy in Encryption Systems," in *TCC*, vol. 5444 of *LNCS*, pp. 457–473, Springer, 2009.

[11] B. Waters, "Functional Encryption: Origins and Recent Developments," in *PKC*, vol. 7778 of *LNCS*, pp. 51–54, Springer, 2013.

[12] A. O'Neill, "Definitional Issues in Functional Encryption." Cryptology ePrint Archive, Report 2010/556, 2010.

[13] D. Boneh, A. Sahai, and B. Waters, "Functional Encryption: Definitions and Challenges," in *TCC*, vol. 6597 of *LNCS*, pp. 253–273, Springer, 2011.

[14] M. Bellare, A. Boldyreva, and A. O'Neill, "Deterministic and Efficiently Searchable Encryption," in *CRYPTO*, vol. 4622 of *LNCS*, pp. 535–552, Springer, 2007.

[15] A. Sahai and H. Seyalioglu, "Worry-Free Encryption: Functional Encryption with Public-Keys," in *CCS*, pp. 463–472, ACM, 2010.

[16] A. Sahai, "Computing on Encrypted Data," in *ICISS*, vol. 5352 of *LNCS*, pp. 148–153, Springer, 2008.

[17] R. Rivest, L. Adleman, and M. Dertouzos, "On Data Banks and Privacy Homomorphisms," in *Foundations of Secure Computation*, 1978.

[18] E. F. Brickell and Y. Yacobi, "On Privacy Homomorphisms (Extended Abstract)," in *EUROCRYPT*, vol. 304 of *LNCS*, pp. 117–125, Springer, 1987.

[19] H. Lipmaa, "On the CCA1-Security of Elgamal and Damgård's Elgamal," in *ISC*, vol. 6584 of *LNCS*, pp. 18–35, Springer, 2010.

[20] Y. Tsiounis and M. Yung, "On the Security of ElGamal Based Encryption," in *PKC*, vol. 1431 of *LNCS*, pp. 117–134, Springer, 1998.

[21] R. Cramer and V. Shoup, "A Practical Public-key Cryptosystem Provably Secure Against Adaptive Chosen Ciphertext Attack," in *CRYPTO*, vol. 1462 of *LNCS*, pp. 13–25, Springer, 1998.

[22] M. Bellare, A. Boldyreva, and J. Staddon, "Randomness Re-use in Multi-recipient Encryption Schemes," in *PKC*, vol. 2567 of *LNCS*, pp. 85–99, Springer, 2003.

[23] B. Chevallier-Mames, P. Paillier, and D. Pointcheval, "Encoding-Free ElGamal Encryption without Random Oracles," in *PKC*, vol. 3958 of *LNCS*, pp. 91–104, Springer, 2006.

[24] S. Goldwasser and S. Micali, "Probabilistic Encryption," *J. Comput. Syst. Sci.*, vol. 28, no. 2, pp. 270–299, 1984.

[25] J. D. Cohen and M. J. Fischer, "A Robust and Verifiable Cryptographically Secure Election Scheme (Extended Abstract)," in *FOCS*, pp. 372–382, IEEE, 1985.

[26] D. Naccache and J. Stern, "A New Public-Key Cryptosystem Based on Higher Residues," in *CCS*, pp. 59–66, ACM, 1998.

[27] T. Okamoto and S. Uchiyama, "A New Public-Key Cryptosystem as Secure as Factoring," in *EUROCRYPT*, vol. 1403 of *LNCS*, pp. 308–318, Springer, 1998.

[28] P. Paillier, "Public-Key Cryptosystems Based on Composite Degree Residuosity Classes," in *EUROCRYPT*, vol. 1592 of *LNCS*, pp. 223–238, Springer, 1999.

[29] D. Boneh, E.-J. Goh, and K. Nissim, "Evaluating 2-DNF Formulas on Ciphertexts," in *TCC*, vol. 3378 of *LNCS*, pp. 325–341, Springer, 2005.

[30] C. Gentry, S. Halevi, and V. Vaikuntanathan, "A Simple BGN-Type Cryptosystem from LWE," in *EUROCRYPT*, vol. 6110 of *LNCS*, pp. 506–522, Springer, 2010.

[31] T. Sander, A. L. Young, and M. Yung, "Non-Interactive CryptoComputing For NC^1," in *FOCS*, pp. 554–567, IEEE, 1999.

[32] C. A. Melchor, P. Gaborit, and J. Herranz, "Additively Homomorphic Encryption with d-Operand Multiplications," in *CRYPTO*, vol. 6223 of *LNCS*, pp. 138–154, Springer, 2010.

[33] C. Gentry, *A Fully Homomorphic Encryption Scheme*. PhD thesis, Stanford University, 2009.

[34] C. Gentry, "Fully Homomorphic Encryption Using Ideal Lattices," in *STOC*, pp. 169–178, ACM, 2009.

[35] C. Gentry, "Toward Basing Fully Homomorphic Encryption on Worst-Case Hardness," in *CRYPTO*, vol. 6223 of *LNCS*, pp. 116–137, Springer, 2010.

[36] M. van Dijk, C. Gentry, S. Halevi, and V. Vaikuntanathan, "Fully Homomorphic Encryption Over the Integers," in *EUROCRYPT*, vol. 6110 of *LNCS*, pp. 24–43, Springer, 2010.

[37] D. Stehlé and R. Steinfeld, "Faster Fully Homomorphic Encryption," in *ASIACRYPT*, vol. 6477 of *LNCS*, pp. 377–394, Springer, 2010.

[38] N. P. Smart and F. Vercauteren, "Fully Homomorphic Encryption with Relatively Small Key and Ciphertext Sizes," in *PKC*, vol. 6056 of *LNCS*, pp. 420–443, Springer, 2010.

[39] Z. Brakerski and V. Vaikuntanathan, "Fully Homomorphic Encryption from Ring-LWE and Security for Key Dependent Messages," in *CRYPTO*, vol. 6841 of *LNCS*, pp. 505–524, 2011.

[40] Z. Brakerski and V. Vaikuntanathan, "Efficient Fully Homomorphic Encryption from (Standard) LWE," in *FOCS 2011*, pp. 97–106, IEEE, 2011.

[41] Z. Brakerski, C. Gentry, and V. Vaikuntanathan, "(Leveled) Fully Homomorphic Encryption without Bootstrapping," in *ITCS*, pp. 309–325, ACM, 2012.

[42] C. Gentry, S. Halevi, and N. P. Smart, "Fully Homomorphic Encryption with Polylog Overhead," in *EUROCRYPT*, vol. 7237 of *LNCS*, pp. 465–482, Springer, 2012.

[43] Z. Brakerski, "Fully Homomorphic Encryption without Modulus Switching from Classical GapSVP," in *CRYPTO*, vol. 7417 of *LNCS*, pp. 868–886, Springer, 2012.

[44] V. Vaikuntanathan, "Computing Blindfolded: New Developments in Fully Homomorphic Encryption," in *FOCS*, pp. 5–16, IEEE, 2011.

[45] C. Gentry, S. Halevi, and V. Vaikuntanathan, "*i*-Hop Homomorphic Encryption and Rerandomizable Yao Circuits," in *CRYPTO*, vol. 6223 of *LNCS*, pp. 155–172, Springer, 2010.

[46] R. Rothblum, "Homomorphic Encryption: From Private-Key to Public-Key," in *TCC*, vol. 6597 of *LNCS*, pp. 219–234, Springer, 2011.

[47] C. Gentry and S. Halevi, "Implementing Gentry's Fully-Homomorphic Encryption Scheme," in *EUROCRYPT*, vol. 6632 of *LNCS*, pp. 129–148, Springer, 2011.

[48] C. Gentry, S. Halevi, and N. P. Smart, "Homomorphic Evaluation of the AES Circuit," in *CRYPTO*, vol. 7417 of *LNCS*, pp. 850–867, Springer, 2012.

[49] M. Naehrig, K. Lauter, and V. Vaikuntanathan, "Can Homomorphic Encryption be Practical?," in *CCSW*, pp. 113–124, ACM, 2011.

[50] O. Goldreich and R. Ostrovsky, "Software Protection and Simulation on Oblivious RAMs," *Journal of the ACM*, vol. 43, no. 3, pp. 431–473, 1996.

[51] A. C.-C. Yao, "How to Generate and Exchange Secrets (Extended Abstract)," in *FOCS*, pp. 162–167, IEEE, 1986.

[52] B. Pinkas, T. Schneider, N. P. Smart, and S. C. Williams, "Secure Two-Party Computation is Practical," in *ASIACRYPT*, vol. 5912 of *LNCS*, pp. 250–267, Springer, 2009.

[53] Y. Huang, D. Evans, J. Katz, and L. Malka, "Faster Secure Two-Party Computation Using Garbled Circuits," in *20th USENIX Security Symposium*, USENIX Association, 2011.

[54] R. Gennaro, C. Gentry, and B. Parno, "Non-Interactive Verifiable Computing: Outsourcing Computation to Untrusted Workers," in *CRYPTO*, vol. 6223 of *LNCS*, pp. 465–482, Springer, 2010.

[55] S. Bugiel, S. Nürnberger, A.-R. Sadeghi, and T. Schneider, "Twin Clouds: Secure Cloud Computing with Low Latency - (Full Version)," in *CMS*, vol. 7025 of *LNCS*, pp. 32–44, Springer, 2011.

[56] A.-R. Sadeghi, T. Schneider, and M. Winandy, "Token-Based Cloud Computing – Secure Outsourcing of Data and Arbitrary Computations with Lower Latency," in *Workshop on Trust in the Cloud*, vol. 6101 of *LNCS*, pp. 417–429, Springer, 2010.

[57] D. Boneh, G. Segev, and B. Waters, "Targeted Malleability: Homomorphic Encryption for Restricted Computations," in *ITCS*, pp. 350–366, ACM, 2012.

[58] R. Rivest, A. Shamir, and L. Adleman, "A Method for Obtaining Digital Signatures and Public-Key Cryptosystems," *Communications of the ACM*, vol. 21, no. 2, pp. 120–126, 1978.

Chapter 5

Remote Data Storage

5.1 REMOTE DATA CHECKING

Contents in Brief

What is this? Interactive assurance that remotely stored data is available and intact.

What can it do? Let a client efficiently verify that a remotely stored file is available (without downloading the file) and can be fully recovered on demand.

How can it be used in cloud computing? Establish trust in cloud storage services by providing proofs to clients that the data is consistent and available at all times.

Interactive certificates of the consistent existence and availability of remotely stored data have been developed independently under the two different yet related notions of *proofs of retrievability* (PoR) and *provable data possession* (PDP). We sketch both techniques separately in Section 5.1.1 and Section 5.1.2, letting a description of the differences and similarities in Section 5.1.3 complete and unify the picture.

Proofs of retrievability, introduced in [1], and provable data possession, introduced in [2], are designed as an apparatus to let a file owner verify the consistent existence of a file at a remote (backup) storage provider (e.g., a cloud storage service). Data owners who outsource data to a remote storage server can then regularly challenge the storage server to check whether outsourced files are still retrievable and intact. Other than the trivial approach of downloading the whole file for checking, PoRs and PDP schemes achieve the same proof with significantly less communication and computational overhead. Furthermore, efficient PoRs and PDP schemes are designed to impose only little storage requirements for the verifier (file owner) – in particular verifiers do not need to store the file anymore – and impose only a small number of memory accesses for the prover (backup file server).

A Simple Yet Unsatisfactory Construction

A very simple scheme is constructed by the file owner choosing a set of keyed hash functions $H(x; k_1), \ldots, H(x; k_t)$ with keys $k_1, \ldots, k_t$ and with x denoting the input data to the hash function.

Now, the backup server storing the file $\mathbf{F}$ can be challenged to provide the hash under a given key k_i, where the verifier (client) stores the t hash values of $\mathbf{F}$ under keys $k_1, \ldots, k_t$. If the server returns the correct value $H(\mathbf{F}; k_i)$, then the verifier has strong evidence that the server actually knows the file. This process can be repeated up to t times. The drawbacks of this simple construction are the storage costs for the verifier, which are proportional to the number of checks, and the need for the server to process the entire file upon every challenge. Furthermore, the number of challenges is limited to t checks. Practical PoRs and PDPs are designed to fix both issues.

A More Efficient Yet Unsatisfactory Construction

Another quite simple approach is to use a cryptographic hash function H and a block cipher $(\texttt{KeyGen}, \texttt{Encrypt}, \texttt{Decrypt})$ like AES. Assume that the data owner outsources a file $\mathbf{F} = (f_1, \ldots, f_n)$ interpreted as a sequence of n blocks and wants to challenge the storage server t times for delivering proofs of intactness of $\mathbf{F}$. Then, the data owner chooses a key k for the block cipher, t random challenges $r_1, \ldots, r_t$ of appropriate bitsize (e.g., 128 bits), and t random index sets $\mathcal{I}_1, \ldots, \mathcal{I}_t \subset \{1, \ldots, n\}$ of size c. Then, prior to outsourcing, the data owner computes tokens $v_i = \texttt{Encrypt}(H(r_i \| f_{i_1} \| \ldots \| f_{i_c}); k)$ for $1 \leq i \leq t$ and $i_j \in \mathcal{I}_i$ and outsources $(\mathbf{F}, v_1, \ldots, v_t)$ to the server. In the ith run of the protocol, the client then sends r_i and $\mathcal{I}_i$ to the server, who computes $h_i = H(r_i \| f_{i_1} \| \ldots \| f_{i_c})$ and sends (v_i, h_i) to the client. The client then checks if $h_i = \texttt{Decrypt}(v_i; k)$ holds, and if the check holds the proof is valid.

This protocol is elegant since it is very simple and can easily be modified to support updates on outsourced files on arbitrary positions [3]. This can be achieved by computing tokens v_i as $v_i = \texttt{Encrypt}(H(r_i\|i_1\|f_{i_1}) \oplus \ldots \oplus H(r_i\|i_c\|f_{i_c}); k)$. Consequently, if some block f_j needs to be modified to f'_j, then all values v_i that include f_j can be updated to

$$v'_i = \texttt{Encrypt}(\texttt{Decrypt}(v_i; k) \oplus H(r_i\|j\|f_j) \oplus H(r_i\|j\|f'_j); k).$$

Actually, in order to hide the information of which tokens include the updated index, all tokens need to be reencrypted by the client on every update operation.

However, since this approach still only supports a limited (predefined) number of t challenges, which may not be desirable or feasible in every application, this is still not optimal.

Spot Checking and Robustness

Ideally, proofs of data availability are of constant length (independent of the size of the data) and the verification of these proofs requires only a small and constant number of computations at the server as well as the client. We note that efficiency at the client is far more important, since the client may be a resource constrained device. For instance, PDPs are typically realized by requiring the client to compute verification metadata (tags) for the data prior to outsourcing and storing the data together with the tags at the server. Furthermore, the server should not need to access the entire data for generating a proof, and therefore, a *probabilistic spot checking* approach is used.

Spot checking means that the client asks the server to prove the possession of a subset of c randomly sampled file blocks of the entire file $\mathbf{F} = (f_1, \ldots, f_n)$. This means that a client challenges the server to prove the possession of a randomly sampled subset of data blocks, such that the server's best strategy to follow is to store the entire data. Otherwise, the client will detect this misbehavior with high probability. Now, one can ask how the choice of c should be made when a file consists of n blocks and we assume that the server has corrupted/deleted β blocks. As Ateniese et al. [4] discuss, the probability P that at least one of c blocks sampled by the client matches one of the blocks corrupted/deleted by the server can be analyzed by an urn experiment and can be shown to be bounded as follows:

$$1 - \left(1 - \frac{\beta}{n}\right)^c \le P \le 1 - \left(1 - \frac{\beta}{n - c + 1}\right)^c \tag{5.1}$$

We will come back to the choice of the parameter c when discussing practical design issues.

Note that when the server only corrupts a small fraction of blocks (e.g., only a single block), this is very unlikely to be detected. Therefore erasure codes can be applied to a file before outsourcing in order to resolve this problem (see Section 5.1.1). This has been considered in the initial PoR construction but not in the original PDP model. PDP schemes that also take resistance against small corruptions into account, typically by means of an erasure code, are called *robust* PDP schemes [4–6].

Static vs Dynamic Proofs

All proofs presented in the following strictly refer to *static* files (e.g., data that does *not* change over the lifetime of the system). Support for updates (modifications, insertions, deletions of data items) between two invocations of a proof protocol yields to *dynamic* PoR or PDP schemes, which appropriately extend – and hence build upon – the static constructions described in the sequel. Explicit literature pointers are given at the end of the respective sections.

We stress that it is usually *not* advisable to straightforwardly modify a static PoR/PDP into a dynamic version of it, since it may introduce security flaws. This effect has been demonstrated by [7] for dynamic proofs using certain homomorphic authenticators.

5.1.1 Proofs of Retrievability (PoR)

PoRs can be *keyless* or *keyed*. A keyless protocol admits an a priori chosen fixed number of challenges, as opposed to a keyed protocol admitting an arbitrary number of challenges [8]. Concerning verifications, those can be private or public. In a PoR with *private verification*, only the file owner can verify the validity of the proof, whereas in a *publicly verifiable* PoR, everyone can verify the existence of the file.

5.1.1.1 General Structure

In general, a PoR consists of six components [9], all of which take the system parameters (security parameters for cryptographic primitives) as an input (omitted in the following):

KeyGen: Generates (from the system parameters) a secret key sk, or a public/secret key-pair (pk, sk) in case of a PoR with public verifiability.

Encode: An algorithm that takes a file $\mathbf{F}$ and a key and returns an encoded version $\tilde{\mathbf{F}}$ of the file and a file handle η.

Challenge: An algorithm executed by the client, taking a file handle η and key sk, to create a challenge message that triggers the proof of retrievability.

Respond: An algorithm executed by the server upon receiving a challenge c and file handle η. Returns a response message for the client.

Verify: The client runs this algorithm on the challenge, response, file handle, and the key sk (pk in case of public verifiability) to check the server's response for validity.

Extract: Determines a sequence of challenges that the verifier can send to the server in order to reconstruct the whole file from the given responses (this is essentially equivalent to downloading the whole file).

We remark that it is possible to make the above algorithms stateful in the sense of taking the client's state into account. However, for practical purposes and to spare the client the burden of tracking past protocol executions, it appears more general to work with stateless verifiers.

5.1.1.2 Adversary and Security Model

PoRs primarily deal with untrusted storage. The adversary is thus assumed to arbitrarily modify (possibly delete) any part of the file, while his or her main goal is to convince the client that the file is still intact. More specifically, there exists an upper bound $N_{\max}$ of challenges that the (hostile) server can receive over the lifetime of the stored file. Enumerating the queries as $1, 2, \ldots, N_{\max}$ with corresponding challenges, we may partition the set C of all challenges into two sets C_i^+, C_i^- for the ith challenge, where C_i^+ comprises all cases in which the server responds correctly, and C_i^- contains all cases in which the server responds incorrectly. Put $\varepsilon_i = |C_i^-| / |C|$ for the likelihood to respond incorrectly on the ith challenge, and write $\varepsilon_A = \max_{i=1,\ldots,N_{\max}} \varepsilon_i$ for the maximal chance of responding incorrectly over all possible challenges. Notice that this definition explicitly covers adaptive adversaries, which may respond correctly or incorrectly to the same challenge but in different rounds.

An ε-adversary is one with $\varepsilon_A \leq \varepsilon$. Presuming uniform distributions, an ε-adversary will thus respond correctly to a fraction of at least $(1 - \varepsilon)$ among all challenges. Security is defined as resilience of the PoR against the following attack:

Attack 5.1. In the first phase, the attacker $\mathcal{A}$ arbitrarily interacts with the verifier V. In particular, $\mathcal{A}$ may create files, have V encode them (properly), and obtain challenges from V. The attacker completes this phase by setting up an archive file $\mathbf{F}^*$. In the second phase, V will execute a PoR to check the existence and retrieve the file through Extract. The attack is successful if Extract successfully recovers a file $\mathbf{F} \neq \mathbf{F}^*$.

The rationale behind this is a scenario in which the prover convinces the verifier to have a file, whereas he or she actually does not have it. Hence, if the extract algorithm successfully recovers $\mathbf{F}^*$ from the adversary, then he or she must somehow possess the file or at least be able to provide enough information to recover it. Otherwise, the corruption must be discovered during the challenge-response cycles. In either case, the PoR worked correctly. The security definition refers to resilience against Attack 5.1 with high probability:

Definition 5.1. For $\varepsilon, \gamma > 0$, a system is called an (ε, γ)-valid PoR, if every polynomially time-bounded adversary $\mathcal{A}$ has a chance of at most γ to succeed in Attack 5.1.

Asymptotic definitions would demand γ as negligible in the security parameter. Intuitively, the security guarantee achieved by Definition 5.1 means that a corrupted server will be discovered upon a challenge-response cycle, or the file can correctly be downloaded (i.e., the file is intact). Notice that this security model implicitly refers to *static* files, and additional security requirements come into play when we allow dynamic variations of the remotely stored data (see Section 5.1.1.8 for references).

Currently, PoR security definitions appear to be still evolving. Here, we have given a general formulation that covers alternative definitions [10] with only slight modifications.

5.1.1.3 General Constructions

The basic idea of a PoR scheme is to embed small (randomly valued) data chunks, called *sentinels*, in a file $\mathbf{F}$, on which subsequent spot checks can be made in order to detect corruptions of $\mathbf{F}$. The verifier (file owner) can execute a spot check by asking the server to return the sentinel values at some specified positions. If the server has deleted *large* parts of the file, then with high probability, he or she will have deleted some of the sentinels too and will be unable to respond correctly. More specifically, if an ε-fraction of the file is corrupted, then an ε-fraction of the sentinels is probably also invalidated.

This idea already suggests a few building blocks, which are found throughout most PoR protocols in the literature:

- To protect against small corruptions of the file, error-correcting block codes are applied prior to the upload of the file at the remote server. This is to meet the practical requirement that changes against any portion of the file must be detectable (and correctable), even a single flipped bit. In the following, let this code be an (n, k, d)-code, or (n, k, d)-*ECC* for short. This code assigns input words with k symbols to output words with n symbols so that up to $d/2$ errors can be corrected (hence d is even).

- To prevent the server from deleting portions of the file while retaining the sentinels only, encryption and permutations are employed to scatter and hide the positions of the sentinels across the file.

For simplicity, we repeat the original protocol of [1], as it is a good starting point for more general constructions. Let the file $\mathbf{F}$ consist of b blocks with ℓ bits, where b is a multiple of the code parameter k (input word size), and we assume padding of F in the last block if needed.

KeyGen: This algorithm depends on what cryptographic primitives have been chosen for the subsequent steps. For brevity, let us write k for the key(s) that this algorithm outputs.

Encode: This algorithm entails four steps:

1. Encoding: split the file $\mathbf{F}$ into k-block chunks, and apply the (n, k, d)-ECC over F_{2^ℓ}. This results in a file $\mathbf{F'}$ with $b' = bn/k$ blocks.

2. Encryption: apply `Encrypt` of an IND-CPA secure symmetric cipher to $\mathbf{F'}$ to get $\mathbf{F''}$, where `Encrypt` operates on the blocks of F' independently, in order to let us later decrypt data blocks in isolation. Practical options include tweakable block ciphers [11] or stream ciphers.

3. Sentinel embedding: let $f : \{0, 1\}^j \times \{0, 1\}^* \to \{0, 1\}^\ell$ be a one-way function. We compute s sentinels $a_1, \ldots, a_s$ with $a_w = f(k, w)$, where k is a key created by `KeyGen`. The sentinels are appended to the file $\mathbf{F''}$, yielding $\mathbf{F'''}$. The client stores the sentinel values locally.

4. Permutation: since the sentinels look random, and thanks to the encryption are practically indistinguishable from the file blocks, we finally apply a pseudorandom permutation [12, 13] $g : \{0, 1\}^j \times \{1, \ldots, b' + s\} \to \{1, \ldots, b' + s\}$ to

the blocks of $\mathbf{F}'''$ and output the file $\widetilde{\mathbf{F}}$. The ith block (for $i = 1, 2, \ldots, b' + s$) is $\widetilde{\mathbf{F}}_i = \mathbf{F}'''_{g(k,i)}$, where k is a key (not necessarily the same one as for the previous step), generated by KeyGen.

Extract: This algorithm simply reverses the operations of Encode after having as many blocks as possible from the server. To handle a possible adversary that randomly rather than deterministically responds to a challenge, Extract uses a majority vote: upon failure of the first recovery attempt, it runs another $\gamma - 1$ queries for each block and makes a majority decision about the correct block. This works under the assumption that the adversary responds correctly to more than half of the challenges. Consequently, the ε-adversary is assumed to obey $\varepsilon < \frac{1}{2}$.

Challenge: This algorithm applies the pseudorandom permutation g to a set of q indices, starting with σ. It yields the positions $p_\sigma, p_{\sigma+1}, \ldots, p_{\sigma+q}$ of the sentinels with numbers $\sigma, \sigma + 1, \ldots, \sigma + q$ in the file; precisely, it outputs $p_i = g(k, b' + i)$.

Respond: This algorithm receives the positions from Challenge, accesses the file $\mathbf{F}'''$ at exactly these positions, and returns the respective file blocks. For bandwidth reduction purposes, it may return the XOR of all return values to condense an otherwise bulky answer.

Verify: This algorithm works in the obvious way, by checking the returned values against the locally stored sentinel values at the client's side.

Obviously, this construction allows only for a limited (finite) number of verifications, which is determined by the number q of challenged sentinels, and the total number s of sentinels embedded in the file. The maximal number of verifications thus comes to

$$N_{\max} = \frac{s}{q}.$$

A scheme that allows an infinite number of verifications will be discussed later, under a more general view and framework. Generically, a limited-use PoR can be cast into an unlimited-use PoR by using PIR (see Section 3.4.2) to avoid disclosing the locations of the sentinels queried. However, in light of the potential increase of communication overhead by the PIR, it appears questionable if such a generic transformation would become more expensive than the trivial approach of simply downloading the entire file.

Fact 5.1 classifies the above construction as a valid PoR under the simplifying assumption that the server upon being queried on the ith block responds correctly with a probability of at least $p = 3/4$ (any likelihood strictly larger than $1/2$ would be sufficient; however, this assumption gives the formulae in the upcoming fact and discussion). It should be noted, however, that all of these statements remain valid asymptotically, under the assumption that $p > 1/2$. Moreover, the server's replies are assumed stochastically independent between challenges and even between different blocks. Under these assumptions, the following holds:

Fact 5.1 ([1]). Assume that the file $\mathbf{F}$ has been encoded using an (n, k, d)-ECC. Let the encoded file have b' blocks, and put $C = b'/n$. For all $0 < \varepsilon < 1$ such that $\mu = n\varepsilon(b' + s)/[b' - \varepsilon(b' + s)] < d/2$, the above scheme is a (ρ, λ)-valid PoR for $\rho \geq C \exp(d/2 - \mu)(d/(2\mu))^{-d/2}$ and $\lambda \geq (1 - \varepsilon/4)^q$.

Concerning the validity of the majority vote potentially required by Extract, the number γ of trials until we reach a reliable decision depends on the likelihood of the server returning a correct block. If this likelihood is, for example, at least $3/4$ (in any case greater than $1/2$), then taking at least $\gamma \geq 24(j \ln 2 + \ln b')$ rounds ensures a likelihood of less than 2^{-j} for the majority vote to fail. The value j can then be chosen large, as the chance to fail is in general negligible in j. However, if the exact fraction of correct responses is presumably unknown in a practical setting, it is advisable to choose a large value for j (e.g., $j \geq 1800$). In the setting given here, this would make the majority vote fail with a probability of less than 2^{-80} under the hypothesis that at least $3/4$ of all responses are correct. Lower likelihoods than $3/4$, but still larger than $1/2$, would call for larger values of j.

Fact 5.1 basically arises from an analysis of an urn experiment in which we calculate the chance to always draw "good balls" (correct sentinels) from the urn upon requests. Hence, the proof in the appendix of [1] may be taken as a guideline to design and analyze sentinel-based variants of this general idea. A different coding-theory inspired framework is reviewed next.

5.1.1.4 Viewing PoRs as (an Application of) Error-Correcting Codes

In a recent work, [8] provides an entirely coding-theoretic framework to construct and analyze PoRs. For its usefulness and to extend the above scheme from bounded-use to an unlimited number of challenges, we briefly recall the general view on PoRs as proposed in [8]. The general framework is the following.

- The file owner (*verifier*) encodes a file $\mathbf{F} \in (\mathsf{F}_q)^k$ into a file $\mathbf{F}' \in (\mathsf{F}_q)^n$ with $n > k$.

- The file $\mathbf{F}$ is given to the storage server (*prover*). In case of an unbounded use scheme, the prover is additionally given a tag that is related to the file and computed by the verifier.

- The verifier constructs appropriate information to check responses against challenges. In case of an unbounded use scheme, this may include a secret key sk, but not necessarily so.

- The verifier (file owner) and the prover (storage provider) run a sequence of challenge-response rounds. In each of these rounds, the verifier checks the prover's responses against the local verification data (in the case of the simple scheme sketched above, this would be the value of the embedded sentinels).

- The success probability for the prover is the likelihood to respond correctly.

- The Extract algorithm interacts with the prover and, in the case of an unbounded use scheme, takes a secret key sk and outputs a decoded file $\widetilde{\mathbf{F}}$. Extraction succeeds if $\widetilde{\mathbf{F}} = \mathbf{F}$.

- The security of a PoR scheme is given as a statement of the form

  The Extract algorithm ("download of the file") succeeds with probability at least δ whenever the cloud provider's response is correct with probability at least ε.

In its simplest form, a PoR is a humble error-correcting encoding of a file, with the challenges only asking to send a portion of the file back to the verifier to do spot checking. The prover's success probability is in that case the chance of the server responding with the correct piece of the file. The previous construction used sentinels for spot checking, whose exact location is hidden by encryption and permutation. However, extending this view to queries on multiple blocks and permitting more general processing by the file owner (in the first step above), allows us to analyze sentinel-based schemes along with other general proposals under the same framework. In particular, [8] introduces a "code" corresponding to a PoR via the set of all valid responses under all possible challenges. Most importantly, the security of such frameworks can be related to the Hamming distance of this code. We will not go further into this direction, but give a modified version of the protocol in [10] given in [8] that fits into this framework of *unconditional security* [14]; not resting security assurances on any number-theoretic or complexity-related intractability assumptions.

5.1.1.5 An Unbounded Use Scheme

KeyGen: This algorithm picks $\alpha \in F_q$ and $\mathbf{b} = (\beta_1, \ldots, \beta_n) \in (F_q)^n$, where q is a prime power, and returns the key $sk = (\alpha, b)$. This key is kept secret by the verifier.

Encode: Takes the file $\mathbf{F} - (f_1, \ldots, f_n) \in (F_q)^n$ and computes a tag $\mathbf{s} = (\sigma_1, \ldots, \sigma_n) \in (F_q)^n$ as $\mathbf{s} = \mathbf{b} + \alpha \cdot \mathbf{F}$. The file $\mathbf{F}$ and tag $\mathbf{s}$ are given to the cloud storage provider.

Challenge: Picks a vector $\mathbf{v} = (v_1, \ldots, v_n) \in (F_q)^n$.

Response: This takes the challenge $\mathbf{v}$, and returns the pair (μ, τ) with $\mu = \langle \mathbf{v}, \mathbf{F} \rangle$ and $\tau = \langle \mathbf{v}, \mathbf{s} \rangle$ (scalar products of the vectors).

Verify: Checks if $\tau \overset{?}{=} \alpha\mu + \langle \mathbf{v}, \mathbf{b} \rangle$ and returns the Boolean result of the comparison.

Extract: This algorithm would run multiple challenges and collect sufficiently many values to set up a system of n equations in n unknowns to recover the file contents. Alternatively, in the coding-theoretic view, one can (theoretically) also apply nearest-neighborhood decoding.

It is easy to see that the verification equation works if the file is intact at the provider's side (since the entire file goes into the response computation). Moreover, besides a response being *acceptable* if the verification equation is satisfied, the response needs to be authentic in the sense that μ, τ have been computed correctly. To verify the latter, one may check if the given response (τ, μ) to a challenge $\mathbf{v}$ is verifiable under *at least two* keys of the form $(\alpha_0, \mathbf{s} - \alpha_0 \cdot \mathbf{F})$ where $\alpha_0 \in F_q$ is arbitrary. If so, then the response is authentic (see [8] for respective proofs).

A modification toward *public verifiability* would employ conventional digital signatures as a replacement for the response equation in the above scheme. This feature allows anyone to act as the verifier in a PoR using publicly available information. See Section 5.1.2 for constructions with public verifiability.

5.1.1.6 Viewing the Adversary as a Noisy Channel

An alternative view on PoRs [9], inspired by coding theory, considers the adversary as a noisy channel between an honest server and the client. This perspective presumes random read errors in the file system, and does not a priori consider a server as malicious. The PoR would employ a two-stage encoding as follows: first, the file owner applies an *outer code* inside Encode, which is basically an error-correcting code. The so-encoded file is given to the server for storage, and the redundancy of the code yields the storage overhead that the server must handle. For the challenge-response phase, the Respond algorithm applies another layer of error-correcting encoding (*inner code*) and responds with a single symbol in the (now doubly) encoded file. The challenge tells which symbol should be returned, and the response is checked on the verifier's side. The server's workload can thus be balanced between storage requirements (induced by the outer code) and computational burden (induced by the inner code). The actual PoR would thus run in two phases: in phase one, the channel error is tested via the inner code and the ability to respond correctly in the presence of the channel noise, respectively. The second phase is then devoted to extracting (downloading) the file by decoding the inner and outer codes.

It can be argued that both of the above schemes fit into this view, as well as the response by sending only a symbol of the encoded file is consistent with the coding-theoretic view of [8]. Hence, it all boils down to applications of error-correcting codes.

5.1.1.7 Practical Design Guidance

Design choices for a PoR implementation primarily concern the construction of error-correcting codes for possibly large message sizes and the suitable selection of cryptographic primitives. In general, it is advisable to stick with standardized cryptographic algorithms and recommended keysizes to meet the hypotheses underlying the security proofs of many PoR schemes. The error-correcting codes should be designed to work with message (block) sizes that are compatible with the chosen cryptographic primitive. For example, if AES is chosen, then the encoding should be over $F_{2^{128}}$. The sentinel values (as being humble random numbers) should as well be chosen sufficiently large to prevent brute force guessing. Taking them with 128 bits (at least) appears advisable.

For designing the codes, one may start from a standard $(255, 223, 32)$-Reed-Solomon code over F_{2^8} (i.e., encoding bytes). A standard procedure to enlarge the message and codeword sizes is to build concatenated codes. A well-written description of this technique is found in [15]. Likewise, the technique of *striping* [16] allows us to construct a $(255, 223, 32)$ code over $F_{2^{128}}$ for example. The particular parameterization of a PoR scheme strongly depends on the chosen scheme, but most literature on PoR contains example parameterizations that can be adapted easily to the application at hand.

To give an impression on how to parameterize the protocol sketched here, consider an encoding using a $(255, 223, 32)$-code over $F_{2^{128}}$, which matches the block size of AES and also prevents brute force guessing of sentinels. A chunk is then a sequence of 255 blocks, and a 2-GB file would have 2^{27} such blocks. The code expands a file by a factor of $255/223 \approx 1.14$ (i.e., 14%). The overall number of challenges is determined by the number of sentinels embedded in the file, so if we seek to run a daily check for the next 5 years involving $q = 1,000$ queries per verification, we end up with $s = 5 \cdot 365 \cdot 1,000 = 1,825,000$ sentinels embedded in the file, each of which is 16 bytes long, creating an overhead of about 30 MB by the sentinels. For a 2-GB file, this would be a further expansion by a factor of 1.015 or 1.5%. Giving precise figures, a 2-GB file with $b = 2^{27}$ blocks is expanded into a file with $b' = b \cdot 255/223 \approx 153,477,672$ blocks. With only $\varepsilon = 0.5\%$ of the blocks being corrupted by the adversary, we get $C = b'/n \approx 601,873$. For Fact 5.1, we find $\mu \approx 1.3 < d/2$, and consequently, $\rho \approx 5.06 \times 10^{-6}$, which is the probability that this adversary can render the file unretrievable. Finally, the probability to detect a corruption during a *single* challenge asking for q sentinels is, by Fact 5.1, $1 - (1 - \varepsilon/4)^q \approx 71.3\%$. This makes repeated challenges necessary to detect a corruption more reliably.

As already mentioned for bandwidth reduction, the responses concerning multiple sentinels may be condensed into a single response by XORing them. This can as well be used to set up the storage service tree-structured in the sense that a single storage server can distribute the contents over multiple subordinate storages. Each of these can provide an XOR-digested response to the higher-level server, which can again XOR all subordinate responses into the final response for the receiver.

5.1.1.8 Dynamic Variants

Dynamic PoRs are usually employ data structures that allow for efficient manipulations, combined with an equally efficiently updateable digital signature. Examples are found in [5, 17, 18]. An interesting additional security requirement is *fairness* [17], which prevents a client from falsely accusing the cloud service provider of having modified the data.

Two general possibilities to support dynamic PoRs are as follows: for sentinel-based spot-checking techniques, one can choose a set of nonces, one for each sentinel, and derive each individual sentinel value from a distinct subset of these nonces. During a challenge-response interaction, some sentinels are used up. When an update needs to be done, the remaining *unused* sentinels can locally be updated to remain consistent with the new file content so that the server can respond correctly after the update. The particular choice of what subsets of nonces make up which sentinels in order to retain enough unused sentinels after a sequence of updates can be leveraged by techniques from statistical planning and block designs (the latter of which are closely related to the theory of error-correcting codes). Details are outside the scope of this book, and we refer the reader to [19–21] for general techniques to create suitable designs.

A different way to support dynamic updates is by organizing the data in structure like a Merkle tree [7,22,23] (where the latter construction uses chameleon hashes) or a skip-list as in [24]. For a Merkle tree, each leaf node corresponds to a data block (record set, single record, attribute, etc.) and each inner node is assigned the hash value of the concatenation of the hashes of its child nodes. The overall hash is the value assigned to the tree's root node. This is the only value that the client needs to store. Any local change to one among n leafs then needs only $\mathcal{O}(\log n)$ inner nodes (hash values) to be updated in order to update the root node consistently. For verification, the server sends the hashes of all siblings along the path from the requested leaf to the root. This information can be used by the client to reconstruct the hash tree and compare it to its locally known root hash value. For an update, the client can use this information obtained by a verification request to compute the updated root value using the new block and send the new data block to the server, which in turn can identically update its internal Merkle tree.

5.1.2 Provable Data Possession (PDP)

PDP schemes always involve a secret key sk and a public key pk. Thereby, sk is only known to the data owner, who outsources the data and can use this key also to perform updates (typically this is restricted to replacements and appending of file blocks; see Section 5.1.2.6 for references to dynamic PDPs) and the pk may be known to any party. As in case of PoRs, a PDP scheme is said to be *privately verifiable* if only the data owner (who is in possession of sk) can verify a proof delivered by a storage server and is said to be *publicly verifiable* if any third party, without having access to sk, can verify the proof.

5.1.2.1 General Structure

A PDP scheme is defined by the following efficient algorithms:

KeyGen: This probabilistic algorithm takes a security parameter, and generates a public and private key pair (pk, sk).

Tag: This deterministic algorithm takes a key pair (pk, sk), a file identifier id, the index i of the file block f_i as input and returns a verification tag T_i.

Prove: This deterministic algorithm gets as input the public key pk, a file $\mathbf{F}$ (whose id is determined by the challenge), the sequence of corresponding tags T_c, and the challenge c. It returns a proof of possession π for the blocks determined by the challenge c.

Verify: This deterministic algorithm takes as input a key pair (pk, sk), a challenge c, and a proof of data possession π. It returns accept if π is a correct proof of possession for the blocks determined by the challenge c and reject otherwise. In case of public verifiability the input sk is not required.

A PDP scheme is called *correct*, if for any honestly generated proof of possession π using honestly generated tags T, the probability that Verify accepts is 1.

Using the definition of a PDP scheme, we can now specify the interaction between a client C and a server S by means of the following generic PDP protocol. A PDP protocol is a tuple of efficient interactive algorithms and defined as follows:

Setup: The client C obtains a key pair (pk, sk) by running KeyGen, publishes pk and keeps sk private.

Store: For a given file $\mathbf{F}$ identified by id, potentially encode the file using a suitable erasure code and obtain the file $\mathbf{F'}$. Then, C divides it into n blocks and executes Tag on every block and sends $(id, \mathbf{F'}, \mathbf{T})$ to S.

Challenge: The challenger V (not necessarily the client C) generates a challenge $c = (id, I, \{\ell_i\}_{i \in I})$, where id is the file identifier, I is a subset of block indexes, and $\{\ell_i\}_{i \in I}$ is a set of randomly chosen coefficients. V sends the challenge c to S and S runs Prove to generate the proof π. S sends π back to V and V checks the proof via Verify.

We emphasize that in a private PDP protocol Store and Challenge can only be run by the data owner, while in a public PDP protocol Challenge can be run by any (third) party and Store only by the data owner. Furthermore, we note that sometimes the Setup and Store protocol are merged into a single Setup protocol. However, since not every file requires a fresh pair of (pk, sk), the above definition seems more natural.

5.1.2.2   Adversary and Security Model

Similar to the case of PoRs, PDPs are concerned with adversaries who try to convince a verifier that a file is still retrievable although the file has been corrupted (i.e., parts of the file have been deleted or modified). In contrast to PoRs, one is not concerned with all queries over the system's lifetime, but either assumes that the parameters and in particular the number of challenged file blocks have been chosen accordingly or an alternate definition is used. Below, we define security as resilience against the following attack and capture both aforementioned cases:

Attack 5.2. In the first phase, the attacker $\mathcal{A}$ interacts with the verifier. In particular, $\mathcal{A}$ can store and run tagging as well as verification queries for arbitrary files. At some point, V generates λ challenges for some previously queried file $\mathbf{F}^*$. $\mathcal{A}$ delivers a proof π for the parts of $\mathbf{F}^*$ identified by the challenges and returns them to V. If $\mathcal{A}$ is able to deliver

Case 1: A valid proof π for $\mathbf{F}^*$, then $\mathcal{A}$ has won. In this case, there is only a single challenge (i.e., $\lambda = 1$).

Case 2: Valid proofs $\pi_1, \ldots, \pi_\lambda$ with respect to file $\mathbf{F}' \neq \mathbf{F}^*$, which can be extracted by an efficient algorithm, then $\mathcal{A}$ has won.

Observe that Case 2 of the above attack is very similar to the PoR Attack 5.1, which succeeds if a different file than the original file is retrieved. The similarity between PoR and PDP emerging from this will become even more evident after looking at the security definitions. The original PDP paper [2] proposes the following:

Definition 5.2. A scheme guarantees (*secure*) *provable data possession* if for any adversary $\mathcal{A}$ the probability that $\mathcal{A}$ wins on a set of file blocks (Case 1 in Attack 5.2) is negligibly close to the probability that V can extract those file blocks by means of a (probabilistic polynomial-time) knowledge extractor.

Roughly speaking, the knowledge extractor is the same as the `Extract` algorithm for a PoR.

An alternative definition focuses on the unforgeability of tags and the extractability and can be stated as follows. Thereby, an adversary is called ϵ-*admissible* if the probability that it is able to convince V to accept a proof in the retrieve phase of the above attack is at least ϵ.

Definition 5.3. A scheme guarantees (*secure*) provable data possession, if it is correct and for any ϵ-admissible probabilistic poly-time adversary $\mathcal{A}$, there is a value λ for the number of queries in the retrieve phase, which is bounded by some polynomial in the number of file blocks, such that the probability that $\mathcal{A}$ succeeds in Case 2 of Attack 5.2 is negligibly small in the security parameter.

This implicitly guarantees that valid proofs can only be given for original files while being in possession of all queried parts of the file and any valid forgery provides an adversary to break some presumably hard problem. Furthermore, by running a sufficient number of challenges the entire file can be reconstructed.

Again, comparing both of these definitions to their common sibling in the PoR framework (Definition 5.1), we see that the definitions are essentially the same, although the notion of an ε-adversary is different for a PoR and a PDP. The apparent mismatch in the definitions is mostly due to a PDP lacking the `Extract` algorithm that a PoR must provide. However, this difference is almost resolved by the security definitions requiring a *knowledge extractor*, which is the theoretical counterpart to `Extract`. We will revisit this comparison in Section 5.1.3.

5.1.2.3 General Constructions

The general idea behind PDP schemes is to apply a preprocessing to a file $\mathbf{F} = (f_1, \ldots, f_n)$ before uploading it. We do not explicitly consider encoding of $\mathbf{F}$ to $\mathbf{F}'$ as preprocessing, although this is used by state-of-the-art PDP schemes. The remaining preprocessing requires the client to compute for every block f_i a so-called *homomorphic verifiable tag* (HVT) T_i. This verification metadata ($\mathbf{T} = (T_1, \ldots, T_n)$) (a tag per block) is then stored at the server together with the file $\mathbf{F}$. For such an HVT one requires two properties [2], namely (1) *blockless verification*, meaning that a server can compute a proof based on these tags without requiring the client to have local access to the corresponding blocks, and (2) *tag homomorphism*, meaning that given two tags T_i and T_j corresponding to file blocks f_i and f_j anyone can compute a tag T_{ij} corresponding to file block $f_i + f_j$. Then a generic PDP scheme runs as follows:

- The client having file $\mathbf{F} = (f_1, \ldots, f_n)$ computes tags $\mathbf{T} = (T_1, \ldots, T_n)$ and stores $(\mathbf{F}, \mathbf{T})$ at the server. Then, the client deletes its local copies of $\mathbf{F}$ and $\mathbf{T}$.

- A PDP amounts to generating a challenge $c = (I, \{\ell_i\}_{i \in I})$ where I is a random subset of $\{1, \ldots, n\}$, and the ℓ_i's are random coefficients. The prover (*server*) responds by computing a homomorphic tag aggregating all tags corresponding to the challenged file blocks $\tau = \sum_{i \in I} \ell_i T_i$ and some linear combination of file blocks $\mu = \sum_{i \in I} \ell_i f_i$, and sends them to the client.

- Toward the proof, the client (*verifier*) checks a certain relation between τ and μ. In the case of a private verifiable PDP, the client therefore requires a secret key sk and in the case of a publicly verifiable PDP, the public key pk is sufficient.

Subsequently, we review the private verifiable version of the first proposed PDP construction [2]. This scheme works in groups of hidden order (i.e., a subgroup of $\mathbb{Z}_n^*$ with $n = pq$ being a special RSA modulus), whose order can only be determined when knowing the factorization of n, and is thus, unfortunately, quite inefficient.

A recent PDP construction (see [6]) first supports simultaneous private and public verifiability, and second constitutes the most efficient PDP constructions to date for private as well as public verifiability. This PDP scheme works in groups of prime order p and thus can take advantage of smaller security parameters and efficient elliptic curve arithmetics and uses pairing friendly elliptic curves to support public verifiability. See also Section 5.1.3 for a comparison and references to other schemes.

5.1.2.4   The Original PDP Construction (S-PDP)

The algorithm KeyGen chooses two prime numbers p, q such that $p = 2p' + 1$ and $q = 2q' + 1$ with p', q' being prime, and $n = pq$ has an appropriate size (e.g., 2048 bits). The choice this special RSA modulus causes the subgroup of quadratic residues (QR_n) of $\mathbb{Z}_n^*$ to be cyclic and being of order $p'q'$. Furthermore, the algorithm chooses e as a large prime and computes d s.t. $ed \equiv 1 \pmod{p'q'}$. Moreover, it chooses a generator g of QR_n, a secret value v of sufficient size (e.g., 128 bits), and defines two cryptographic hash functions $H_1 : \{0,1\}^* \rightarrow \{0,1\}^\ell$ (e.g., SHA-2, and $H_2 : \{0,1\}^* \rightarrow QR_n$; see Section 2.5.4). It sets the public key to be $pk = (n, g)$ and the secret key to be $sk = (e, d, v)$.

The algorithm Tag produces for every block in $\mathbf{F} = (f_1, \ldots, f_n)$ a tag, where in this construction blocks may be some KB in size (in [2] the authors suggest 4-KB blocks). In other constructions, blocks typically need to be group elements or vectors thereof, but due to the hidden order of the group QR_n in this construction, they can be of arbitrary size without sacrificing security. A tag is then computed as $T_i = (H_2(v\|i) \cdot g^{f_i})^d \text{ MOD } n$. Thereby, the hash function H_2 is used to guarantee that $v\|i$ is invertible in QR_n and exponentiation with the unknown value d prevents forgery and malleability of tags. After the preprocessing, $(\mathbf{F}, \mathbf{T})$ along with pk is stored at the server.

In the Prove algorithm, the server is then required to prove to the client that all file blocks corresponding to the indices in the challenged index set I are still stored and retrievable. From the challenge $c = (I, \{\ell_i\}_{i \in I}, g_s = g^s)$, where g_s is a random challenge base (which is more or less required to get the security proof to work), the server computes the response (τ, ρ) as follows:

$$\tau = \prod_{i \in I} T_i^{\ell_i} \text{ MOD } n,$$

$$\rho = H_1 \left(g_s^{\sum_{i \in I} \ell_i f_i} \text{ MOD } n \right)$$

The `Verify` algorithm then computes

$$\tau' = \left(\frac{\tau^e}{\prod_{i \in I} H_2(v \| i)^{\ell_i}} \right) \text{ MOD } n,$$

and checks whether the relation

$$\rho \stackrel{?}{=} H_1(\tau'^s \text{ MOD } n)$$

holds. It is straightforward to verify that the S-PDP scheme is correct, since

$$
\begin{aligned}
H_1(\tau'^s) = H_1 \left(\left[\frac{\tau^e}{\prod_{i \in I} H_2(v \| i)^{\ell_i}} \right]^s \right) &= H_1 \left(\left[\frac{(\prod_{i \in I} T_i^{\ell_i})^e}{\prod_{i \in I} H_2(v \| i)^{\ell_i}} \right]^s \right) \\
&= H_1 \left(\left[\frac{(\prod_{i \in I} ((H_2(v \| i) g^{f_i})^d)^{\ell_i})^e}{\prod_{i \in I} H_2(v \| i)^{\ell_i}} \right]^s \right) \\
&= H_1 \left(\left[\frac{\prod_{i \in I} H_2(v \| i)^{\ell_i} \cdot \prod_{i \in I} g^{f_i \ell_i}}{\prod_{i \in I} H_2(v \| i)^{\ell_i}} \right]^s \right) \\
&= H_1 \left((g^{\sum_{i \in I} f_i \ell_i})^s \right) \\
&= H_1 \left(g_s^{\sum_{i \in I} f_i \ell_i} \right) = \rho.
\end{aligned}
$$

Note that we have omitted to write the reductions modulo n above explicitly for brevity. Security of this scheme can be shown under the RSA assumption and the somewhat controversial KEA-1 assumption in the random oracle model, and we refer the reader to [4] for details. Although elegant, this RSA-style construction imposes a rather large computational burden on the verifier/client (i.e., a number of large integer exponentiations and inversions linear in the number of challenged file blocks). Furthermore, although [2] also provide a public verifiable version this version is extremely inefficient when compared to other schemes providing public verifiability.

5.1.2.5   Practical Design Guidance

We did not consider details of erasure/error-correcting codes applied to $\mathbf{F}$ before running the PDP scheme, and we refer the reader to Section 5.1.1 for a discussion of the choice of suitable parameters.

We have represented the challenge sent to the server via an index set I, as well as the set of random coefficients $\{\ell_i\}_{i \in I}$, in the case of S-PDP. Note, however, that the challenges as well as the index sets can be computed from short seeds and thus the bandwidth overhead can be kept minimal. These sets can for instance be generated by using pseudorandom functions (PRFs) as in [4].

Now, we come back to the choice of the parameters for the spot checking. Recall that in Equation (5.1), c represents the number of indexes used by the Prove algorithm, n the number of blocks in $\mathbf{F}$, and β the number of corrupted/deleted blocks. Now, when given n one can use β as an assumption about the adversary's behavior and c to adjust the probability of detecting a cheating adversary. For instance, let us assume that we have a file consisting of 10^6 file blocks (of t elements each) and we assume that the server has corrupted $\beta = 10^3$ of these blocks (i.e., 0.1% of all blocks), then to achieve $P \approx 0.99$ we have to set the challenge size to $c = |\mathcal{I}| = 4600$.

5.1.2.6   Dynamic Variants

Various other PDP treatments, including dynamic versions, are found in [3, 5, 6, 10, 24–26] and [27].

5.1.3   Comparison of PoR and PDP

As mentioned in Section 5.1, PoRs were initially designed such that they only support a limited number of challenges (although, by now, there exist constructions for an unlimited number of challenges). In contrast, PDPs were particularly designed to support an unlimited number of challenges. Furthermore, while PoRs employ a coding theoretic approach (i.e., a file is encoded prior to outsourcing), PDPs initially were not concerned with encoding and thus corrections of minor corruptions, but only handled corruptions of larger parts of the outsourced file. However, we note that in recent works both approaches seem to converge to a single unified approach as it is quite straightforward to combine PDPs with suitable codes and thus obtain robustness against small corruptions as well.

While PoRs come with an explicit knowledge extraction algorithm `Extract` to retrieve the file from a sequence of challenges, PDPs only implicitly require such a knowledge extractor in the course of their security proofs (see Definition 5.2). Therefore, the security guarantees made by a PDP are slightly weaker than those of a PoR, since the latter certifies correctness of *all* the data, whereas a PDP assures correctness of *most* of the data [18].

For guidance when a PoR or PDP protocol should be selected for practical implementation, we give a comparison of existing approaches in terms of storage and communication overhead as well as computational effort. We point out that existing literature typically uses too small security parameters for the intended use of PoRs/PDPs (i.e., outsourcing large datasets for long-term storage). In particular, RSA-based/DL-based approaches typically use 1024 bits and 160 bits for elliptic curve-based approaches. However, having the long-term characteristic in mind, it is more natural to choose at least 2048 and 224 bits security, respectively, as suggested by NIST in [28]. Subsequently, κ, t, and ℓ stand for the security parameter, the number of file elements, which are aggregated into one tag, and $\ell = n/t$ is the number of file blocks (vectors), respectively. Furthermore, let the challenged index set of file blocks (vectors) I be of size c.

Computational Effort

Table 5.2 lists existing approaches along with their computational costs. The symbols for the operands and their respective meanings are illustrated in Table 5.1.

Table 5.1

Symbols for Costs of Arithmetical Operations

Operation	Semantics	Operand Size	Description
P	$e(P_1, P_2')$	224	Pairing computation
E	b^d	2048	Large integer exponentiation
S	$d \cdot P$	224	Scalar multiplication
A	$P_1 + P_2$	224	Point addition
I	$b^{-1} \pmod{N}$	2048	Large integer modular inversion
M	$b_1 \cdot b_2$	2048	Large integer multiplication
i	b^{-1}	224	Field inversion
m	$b_1 \cdot b_2$	224	Field multiplication
H	$H(m)$	224	Hash or PRF function evaluation

Table 5.2

Comparison of Computational Complexity of PDP/PoR Schemes

Scheme	Key Size	Tagging	Server	Client
Private Verifiability				
S-PDP [4]	$\kappa = 2048$	$\ell(2\kappa E + 2M + H)$	$(2ct + c)E + 2(c-1)M + H$	$(c+2)E+I+cM+(c+1)H$
SPOR [10]	$\kappa = 2048$	$\ell t M + (\ell + 1)H$	$c(t+1)M$	$(c+t)M+(c+1)H$
EPOR [26]	$\kappa = 224$	$\ell(t+1)m + \ell H$	$(t-1)(S + A) + (ct + c + t)m$	$2S+i+(c+1)m+cH$
SRPDP [6]	$\kappa = 224$	$\ell(S+(t+3)m+2H)$	$cS + (c-1)A + c(t+2)m + cH$	$S+(c+t+2)m+cH$
Public Verifiability				
P-PDP [4]	$\kappa = 2048$	$2n(\kappa E + M + H)$	$cE + 2(c-1)M$	$(c+2)E + I + 2(c-1)M + 2cH$
PPOR [10]	$\kappa = 224$	$\ell((t+1)S+tA+H)$	$cS+(c-1)A+ctm$	$2P + (c+t)S + (c+t-1)A$
SRPDP [6]	$\kappa = 224$	$\ell(S+(t+3)m+2H)$	$cS + (c-1)A + c(t+2)m + cH$	$3P + (t+1)S + (t-1)A+cm+cH$

Storage Overhead

Table 5.3 gives an overview of the storage and communication overhead of existing approaches. In the following, h stands for the output length of a hash function or HMAC of suitable size. Here, we need to note that when one wants to have private and public verifiability simultaneously, then for all other schemes except the scheme from [6] the storage overhead will be the sum of the storage overheads of the respective privately and publicly verifiable PDP schemes.

Table 5.3

Communication and Storage Overhead of PDP Schemes

Scheme	Key Size	Communication	Storage
Private Verifiability			
S-PDP [4]	$\kappa = 2048$	$(c+1)\kappa + h$	$\ell\kappa$
SPOR [10]	$\kappa = 2048$	$(2t+c+1)\kappa + h$	$\ell\kappa + t\kappa$
EPOR [26]	$\kappa = 224$	$(c+3)\kappa$	$\ell\kappa$
SRPDP [6]	$\kappa = 224$	$(t+1)\kappa$	$\ell\kappa$
Public Verifiability			
P-PDP [4]	$\kappa = 2048$	$(c+2)\kappa$	$\geq n\kappa$
PPOR [10]	$\kappa = 224$	$(2t+c+2)\kappa$	$\ell\kappa + (t+1)\kappa$
P-SRPDP [6]	$\kappa = 224$	$(t+1)\kappa$	$\ell\kappa$

5.2 SECURE DATA DEDUPLICATION

Contents in Brief

What is this? Methods that prevent misuse of cloud storage and allow secure deduplication at cloud services.

What can it do? Clients can be sure that their outsourced data is kept confidential.

How can it be used in cloud computing? Help cloud providers to save storage space while at the same time preserving confidentiality of client data.

Data deduplication is a means to reduce the storage overhead for a provider of outsourced storage services such as cloud storage services. Basically, the storage system attempts to host only a single copy of a file regardless of how many users refer to it. Essentially, this means that a physical storage only happens when the initial (first) user uploads the file. For any subsequent storage request for the same file, the server creates only a reference to the initial file.

There are four different strategies for deduplication; namely it can either be applied on a *file level* or *block level*, and it can either be performed on the *client* or at the *server*. Client-side deduplication is typically performed by having the server look up the file before uploading it (e.g., by asking if the server knows a file with the given hash value). In server-side deduplication, the upload always happens, letting the server handle redundant copies of the same file. Consequently, client-side deduplication is the most rewarding solution, applied by many popular storage services such as Dropbox and Mozy, and can be shown to result in enormous bandwidth and disk savings [29].

However, from the security and privacy perspective, various issues emerge through introduction of client-side deduplication, as it was first observed in [30]. When deduplication is demanded, then confidentiality with respect to *insider attacks* (the storage provider) is hard to achieve. Suppose that a client encrypts a file prior to uploading the file; how can the server check when another client wants to upload the same file, typically encrypted under a different key, whether the file is already stored? This question will be discussed in Section 5.2.1. On the other hand, since only a small piece of information about the file is required to obtain access to a file (i.e., pretending to upload it by presenting the hash value), and then download the entire file, various potential *outsider attacks* are introduced. This motivates proofs of ownership (see Section 5.2.2).

5.2.1   Convergent or Message-Locked Encryption

Encrypting files before uploading them to a storage service allows us to guarantee confidentiality with respect to insider attacks of the storage provider (SP) or any outsider that breaks into the system, since neither the SP nor the outsider gets to know the respective decryption keys (they are managed by the clients). We note that today several cloud SPs like Amazon S3 [31] provide means to server-side encryption. However, this can at most provide confidentiality with respect to external attackers (assuming the decryption keys are appropriately secured at the storage provider), but not against insider attacks, because the SP has access to the outsourced data in plaintext, as all decryption keys are available to the SP.

In [32], the authors discussed whether it is possible to use client-side encryption with the following feature: if the same file is encrypted by two different clients who do not share any internal state nor any secret key, can the resulting ciphertext always be identical? Therefore, they introduced what they call a *convergent encryption scheme*, which produces identical ciphertext (files) from identical plaintext (files), irrespective of their encryption keys and should provide reasonable confidentiality guarantees with respect to insiders (i.e., the storage server in our scenario).

The basic idea behind their construction is very simple and shares some similarities with turning probabilistic into deterministic public key encryption schemes (see Section 3.1.2 and Section 4.1.3). Therefore, let (KeyGen,Encrypt,Decrypt) be a secure symmetric encryption scheme and let H be a secure hash function. The idea is not to use KeyGen to generate a random key, but to compute a key k as $k = H(F)$ where F is the file to be stored. Consequently, the ciphertext F' (the encrypted file) is computed as $F' = \text{Encrypt}(F; H(F))$. Note that everybody having the file F can compute $k = H(F)$, and thus produce the deterministic ciphertext F', which allows deduplication at the server without compromising the confidentiality. Note that the server does not know F, and thus the key k required to decrypt F'.

Although convergent encryption has been around for some years and is already used in deployed applications and proposed for the use in deduplication [33], a formal study of what the authors call *message-locked encryption* has only been performed very recently [34]. This work, from a practical side, essentially shows that convergent encryption, as introduced above in the context of deduplication, is secure.

This construction works out of the box when using server-side deduplication. However, care must be taken when using convergent encryption with client-side deduplication. Basically, just sending the hash value $H(k) = H(H(F))$ of the key (the hashed file F) to the server (called HCE1 in [34]) or the hash value of F' (called CE in [34]) for checking, then some of the attacks discussed below are still possible. Consequently, one should use more sophisticated proofs of ownership (PoW) protocols, as also discussed below.

5.2.2 Proofs of Ownership

When applying client-side deduplication with the approach discussed in the introduction; that is by simply sending the hash value of the file for the check, two main classes of potential attacks are introduced [30], for which we provide some illustrating examples:

Privacy and confidentiality: Fraudulent users can check whether someone has stored a specific file. For example, think of some privacy intrusive file or some whistleblowing activity. Furthermore, if a file is highly structured and only a small space of varying content is left, someone can simply brute force all potential files by computing their hash values and check whether the respective file has been stored – think of contract backups. Moreover, if someone just learns the hash values of files (e.g., reports containing sensitive information), then this person can illegally get access to the file.

Misuse of storage service: Fraudulent users may use a storage service as a low bandwidth covert channel. For example, by choosing two files, and assigning them bit values, a bit can be communicated via the information whether or not a file is already present at the SP. Another misuse is by uploading a file to the storage service and then distributing its hash value such that other users can download such files. This would actually let the SP unknowingly act as a content distribution network.

Note that in all above examples, access control does not prevent any of these attacks, since deduplication is performed over all users irrespective of access rights to particular files. We also refer the interested reader to [30,35] for further examples and potential threats.

As already outlined above, the problem yielding to attacks is that short information from the file is sufficient to download the file. In [30], the authors propose to weaken this correlation between deduplication and the existence of files by assigning a random threshold for every file and performing deduplication only if the number of copies of the file exceeds this threshold. However, this solution is far from optimal, since it produces high bandwidth costs and does not really tackle the problem as it as.

Essentially, the solution to the problem is to force users to prove that they know much more information about the file at hand and not only its hash value. Thus, such a solution is called a *proof of ownership* (PoW), and more sophisticated proposals than the threshold solution have been given in [35], which we briefly sketch below. The security model requires that a client succeeds only with negligible probability in a PoW, as long as the client has enough uncertainty about the file (i.e., an attacker is allowed to have partial information about the file). The security guarantees in the subsequent constructions are increasingly relaxed for the sake of efficiency.

- The first construction takes a file, uses an erasure code to produce an encoded file, and then computes a Merkle tree over the encoded file. The server stores the root hash of the Merkle tree along with the file. A PoW then amounts to challenge the client to send the authentication paths (i.e., siblings of a leaf on the path to the root) for a randomly sampled (superlogarithmic) number of leaf indices.

- The second construction avoids such costly and disk access intensive erasure coding. Instead, this solution uses a universal hash function to hash the file into a so-called reduction buffer, which is much smaller than an encoded file, but still too large to share it with other users, say, 64 MB. Then the Merkle tree approach is implemented on this reduction buffer instead of the encoded file.

- The third schemes replaces universal hashing, which is costly to compute for such a large output space, with a more efficient mixing and reduction procedure. Essentially, the mixing phase builds the reduction buffer by XORing each block of the original file with four random positions in the buffer (after performing a bit shift). The mixing phase then amplifies confusion and diffusion in the reduction buffer by XORing together random positions of the reduction buffer. Finally, the reduction buffer is used as a basis for the Merkle tree approach.

The problem with all the above-mentioned constructions is that the client needs to process the entire file for conducting a PoW. In [36], the authors improve the third construction of [35] such that the I/O and computational costs of the client no longer depend on the file size (thus improving the efficiency), and prove the security in an information-theoretic framework. Basically, instead of using a Merkle tree such that the server only has to store the root hash of a file, the server precomputes answers to challenges that are sent to clients. More precisely, the client sends the hash value of the file to the server and the server then sends as challenge a seed for a pseudorandom generator, which is used by the client to generate k random positions of bits in the file and send the concatenation of the respective bits to the server, who compares them to the precomputed value. In [36], further optimizations by replacing the cryptographic hash functions and by introducing a more efficient indexing function are proposed.

Finally, we stress that the aim of PoWs is diametrically opposed to that of PoR/PDP, as in the former case the client proves the possession of a file. However, although these concepts are somewhat related, one cannot use PoR/PDP protocols to construct PoW for various reasons, most importantly, since clients would need to share a common state (tag metadata or sentinel metadata), which is impractical in this scenario.

5.3 SEARCHABLE ENCRYPTION

Contents in Brief

What is this? Encryption that allows keyword search over encrypted files.

What can it do? Clients can outsource their data to a server and run queries that the server can correctly execute without learning anything about the query or the data.

How can it be used in cloud computing? Use of highly available cloud storage without revealing the files in plaintext to the storage provider.

A naive approach for enabling search capabilities in outsourced storage would be to store documents in plaintext and to run queries with conventional search techniques. This is permissible as long as the storage provider is fully trustworthy. For cloud storage/computing, outsourcing encrypted files seems to be the sine qua non [37], as it guarantees confidentiality of the client's data. However, the usual search algorithms are as well no longer applicable. Another naive solution is to download all the encrypted data, decrypt it, and do the search locally. For large data sets, this is impractical for obvious reasons.

Searchable encryption combines confidentiality with respect to the storage provider with search functionality and enables the storage server to search the encrypted data by virtue of a *trapdoor information* that the client provides. The server thereby neither learns the exact query nor the underlying data (search space). The storage server can then retrieve and respond with all the data (encrypted documents) that matched the query, and the client can decrypt the results locally. This vastly cuts the bandwidth consumption, compared to the trivial download of all encrypted content. Over the last years, this field has seen a considerable amount of research activity [38], and various constructions with quite different features and security guarantees have been proposed. Still, it is a very active research field.

As mentioned in Section 4.1.3, searchable encryption is a special case of functional encryption. Also, fully homomorphic encryption schemes (see Section 4.2.3) allow the construction of searchable encryption. Moreover, oblivious RAM as discussed in Section 3.4.3 allows a straightforward (although impractical) search on encrypted data. In the following, we are only interested in encryption schemes specifically designed for searching on encrypted data, and thus being much more efficient than these alternative generic constructions.

5.3.1 Categorization

Searchable encryption schemes can be divided into three major categories.

Symmetric vs Asymmetric Searchable Encryption

In a symmetric searchable encryption scheme [39,40], only the owner of a secret key (data owner) can store encrypted data to the storage provider and generate encrypted search queries as well as decrypt the outsourced data. Contrary to this, asymmetric searchable encryption [41], often called *public key encryption with keyword search* (PEKS), allows everyone to store encrypted data on behalf of the owner, but (in the default setting) only the owner of the respective secret key can issue search queries and decrypt the outsourced data.

Fulltext vs Index Search

When speaking of search on data, we can distinguish *fulltext* search from *index-based* search. In the former, the entire content of a data file is searched item by item, where every item is tested for some condition (e.g., equality with a given keyword). Clearly, the complexity of fulltext search increases with the size of the respective data file, and can thus quickly become impractical. Index search does not search on the data itself, and instead runs the query on a separate encrypted index file. How this index is built (i.e., which subsets of data items such as words it includes) depends on the application and is not discussed here. Furthermore, the index can be *forward* or *inverted*. Thereby, a forward index stores a list of keywords per file, whereas an inverted index maintains a list of matching files for every keyword.

Types of Queries

One can generally model a query as a predicate f that needs to be satisfied by data matching the query. The most common predicate used in searchable encryption is the equality predicate; that is, to test whether a given keyword (the query) matches a keyword in the encrypted plaintext or index, respectively. While given more than a single keyword, a conjunctive keyword search is easy by doing equality tests for every single keyword, and computing the intersection of all resulting sets of matches. Some constructions [42–44] improve this by concealing the number of searched keywords in such a conjunctive query by always issuing a query of the same size. Such an approach for disjunctive queries has only been recently introduced in the symmetric setting in [45]. Another perhaps practically useful kind of predicate checks the similarity of keywords [46, 47] based on some given similarity metric.

5.3.2 Symmetric Searchable Encryption

In the following, we present a candidate construction of a fulltext as well as an index-based symmetric searchable encryption scheme.

Fulltext Symmetric Searchable Encryption

Let us consider a file to be a sequence $F = (w_1, \ldots, w_k)$ of n-bit keywords and we want to achieve sequential search capabilities. Intuitively, the basic construction in [39] works by computing the bitwise XOR of the plaintext with a sequence of pseudorandom bits (having a special structure, which allows us to search on the data without revealing anything else about the plaintext.).

The basic scheme is very simple: To encrypt a file $F = (w_1, \ldots, w_k)$ of n-bit words, the data owner chooses a pseudorandom sequence $(S_1, \ldots, S_k)$ used as seeds of adequate size (where this sequence can be constructed from a single compact seed). In order to encrypt w_i, the data owner computes $T_i = S_i \| F_{k_i}(S_i)$ where F_{k_i} is a pseudorandom generator taking the key k_i, and the ciphertext is $c_i = w_i \oplus T_i$. The encrypted file $F' = (c_1, \ldots, c_k)$ is then stored at the server. Searching can be performed as follows: If the data owner wants to search for a word w, it gives w, k_i, and the location i where w potentially occurs to the server. The server can then check whether $c_i \oplus w = s \| t$ is of the form $(s, t = F_{k_i}(s))$. Obviously, this solution is not really satisfying, since it reveals the query, and either the data owner must know the positions where a potential keyword has to be searched for (which is not really realistic) or needs to reveal all the secrets k_i for a single search query.

The second scheme supporting controlled searching in [39] mitigates this problem. The main idea here is to choose the values k_i of a specific form, namely to compute them as $k_i = f_{k'}(w_i)$ where k' is chosen uniformly at random from the keyspace of another pseudorandom function f. Basically, the data owner can reveal $k_i = f_{k'}(w_i)$ to the server, and this allows the server to check all locations for an occurrence of a keyword w_i, without learning or revealing anything about the other locations j where $w_j \neq w_i$. Nevertheless, from a match, the server still learns w_i.

The third construction in [39] supports hidden searches; that is, searches where the data owner no longer has to reveal w to the server (which is clearly desirable in a practical application). Therefore, every keyword w needs to be encrypted using a deterministic symmetric encryption scheme (KeyGen, Encrypt, Decrypt) prior to applying the above construction. In particular, the above construction is applied no longer to the keywords, but to ciphertexts $c'_i =$

$\mathrm{Encrypt}(w_i; k'')$, where k'' is another key and $T_i = S_i \| F_{k_i}(c_i')$. The search remains the same with the exception that the data owner gives $(f_{k'}(c_i'), c_i')$ instead of $f_{k'}(w)$ to the server. Actually, in the initial construction of the third scheme, the data owner is unable to decrypt the full ciphertexts again, since he or she would need to know $F_{k_i}(c_i')$ and in particular $c_i' = \mathrm{Encrypt}(w_i; k'')$ for every encrypted block $c_i = c_i' \oplus T_i$ in the ciphertext of the entire file. This, however, can easily be fixed as shown in [39] (we do not discuss this modification here in detail).

We note that [48] reviews security definitions in the setting of symmetric searchable encryption, which are not going to be discussed here. Recently, [49] presented the first fully secure dynamic searchable symmetric encryption scheme that supports efficient updates of indexes (i.e., add and remove keywords from an existing index).

Index-Based Symmetric Searchable Encryption

An abstract definition of an index-based symmetric searchable encryption scheme comprises the following algorithms:

KeyGen: This probabilistic algorithm generates a secret key sk.

BuildIndex: This algorithm takes a list of keywords $W = \{w_1, \ldots, w_k\}$ for a file F and a secret key sk and returns an index $\mathcal{I}$, which encodes the set of keywords W for file F.

Trapdoor: This algorithm takes a keyword w_j and a secret key sk and produces a trapdoor T_{w_j} for this keyword.

Test: This algorithm takes an index $\mathcal{I}$, a trapdoor T_{w_j} and outputs true if $w_j \in W$ and false otherwise.

As a representative of this class of schemes, we now sketch the construction of [40] (and refer the reader to [50] for an alternative construction), which uses Bloom filters [51] as a per file index.

A Bloom filter represents a set $W = \{w_1, \ldots, w_n\}$ of n elements by an array of m bits, initially all set to 0. Furthermore, we require k independent hash functions $H_1, \ldots, H_k$, with $H_i : \{0, 1\}^* \to \{1, \ldots, m\}$. In order to map an item $w_j \in W$ to the Bloom filter, one computes $H_1(w_j), \ldots, H_k(w_j)$ and sets the corresponding positions of the array to 1. If a bit at a specific position is set multiple times to 1, only the first change takes effect. In order to verify if a given element w is an element of W, the bits at all positions $H_1(w), \ldots, H_k(w)$ of the array must be set to 1. Obviously, there is a chance of false positives (i.e., elements that seem to be in W but have not been included in the Bloom filter, since it may accidentally happen that all bits of interest are set to 1). A Bloom filter's false positive probability P can thereby be approximated as $P \approx (1 - e^{-\frac{kn}{m}})^k$.

The scheme of [40] works as follows. We omit discussing the encryption of the file itself, since this can be considered decoupled from the encryption of the index and only focus on the index. The KeyGen algorithm chooses a pseudorandom function $f : \{0,1\}^n \times \{0,1\}^\kappa \rightarrow \{0,1\}^\kappa$ for security parameter κ and a parameter n and a secret key $sk = (k_1, \ldots, k_k)$ for $k_i \in_R \{0,1\}^\kappa$. Given a file F with identifier id_F and associated keywords $W = \{w_1, \ldots, w_\ell\}$, the BuildIndex algorithm computes for each keyword w_i values $x_j = f(w_i, k_j)$ and $y_j = f(id_F, x_j)$ for $1 \leq j \leq k$, and inserts the values $y_1, \ldots, y_k$ into the Bloom filter. Furthermore, the Bloom filter is blinded by inserting a suitable number of random keywords into it (see [40] for the choice of parameters). Consequently, to produce a trapdoor T for a keyword w, the Trapdoor algorithm simply computes $T = (x_1, \ldots, x_k)$ with $x_j = f(w, k_j)$ for $1 \leq j \leq k$. In order to perform the search, the server runs the Test algorithm upon input of T and id_F, computes $y_j = f(id_F, x_j)$ for $1 \leq j \leq k$, and tests whether $y_1, \ldots, y_k$ are contained within the Bloom filter. Note that when inserting the trapdoors directly into the Bloom filter, the index would become vulnerable to correlation attacks (i.e., it would be possible to deduce similarities of files by comparing different indices).

5.3.3 Asymmetric Searchable Encryption

In [41], the authors introduce the notion of PEKS, which allows everyone to build an encrypted keyword index for files that can then be stored along with the encrypted file at some untrusted server. However, only the holder of the secret key can then generate search queries for a keyword (trapdoors), which allow the server to perform an equality test for the keyword in encrypted indexes. As above, we omit discussing the encryption of the file itself for obvious reasons. We assume that for every file F there is a set of keywords $W = \{w_1, \ldots, w_k\}$. A PEKS is defined as follows:

KeyGen: This probabilistic algorithm generates and returns a public and secret key (pk, sk).

Tag: This algorithm takes a list of keywords $W = \{w_1, \ldots, w_k\}$ for a file F and a public key pk and returns an index $\mathcal{I} = \{I_1, \ldots, I_k\}$, which encodes the set of keywords W for file F.

Trapdoor: This algorithm takes a keyword w_j and a secret key sk and produces a trapdoor T_{w_j} for this keyword.

Test: This algorithm takes an index $\mathcal{I}$, a trapdoor T_{w_j} and a public key pk and outputs true if $w_j \in W$ and false otherwise.

A concrete instantiation of PEKS can be realized via bilinear maps. Therefore, let G, G_T be two groups of prime order p, $e : G \times G \rightarrow G_T$ be a bilinear map, and $H_1 : \{0,1\}^* \rightarrow G$ and $H_2 : G_T \rightarrow \{0,1\}^{\log p}$ be two hash functions. Then, the KeyGen algorithm chooses a random $\alpha \in \mathbb{Z}_p$ and a random generator $g \in G$. It sets $sk = \alpha$ and $pk = (g, h = g^\alpha)$.

The Tag algorithm takes a list of keywords $W = \{w_1, \ldots, w_k\}$ for some file F, chooses random $r_i \in \mathbb{Z}_p$, computes $t_i = e(H_1(w_i), h^{r_i})$, and sets $I_i = (g^{r_i}, H_2(t_i))$ for $1 \leq i \leq k$. It returns $\mathcal{I} = \{I_1, \ldots, I_k\}$.

Given a search query being a keyword w, the Trapdoor algorithm computes $T_w = H_1(w)^\alpha$, which is then sent as a search query to the server. For every encrypted index $\mathcal{I}$ corresponding to file F, the server then runs Test. This amounts to checking for each element $I_i = (g^{r_i}, H_2(t_i))$ of each encrypted index, if $H_2(e(T_w, g^{r_i})) \stackrel{?}{=} H_2(t_i)$ holds. Observe that if Test returns true, then we have $w = w_i$, and consequently

$$H_2(e(T_w, g^{r_i})) = H_2(e(H_1(w)^\alpha, g^{r_i})) = H_2(e(H_1(w), h^{r_i})) = H_2(t_i).$$

This PEKS scheme can be proven semantically secure under the bilinear CDH assumption.

In [52] the authors argue that this semantic security notion might be too weak for practical applications and propose *PEKS with registered keywords* (PERKS) in order to make PEKS secure against (partial) off-line keyword guessing attacks by the server. We briefly review the ideas subsequently that typically emerge since the keyword set is public and comes from a "small" (polynomially bounded) message space.

Off-line keyword guessing attack: Since in a PEKS the server can generate tags for every potential keyword (the computation of Tag does not require the secret key), it may figure out the relationships between keywords and the trapdoors (queries) by generating a tag for each keyword of interest and test it with the trapdoors it has already received. With the knowledge of the relationships between keywords and the trapdoors, given a tag, the server can straightforwardly determine keywords in an index.

Partial off-line keyword guessing attack: In this case, we do not assume that the set of potential keywords is polynomially bounded, and thus it may not be efficiently possible to determine the entire set of keywords corresponding to one index, hence it is a partial keyword guessing attack. Apart from this fact, the attack works as above.

The construction in [52], PERKS, mitigates this problem by introducing a keyword registration phase, which is run by the owner of the secret key and every other party that should be able to generate trapdoors for querying the server. Clearly, this introduces an additional overhead while mitigating the problems of (partial) off-line keyword guessing attacks. The instantiation proposed in [52] is a quite straightforward modification of the original PEKS scheme of [41]. Before we present the modification, we give an abstract description of a PERKS scheme for the sake of completeness:

KeyGen: This probabilistic algorithm generates and returns a public and secret key pair (pk, sk). This algorithm also generates a public keyword set with cardinality N.

KeywordReg: This algorithm takes a keyword w and a secret key sk and returns a pretag s_w.

Tag: This algorithm takes a list of keywords $W = \{w_1, \ldots, w_k\}$ for a file F and pretags $s_{w_1}, \ldots, s_{w_k}$ corresponding to the keywords and a public key pk and returns an index $\mathcal{I} = \{I_1, \ldots, I_k\}$ (set of tags), which encodes the set of keywords W for file F.

Trapdoor: This algorithm takes a keyword w_j and a secret key sk and outputs a trapdoor T_{w_j} for this w_j.

Test: This algorithm takes an index $\mathcal{I}$, a trapdoor T_{w_j}, the corresponding pretag s_{w_j}, and a public key pk, and outputs true if $w_j \in W$ and false otherwise.

In contrast to the PEKS scheme of [41], the PERKS scheme of [52] generates a secret key $sk = (\alpha, \beta)$ for $\alpha, \beta \in_R \mathbb{Z}_p$. The KeywordReg algorithm computes a pretag for a keyword w as $s_w = H_1(w\|\beta)$ and the computation of a tag (an element of the index $\mathcal{I}$) by the Tag algorithm amounts to computing $(S_{w_1}, S_{w_2}) = (g^r, e(g^\alpha, s_w)^r)$ (note that the hash function H_2 for the PEKS scheme is no longer used). The Trapdoor algorithm computes $T = H_1(w\|\beta)^\alpha = s_w^\alpha$, and the Test algorithm checks whether $S_{w_2} = e(S_{w_1}, T)$ holds, which can easily be verified for correctness. The basic trick behind this construction is that the server can no longer compute tags since it does not know the secret β.

5.3.3.1 Conjunctive Keyword Search

A drawback of the simple PEKS scheme is that it is not possible to search for multiple keywords at the same time. The PEKS scheme could provide this functionality by using intersections of search results from single keyword searches or meta keywords. Using intersections, however, enables the server to learn all documents matching the individual keywords. The other option, meta keywords, requires exponential storage proportional to the number of keyword fields.

In [43], Park et al. proposed *public key encryption with conjunctive field keyword search* (PECK), a model that extends PEKS and enables a conjunctive keyword search on encrypted data. The proposed scheme works under the assumptions that (1) the same keyword never appears in two different keyword fields in the same document and (2) every keyword field is defined for every document. These assumptions, however, can easily be satisfied by tagging (prepending a field name) and using default (null) values for keywords that do not appear in a specific document respectively.

As above, we assume that for every file F there is a set of keywords $W = \{w_1, \ldots, w_k\}$ and note that due to the assumptions we consider all indices to be of equal size (i.e., they contain all keywords whose values have a default value unless they appear in that specific file). To enable conjunctive search capabilities, the query format is defined as $Q = (I_1, \ldots, I_k, \Omega_1, \ldots, \Omega_k)$ where the values of I_i are the positions of the keywords in the keyword vector and the Ω_i are the values of the keywords to be searched for. The corresponding trapdoor that is used to test if a document has the specified keywords in its keyword fields is denoted by T_Q.

A so-called noninteractive PECKS is defined by the following algorithms:

KeyGen: This probabilistic algorithm generates and returns a public and secret key pair (pk, sk).

Tag: This algorithm takes a list of keywords $W = \{w_1, \ldots, w_k\}$ for a file F and a public key pk and returns an index $\mathcal{I} = \{I_1, \ldots, I_k\}$, which encodes the set of keywords W for file F.

Trapdoor: This algorithm takes a query Q and a secret key sk to output a trapdoor T_Q for this query.

Test: This algorithm takes an index $\mathcal{I}$, a trapdoor T_Q, and a public key pk, and outputs true if $\{(w_{I_1} = \Omega_1), \ldots, (w_{I_k} = \Omega_k)\}$ and false otherwise.

For the concrete instantiation in [43], let G, G_T be two groups of prime order p, $e : \mathsf{G} \times \mathsf{G} \to \mathsf{G}_T$ be a bilinear map, and $H : \{0, 1\}^* \to \mathsf{G}$ be a suitable hash function. The KeyGen algorithm chooses a random generator g of G and two values $s_1, s_2 \in_R \mathbb{Z}_p$ and outputs $pk = (y_1 = g^{s_1}, y_2 = g^{s_2})$ and $sk = (s_1, s_2)$.

The Tag algorithm gets a list of keywords $W = \{w_1, \ldots, w_k\}$ for a file F and the public key $pk = (y_1 = g^{s_1}, y_2 = g^{s_2})$. It chooses a value $r \in_R \mathbb{Z}_p$ and computes the index $\mathcal{I}$ as

$$\mathcal{I} = (e(H(w_1)^r, y_1), \ldots, e(H(w_k)^r, y_k), y_2^r, g^r).$$

The Trapdoor algorithm takes a query $Q = (I_1, \ldots, I_k, \Omega_1, \ldots, \Omega_k)$, and a secret key $sk = (s_1, s_2)$, and works as follows. It chooses $u \in_R \mathbb{Z}_p$ and computes the trapdoor $T_Q = (T_1, T_2, I_1, \ldots, I_k)$ as

$$T_1 = \left(\prod_{j=1}^{k} H(\Omega_j) \right)^{\frac{s_1}{u+s_2}}$$

$$T_2 = u$$

and the I_i are such as in the query Q.

The Test algorithm takes an index $\mathcal{I} = (e(H(w_1)^r, y_1), \ldots, e(H(w_k)^r, y_k), y_2^r, g^r)$, a trapdoor $T_Q = (T_1, T_2, I_1, \ldots, I_k)$, and a public key $pk = (y_1 = g^{s_1}, y_2 = g^{s_2})$, and checks whether the following relation holds:

$$\prod_{j=1}^{k} e(H(w_j)^r, y_j) = e(T_1, y_2^r(g^r)^{T_2})$$

and outputs true if this is true and false otherwise. The equality of Test holds if $w_{I_i} = \Omega_i$ for $1 \leq i \leq k$. It can be seen that:

$$e(T_1, y_2^r(g^r)^{T_2}) = e\left(\left(\prod_{j=1}^{k} H(\Omega_j) \right)^{\frac{s_1}{u+s_2}}, y_2^r(g^r)^{T_2} \right)$$

$$= \prod_{j=1}^{k} e\left(H(\Omega_j), y_2^r(g^r)^{T_2} \right)^{\frac{s_1}{u+s_2}}$$

As a consequence, we see that for all $1 \leq i \leq t$ it holds that:

$$
\begin{aligned}
e(H(\Omega_i), y_2^r (g^r)^{T_2})^{\frac{s_1}{u+s_2}} &= e(H(\Omega_i)^r, y_2 g^{T_2})^{\frac{s_1}{u+s_2}} \\
&= e(H(\Omega_i)^r, g^{s_2} g^u)^{\frac{s_1}{u+s_2}} \\
&= e(H(\Omega_i)^r, g)^{s_1} \\
&= e(H(\Omega_i)^r, y_1),
\end{aligned}
$$

which shows the correctness of the construction.

5.3.4 Security of Searchable Encryption

In the context of searchable encryption, one assumes that the server is honest but curious, meaning that the server wants to learn information about the search queries but faithfully follows the protocol specifications. The information this adversarial server can infer can be with respect to the *index*, the *trapdoor* (the search query), or the *query result*. Below we briefly discuss these issues:

Index privacy: A server given an encrypted index should be unable to obtain information about the keywords in the index and in particular should be unable to reconstruct the keywords. Ideally, a server given a trapdoor only learns whether the predicate in the trapdoor is satisfied.

Trapdoor privacy: Given a trapdoor any third party and in particular the server performing the search should be unable to infer information encoded in the trapdoor (i.e., the predicate).

Query result privacy: The query result should not leak any information beyond the fact that the predicate matches.

When speaking of security of searchable encryption, there are quite different security models that have been proposed over time. Here, we limit ourselves to the security for searchable encryption based on index searches, which seem to be the most relevant schemes for practical applications, and refer the reader to [38] for an overview of state-of-the-art security models for fulltext search on encrypted data.

In the symmetric setting, security is defined as resistance against the following attack, referring to index, as well as trapdoor privacy explicitly.

Attack 5.3. The challenger chooses a bit b at random and the adversary $\mathcal{A}$ is allowed to adaptively issue index queries as well as trapdoor queries. The jth index query contains data items m_{j_0} and m_{j_1} with corresponding index sets of the same cardinality, and $\mathcal{A}$ obtains in return an encrypted index for m_{jb}. The ith trapdoor query from $\mathcal{A}$ contains predicates f_{i_0} and f_{i_1}, and $\mathcal{A}$ obtains in return a trapdoor for f_{i_b}. Thereby, $\mathcal{A}$ is restricted to predicates which are satisfied by the index sets corresponding to the respective m_{j_0} and m_{j_1}. At some point $\mathcal{A}$ outputs a bit b'.

The adversary $\mathcal{A}$ succeeds if $b = b'$ and an index-based symmetric searchable encryption scheme is said to be secure if any poly-time bounded adversary $\mathcal{A}$ has a negligible probability of succeeding in Attack 5.3.

In the asymmetric setting, security is defined by the following attack, where this attack only considers index privacy explicitly.

Attack 5.4. In the first phase, the attacker $\mathcal{A}$ can adaptively issue trapdoor queries and at some point outputs two data items m_0 and m_1 such that the index sets corresponding to the two data items have the same cardinality. Then, the attacker can make further trapdoor queries with the restriction that for any queried predicate f queried, both index sets need to satisfy the predicate. Then, the challenger chooses a random bit b, builds and gives the index I_b corresponding to m_b to $\mathcal{A}$. In the second phase, the adversary $\mathcal{A}$ can issue the same queries with the same restrictions as in the first phase and at the end, $\mathcal{A}$ outputs a bit b' as its guess.

The adversary $\mathcal{A}$ succeeds if $b = b'$, and an index-based asymmetric searchable encryption scheme is said to be secure if any poly-time bounded adversary $\mathcal{A}$ has a negligible probability of succeeding in Attack 5.4.

5.4   AVAILABILITY IN THE CLOUD

Contents in Brief

What is this? Methods to achieve availability by data redundancy and distribution.

What can it do? Distribute a data item across several hosts so that only a subset of which is sufficient to reconstruct the message (resilience against server outages).

How can it be used in cloud computing? Lets a client securely and with high availability store data remotely in a cloud or across a cloud of clouds.

Availability is traditionally achieved by redundancy, in the simplest case meaning that we humbly replicate a file over several hosts in order to recover from failures. In particular, the *cloud-of-clouds* approach would in fact replicate the data over several subordinate clouds. For matters of such distribution to be efficient and secure, several schemes of *information dispersion* have been proposed under different disguises, yet mostly resting on the fundament of error-correcting codes and encryption.

Information Dispersal Algorithms

To avoid the n-fold blowup in size of the shared data (as would happen for secret-sharing), an alternative has been introduced by Rabin [53] under the name *information dispersal algorithm* (IDA). As for any encoding, the data to be distributed is assumed as a vector of symbols (e.g., bytes) $\mathbf{F} = (f_1, \ldots, f_k)$. For illustration, let us say that $f_1, \ldots, f_k$ are *bytes*, so we work in the field F_{2^8}, say with $p(x) = 1 + x^4 + x^5 + x^7 + x^8$ as our irreducible polynomial. However, we emphasize that any finite field would work (in case that one encodes unicode symbols for instance).

The sharing is done by supplying a set of n servers with individual linear combinations of the information word (i.e., the ith server gets the value)

$$s_i = a_{i1}f_1 + a_{i2}f_2 + \cdots + a_{ik}f_k, \tag{5.2}$$

where the vector $\mathbf{a}_i = (a_{i1}, \ldots, a_{ik})$ is to be chosen carefully (we come back to this below). To retrieve a file from k (honest) servers, we simply set up a system of k equations in k unknowns $f_1, \ldots, f_k$, with the right-hand side values provided by the servers. In other words, when querying the server j, the user retrieves the vector $\mathbf{a}_j$ associated with this server, and the data item s_j that this server has stored. Having k equations like (5.2), reconstructing the data $\mathbf{F}$ boils down to solving a system of k equations in k unknowns.

In order to put this to work, we need to assure that any such system can be solved; that is, any selection of k out of n vectors $\mathbf{a}_1, \ldots, \mathbf{a}_n$ leads to a nonsingular coefficient matrix. The original work [53] proposed the following procedure to construct these vectors appropriately: choose distinct random values $x_1, \ldots, x_n \in \mathsf{F}_{2^8}$ and distinct $y_1, \ldots, y_k \in \mathsf{F}_{2^8}$, subject to the condition that for all i and all j, we have

$$x_i + y_j \neq 0, \quad \text{and } i \neq j \text{ implies } (x_i \neq x_j \text{ as well as } y_i \neq y_j).$$

Define the ith vector $\mathbf{a}_i$ as

$$\mathbf{a}_i := \left(\frac{1}{x_i + y_1}, \frac{1}{x_i + y_2}, \ldots, \frac{1}{x_i + y_k} \right) \quad \text{in } \mathsf{F}_{2^8},$$

then any selection of k such vectors will work to solve the arising system of equations.

This technique technically falls into the larger class of error-correcting codes, and does by itself achieve only weak security guarantees. Hence, it is advisable to encrypt the file before applying this kind of dispersal. A simple method to handle the necessary key management is to implicitly include the key in the file, as an encrypted $(k+1)$th block, where the encryption key is derived from all the preceding file blocks. This encrypted file is then put through an error-correcting encoding. This trick spares the need to share the key in advance, and enforces that all file blocks must be available to properly decrypt the file. Details are found in [54].

Gaining Efficiency from Encryption Combined with Secret-Sharing

For efficiency [55, 56], it is possible to combine information dispersal with secret-sharing to achieve short shares and high security. The idea is a simple three-step approach:

1. Encrypt the file symmetrically under a key sk and using an IND-CPA secure symmetric encryption scheme. Apply an IDA to the resulting ciphertext, giving the shares $c_1, \ldots, c_n$.

2. Apply a k-out-of-n-secret-sharing scheme (see Section 2.5.6) to the secret key sk, giving the shares $sk_1, \ldots, sk_n$.

3. To the ith server (among $i = 1, 2, \ldots, n$), give the share (c_i, sk_i).

Reconstruction is straightforward by obtaining k shares $(c_{i_1}, sk_{i_1}), \ldots, (c_{i_k}, sk_{i_k})$ and reconstructing the key sk using Lagrange interpolation (potentially invoking an error correction algorithm first). Then recover the encrypted file by solving the linear system with rows given by (5.2) for the IDA algorithm, and finally decrypt the file using the secret key sk. Reference [56] proves the above construction secure under one-query unrecoverability of the key, which holds for practical encryption schemes.

References

[1] A. Juels and B. S. J. Kaliski, "PoRs: Proofs of Retrievability for Large Files," in *CCS*, pp. 584–597, ACM, 2007.

[2] G. Ateniese, R. Burns, R. Curtmola, J. Herring, L. Kissner, Z. Peterson, and D. Song, "Provable Data Possession at Untrusted Stores," in *CCS*, pp. 598–609, ACM, 2007.

[3] G. Ateniese, R. Di Pietro, L. V. Mancini, and G. Tsudik, "Scalable and Efficient Provable Data Possession," in *SecureComm*, pp. 9:1–9:10, ACM, 2008.

[4] G. Ateniese, R. Burns, R. Curtmola, J. Herring, O. Khan, L. Kissner, Z. Peterson, and D. Song, "Remote Data Checking Using Provable Data Possession," *ACM Trans. Inf. Syst. Secur.*, vol. 14, pp. 12:1–12:34, June 2011.

[5] B. Chen and R. Curtmola, "Robust Dynamic Provable Data Possession," in *ICDCS Workshops*, pp. 515–525, IEEE, 2012.

[6] C. Hanser and D. Slamanig, "Efficient Simultaneous Private and Public Verifiable Robust Provable Data Possession from Elliptic Curves," in *SECRYPT)*, SciTePress, 2013.

[7] Q. Wang, C. Wang, J. Li, K. Ren, and W. Lou, "Enabling Public Verifiability and Data Dynamics for Storage Security in Cloud Computing," in *ESORICS*, vol. 5789 of *LNCS*, pp. 355–370, Springer, 2009.

[8] M. B. Paterson, D. R. Stinson, and J. Upadhyay, "A Coding Theory Foundation for the Analysis of General Unconditionally Secure Proof-Of-Retrievability Schemes for Cloud Storage," *CoRR*, vol. abs/1210.7756, 2012.

[9] K. D. Bowers, A. Juels, and A. Oprea, "Proofs of Retrievability: Theory and Implementation," in *CCSW*, pp. 43–54, ACM, 2009.

[10] H. Shacham and B. Waters, "Compact Proofs of Retrievability," in *ASIACRYPT*, vol. 5350 of *LNCS*, pp. 90–107, Springer, 2008.

[11] M. Liskov, R. L. Rivest, and D. Wagner, "Tweakable Block Ciphers," in *CRYPTO*, vol. 2442 of *LNCS*, pp. 31–46, Springer, 2002.

[12] M. Luby and C. Rackoff, "How to Construct Pseudo-random Permutations from Pseudo-random Functions," in *CRYPTO* (H. C. Williams, ed.), vol. 218 of *LNCS*, pp. 447–447, Springer, 1986.

[13] J. Black and P. Rogaway, "Ciphers with Arbitrary Finite Domains," in *CT-RSA*, vol. 2271 of *LNCS*, pp. 114–130, Springer, 2002.

[14] Y. Dodis, S. P. Vadhan, and D. Wichs, "Proofs of Retrievability via Hardness Amplification," in *TCC*, vol. 5444 of *LNCS*, pp. 109–127, Springer, 2009.

[15] W. W. Peterson and E. J. Weldon, *Error-Correcting Codes*. MIT Press, 1972.

[16] C. Cachin and S. Tessaro, "Asynchronous Verifiable Information Dispersal," in *DISC*, vol. 3724 of *LNCS*, pp. 503–504, Springer, 2005.

[17] Q. Zheng and S. Xu, "Fair and Dynamic Proofs of Retrievability," in *CODASPY*, pp. 237–248, ACM, 2011.

[18] D. Cash, A. Küpçü, and D. Wichs, "Dynamic Proofs of Retrievability via Oblivious RAM," in *IACR Cryptology ePrint Archive*, 2012. Report 2012/550.

[19] P. J. Cameron and J. H. van Lint, *Designs, Graphs, Codes and Their Links*. Cambridge University Press, 1991.

[20] D. R. Stinson, *Combinatorial Designs: Constructions and Analysis*. Springer, 2003.

[21] C. J. Colbourn and J. H. Dinitz, *Handbook of Combinatorial Designs*. Chapman & Hall, 2007.

[22] E. Stefanov, M. van Dijk, A. Oprea, and A. Juels, "Iris: A Scalable Cloud File System with Efficient Integrity Checks," in *ACSAC*, pp. 229–238, ACM, 2012.

[23] S. Rass, "Dynamic Proofs of Retrievability from Chameleon-Hashes," in *SECRYPT*, SciTePress, 2013.

[24] C. Erway, A. Küpçü, C. Papamanthou, and R. Tamassia, "Dynamic Provable Data Possession," in *CCS*, pp. 213–222, ACM, 2009.

[25] R. Curtmola, O. Khan, R. C. Burns, and G. Ateniese, "MR-PDP: Multiple-Replica Provable Data Possession," in *ICDCS*, pp. 411–420, IEEE, 2008.

[26] J. Xu and E.-C. Chang, "Towards Efficient Proofs of Retrievability," in *ASIACCS*, pp. 79–80, ACM, 2012.

[27] G. Ateniese, S. Kamara, and J. Katz, "Proofs of Storage from Homomorphic Identification Protocols," in *ASIACRYPT*, vol. 5912 of *LNCS*, pp. 319–333, Springer, 2009.

[28] E. Barker, W. Barker, W. Burr, W. Polk, and M. Smid, "NIST SP800-57: Recommendation for Key Management Part 1: General(Revised)," tech. rep., 2007.

[29] M. Dutch, "Understanding Data Deduplication Ratios." www.snia.org, 2008.

[30] D. Harnik, B. Pinkas, and A. Shulman-Peleg, "Side Channels in Cloud Services: Deduplication in Cloud Storage," *IEEE Security & Privacy*, vol. 8, no. 6, pp. 40–47, 2010.

[31] A. W. S. Blog, "Amazon S3 Server Side Encryption for Data at Rest." http://aws.typepad.com/aws/2011/10/new-amazon-s3-server-side-encryption.html, 2013.

[32] J. R. Douceur, A. Adya, W. J. Bolosky, D. Simon, and M. Theimer, "Reclaiming Space from Duplicate Files in a Serverless Distributed File System," in *ICDCS*, pp. 617–624, IEEE, 2002.

[33] M. W. Storer, K. M. Greenan, D. D. E. Long, and E. L. Miller, "Secure Data Deduplication," in *StorageSS*, pp. 1–10, ACM, 2008.

[34] M. Bellare, S. Keelveedhi, and T. Ristenpart, "Message-Locked Encryption and Secure Deduplication," in *EUROCRYPT*, vol. 7881 of *LNCS*, pp. 296–312, Springer, 2013.

[35] S. Halevi, D. Harnik, B. Pinkas, and A. Shulman-Peleg, "Proofs of Ownership in Remote Storage Systems," in *CCS*, pp. 491–500, ACM, 2011.

[36] R. Di Pietro and A. Sorniotti, "Boosting Efficiency and Security in Proof of Ownership for Deduplication," in *ASIACCS*, pp. 81–82, ACM, 2012.

[37] S. Kamara and K. Lauter, "Cryptographic Cloud Storage," in *Financial Cryptography Workshops*, vol. 6054 of *LNCS*, pp. 136–149, Springer, 2010.

[38] Q. Tang, "Search in Encrypted Data: Theoretical Models and Practical Applications." Cryptology ePrint Archive, Report 2012/648, 2012. http://eprint.iacr.org/.

[39] D. X. Song, D. Wagner, and A. Perrig, "Practical Techniques for Searches on Encrypted Data," in *IEEE Symposium on Security and Privacy*, pp. 44–55, IEEE, 2000.

[40] E.-J. Goh, "Secure Indexes." Cryptology ePrint Archive, Report 2003/216, 2003. http://eprint.iacr.org/.

[41] D. Boneh, G. Di Crescenzo, R. Ostrovsky, and G. Persiano, "Public-Key Encryption with Keyword Search," in *EUROCRYPT*, vol. 3027 of *LNCS*, pp. 506–522, Springer, 2004.

[42] P. Golle, J. Staddon, and B. R. Waters, "Secure Conjunctive Keyword Search over Encrypted Data," in *ACNS*, vol. 3089 of *LNCS*, pp. 31–45, Springer, 2004.

[43] D. J. Park, K. Kim, and P. J. Lee, "Public Key Encryption with Conjunctive Field Keyword Search," in *WISA*, vol. 3325 of *LNCS*, pp. 73–86, Springer, 2004.

[44] L. Ballard, S. Kamara, and F. Monrose, "Achieving Efficient Conjunctive Keyword Searches over Encrypted Data," in *ICICS*, vol. 3783 of *LNCS*, pp. 414–426, Springer, 2005.

[45] T. Moataz and A. Shikfa, "Boolean Symmetric Searchable Encryption," in *ASIACCS*, pp. 265–276, ACM, 2013.

[46] M. Kuzu, M. S. Islam, and M. Kantarcioglu, "Efficient Similarity Search over Encrypted Data," in *ICDE*, pp. 1156–1167, IEEE, 2012.

[47] M. Raykova, A. Cui, B. Vo, B. Liu, T. Malkin, S. M. Bellovin, and S. J. Stolfo, "Usable, Secure, Private Search," *IEEE Security & Privacy*, vol. 10, no. 5, pp. 53–60, 2012.

[48] R. Curtmola, J. A. Garay, S. Kamara, and R. Ostrovsky, "Searchable Symmetric Encryption: Improved Definitions and Efficient Constructions," in *CCS*, pp. 79–88, ACM, 2006.

[49] S. Kamara, C. Papamanthou, and T. Roeder, "Dynamic Searchable Symmetric Encryption," in *CCS*, pp. 965–976, ACM, 2012.

[50] Y.-C. Chang and M. Mitzenmacher, "Privacy Preserving Keyword Searches on Remote Encrypted Data," in *ACNS*, vol. 3531 of *LNCS*, pp. 442–455, Springer, 2005.

[51] B. H. Bloom, "Space/Time Trade-Offs in Hash Coding with Allowable Errors," *Communications of the ACM*, vol. 13, no. 7, pp. 422–426, 1970.

[52] Q. Tang and L. Chen, "Public-Key Encryption with Registered Keyword Search," in *EuroPKI*, vol. 6391 of *LNCS*, pp. 163–178, Springer, 2009.

[53] M. O. Rabin, "Efficient Dispersal of Information for Security, Load Balancing, and Fault Tolerance," *Journal of the ACM*, vol. 36, pp. 335–348, Apr. 1989.

[54] J. K. Resch and J. S. Plank, "AONT-RS: Blending Security and Performance in Dispersed Storage Systems," in *USENIX FAST*, pp. 14–14, USENIX Association, 2011.

[55] H. Krawczyk, "Secret Sharing Made Short," in *CRYPTO*, vol. 765 of *LNCS*, pp. 136–146, Springer, 1994.

[56] P. Rogaway and M. Bellare, "Robust Computational Secret Sharing and a Unified Account of Classical Secret-Sharing Goals," in *CCS*, pp. 172–184, ACM, 2007.

Chapter 6

Practical Issues

6.1 THE ROLE AND LIMITS OF CRYPTOGRAPHY

Cryptography is necessary, but not sufficient to protect sensitive information. Limitations exist in the theoretical as well as practical domain, both of which are worthwhile to look at.

Theoretical Limitations and Issues

Remember that fully homomorphic encryption (FHE), discussed in Section 4.2.3, enables a cloud provider to compute arbitrary functions on encrypted data only, while leaving the ability to decrypt the results exclusively to the holder of the secret key. Concerning computations, this is arguably one of the most powerful primitives known. However, taken on its own it cannot enforce the privacy demands of common cloud services, as has been proven by [1]. In brief, their line of arguments rests on a hierarchy of privacy levels for cloud applications, for which they can prove any cryptographic primitive unable to achieve it. Starting this hierarchy with single-client computing (see Figure 6.1a), in which a single client u_1 has a cloud provider compute a function on the data x_1, subject to the access policy that only u_1 may learn any outputs (e.g., computation of taxes). It is easy to argue that FHE can realize this (first level of the hierarchy), however, it fails to achieve the same goal for a multiclient computation (second level of the hierarchy; see Figure 6.1b): here, the application executes over data items $x_1, x_2, \ldots, x_n$ of multiple clients $u_1, \ldots, u_n$, subject to the access policy that release of information is selective and specific for each client; for example, u_i may be entitled to learn the computation result $f(x_i, x_j)$, while u_j – who provided x_j – is not. Proving that this is impossible

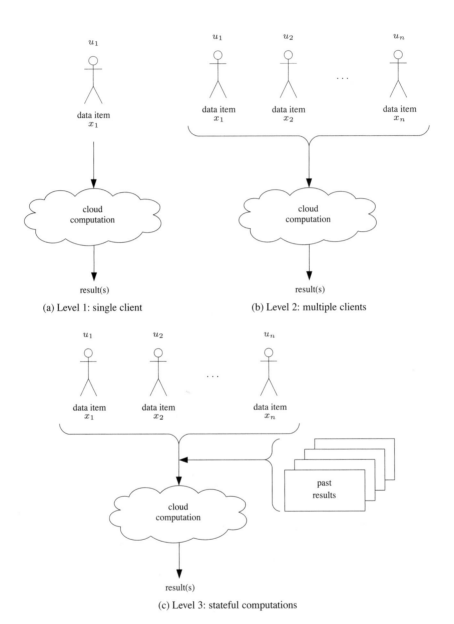

(a) Level 1: single client

(b) Level 2: multiple clients

(c) Level 3: stateful computations

Figure 6.1 Computing hierarchy of [1].

happens by showing that the possibility would lead to a general circuit-obfuscator, which is known to be unachievable in software alone [2], except in some restricted special cases. The same conclusion holds for the third level of [1]'s hierarchy, in which the computation is made stateful (i.e., dependent on past computations and results as illustrated in Figure 6.1c). Concerning computational complexity as a fundament for security, homomorphic encryption cannot be based on problems of "arbitrary strong intractability" [3], fortunately however, this finding does not limit their practical usefulness or security.

The conclusion to be drawn from this is that multiclient computations inevitably require trusted hardware at some point. Following this approach, a potential way out of the dilemma is to use *secure multiparty computation* (SMC). Roughly speaking, SMC allows several clients to collaborate in an attempt to compute any function (of bounded complexity) over private inputs only, often based on variations of secret-sharing (see Section 2.5.6). The crux is that no coalition (up to a fixed bounded size or from an a priori specified family of sets) can learn the entire input, intermediate results, or output. This technique is theoretically capable of carrying out the actions of any trusted third party as a team, thus distributing trust across several instances, and providing security guarantees via the assumption that no more than some threshold number of entities are adversaries or otherwise corrupted. This ability, however, comes not for free and is bought at the cost of pairwise secure channels and a secure broadcast channel, neither of which is trivial or cheap to achieve. However, SMC is as well subject to theoretical limitations:

Fact 6.1. Assuming that up to t out of n participants collude, we have the following maximal security achievable (see [4]):

- Against passive adversaries, assuming secure channels if and only if $t < n/2$ [5,6].

- Against active adversaries, assuming secure channels if and only if $t < n/3$ [5,6]. Equipped with a secure consensus broadcast channel, security against active adversaries holds if and only if $t < n/2$ for computational security, or $t < n/3$ for perfect security.

If attacks are described by a collection Σ of possibly compromised subsets (an adversary structure; see Definition 4.1), then the following general limits are known [7]:

Fact 6.2. Assume that the players have pairwise secure channels.

- SMC is possible against passive adversaries if and only if for all $A, B \in \Sigma$ we have $A \cup B \in \Sigma$.

- Assuming an additional secure broadcast consensus channel, SMC is possible against active adversaries if and only if for all $A, B, C \in \Sigma$ we have $A \cup B \cup C \in \Sigma$.

Often, the evaluation of a function via an interactive protocol carried out between n participants (clients) comes at unpleasantly high costs in terms of computation and communication. Hence, SMC is usually considered as impractical and cumbersome to implement. Moreover, the problem of setting up the secure pairwise channels and the secure broadcast channel is not straightforwardly solvable by public key cryptography, unless one is willing to accept computational security of SMC only, whereas SMC can theoretically provide perfect security [8] (setting up SMC with this highest known security level requires secure channels via means of multipath communication [9, 10], which adds another layer of considerable overhead to the overall system).

Other aspects of security like anonymous communication or data anonymization are as well subject to theoretical limitations. For example, it is easy to see that perfect anonymity is basically unachievable without a set of proxies in between. The number of layers required to sufficiently "blur" the message's origin and relations to other channels (unlinkability) is at least $\mathcal{O}(\log n)$, if n nodes exist in the network in total [11].

Theoretical limitations may as well concern computational overhead: for example, it is known that the general problem of achieving k-anonymity (and hence any property building upon) by suppression is NP-hard, thus intractable for large databases [12]. The same reference, however, provides more efficient approximations, which may be the way to go in practice, besides other practical proposals, such as [13].

Practical Limitations and Issues

Formal security assurances like those provided by cryptographic research (papers) are, according to Kerckhoff's principle [14], only as good as the protection of the respective cryptographic keys. This protection is usually made up of access control and key entropy; that is, the uncertainty when the key is simply guessed. Although cryptographic keys, say an AES key, usually come with 128 bit, and can hardly be guessed as such, they are nevertheless stored in devices that grant access to the key using a considerably shorter password. Taking that passwords of sufficient complexity to thwart guessing are hard to remember, the "effective" uncertainty about a cryptographic key often boils down to the uncertainty in guessing the protective password. Though the cryptographic protection may be good, cryptography remains strong only if its keys remain hidden, which is the point where nontechnical techniques like social engineering come into play. Concerning passwords, several alternatives to conventional alphanumeric passwords (graphical passwords) have been proposed, some of which are resistant to shoulder-surfing (see [15–18]). Besides, one technical measure to lower the risk is the use of SMC to bring multiple instances into the game, so that no single (or no number of t) compromised machine(s) suffice to penetrate the system's protection. This would be a form of risk diversion; however, given viruses, worms, and trojans that spread like epidemics, the theoretical assumptions underneath most SMC research seem to yet poorly match the way in which real-life hackers conquer parts of a system. The extent to which a technical system can recover from human failure is thus highly questionable, and well-defined business processes and security models need to be implemented on top of pure cryptographic or technical protections.

Cloud implementations, insofar they are based on virtualization, have been discovered as vulnerable to side-channel-like attacks [19, 20]. The idea is the very same one that works for smartcard attacks, which uses a coresident virtual machine or sniffer to monitor the activity of a cloud VM in an attempt to discover what happens internally. In the laboratory setting, [19] has demonstrated how ElGamal decryption keys can be drained from a VM. Likewise, [20] describes how to measure times between keystrokes (to infer passwords), measure the cache usage (to establish covert channels to penetrate the VM towards the outside), and to discover traffic patterns. Countermeasures against such attacks are rare, but two important ones are: (1) use side channel resistant algorithms, and (2) avoid coresidency of tasks that should run in isolation from each other. However, neither may be easy to assure in practice.

As a final practical advice, it appears reasonable to minimize the user's burden when using security mechanisms. PKIs were originally intended to handle problems of key management, say if an encrypted file will be accessed by many people in the organization. However, the resulting processes occasionally reach a level of complexity that makes users invent workarounds to ease their daily work while unintendedly defeating security at the same time. Fortunately, many security precautions can be done transparently for cloud customers, such as protection against malware, viruses, worms, and so forth, and the use of trusted computing hardware. However, in cases where clouds are opened to the public in an attempt to minimize idle times and better utilize hardware that exists anyway, systems that have not been designed from scratch towards secure cloud service provisioning may be difficult to endow with such security functionality a posteriori.

6.2   IMPLEMENTATIONS AND STANDARDIZATION

As we have presented various cryptographic primitives and different kinds of cryptographic protocols in this book, this section is devoted to a brief overview of different standardization attempts as well as available cryptographic toolkits. The following list is not intended to be complete or exhaustive. It should, however, provide sufficient pointers to standards and available software libraries to serve the interested reader as a starting point to dive deeper into implementation issues of various cryptographic concepts presented in this volume. The section finishes with some discussion and information on standardization attempts in the cloud computing area.

6.2.1   Implementations

For efficient implementations, libraries are available for performing basic arithmetic required for cryptographic constructions as well as for elliptic curves and pairing computations. On top of these, we give a selection of cryptographic toolkits providing functionality for various cryptographic constructions.

Basic Arithmetic

The GNU Multiple Precision Arithmetic Library (GMP) is a free library for arbitrary precision arithmetic, operating on signed integers, rational numbers, and floating point numbers and is available at http://gmplib.org/. The library is written in C, but there are wrappers available for other languages including Ada, C++, C#, OCaml, Perl, PHP, and Python.

NTL is a high-performance, portable C++ library developed and maintained by Victor Shoup and is freely available at http://www.shoup.net/ntl under the GPL license. It provides data structures and algorithms for arbitrary length integers, for vectors, matrices, and polynomials over the integers and over finite fields and for arbitrary precision floating point arithmetic. NTL may also be used in conjunction with the GMP library for enhanced performance in basic long integer arithmetics.

The Multiprecision Integer and Rational Arithmetic C Library (MIRACL) is a C/C++ library that implements all arithmetic and functionality for public key cryptography, including elliptic curve cryptography. It can be used without charge for academic and noncommercial purposes and is available at http://www.compapp.dcu.ie/~mike/shamus.html.

Furthermore, we note that today typically all programming languages support basic large integer arithmetics, but the above-mentioned libraries are usually orders of magnitudes faster.

Elliptic Curves and Pairings

There are various elliptic curve implementations available today. We focus on C/C++ as well as Java implementations, since those seem to be the most prevalent ones. Furthermore, we note that all these libraries also provide functionality for other (not elliptic curve based) cryptographic algorithms such as RSA, symmetric cryptography, and so forth.

The MIRACL C/C++ library (see above) as well as the OpenSSL library (`http://www.openssl.org/`), which is written in C, provide functionality for elliptic curve cryptography.

Well-known Java implementations are the ECCelerate library, which is available from (`http://jce.iaik.tugraz.at`) and can be freely used for academic and noncommercial purposes. Another Java library is the FlexiProvider, which is available under the GPL from `http://www.flexiprovider.de/`. The latter one additionally provides some postquantum schemes like code-based cryptosystems.

One of the first available and comprehensive pairing libraries has been the pairing-based cryptography (PBC) library, which is implemented in C, based on the GMP and created by Ben Lynn, and is available from `http://crypto.stanford.edu/pbc/`. There also exists a Java wrapper and a Java porting (jPBC) created by Angelo De Caro and is available from `http://gas.dia.unisa.it/projects/jpbc/`. Two other notable implementations of Type-3 Pairings on Baretto-Naehrig curves are the bnpairings library, which is written in Java and available from `http://code.google.com/p/bnpairings` and the ate − pairing library, written in C++, which is available from `https://github.com/herumi/ate-pairing`.

Cryptographic Toolkits

The Advanced Crypto Software Collection (ACSC) is a collection of cryptographic tools accessible for system developers, which comprises among others ABE. Idemix and U-Prove are implementations of multishow and one-show anonymous credentials, respectively, and ABC4Trust is a project that aims at developing an easy accessible abstract interface for these two aforementioned anonymous credential systems at an application level. The libfenc library is a functional encryption library that currently provides an implementation of various ABE schemes. HElib is a recently released library for fully homomorphic and somewhat homomorphic encryption written in C++ and based on the NTL library. Percy++ is a C++ library implementing PIR and is also based on NTL. ORAM is the first ever implementation of oblivious random access memory, which incorporates many recent advances and is written in C#.

We also want to draw the readers attention to Charm, a framework written in Python to assist the rapid prototyping of (complex) cryptographic protocols. Furthermore, there are some cryptographic compilers, ZKPDL and CACE, which can be useful when relying on (complex) zero-knowledge proofs and automatically generate program code from abstract specifications of such proofs. Further interesting tools are TASTY [21], VIFF, as well as the project *Might Be Evil* [22], which provide optimized solutions to secure multiparty computations (SMC).

Table 6.1 provide an overview of all those tools and respective download locations.

Table 6.1

Overview of Available Toolkits for Relevant Cryptographic Tasks

Description	URL
ACSC	`http://hms.isi.jhu.edu/acsc`
Idemix	`http://www.zurich.ibm.com/idemix`
U-Prove	`http://research.microsoft.com` `/en-us/projects/u-prove`
ABC4Trust	`https://abc4trust.eu`
libfenc	`http://code.google.com/p/libfenc`
Helib	`https://github.com/shaih/HElib`
Percy++	`http://percy.sourceforge.net`
ORAM	`http://www.emilstefanov.net` `/Research/ObliviousRam`
Charm	`http://www.charm-crypto.com`
ZKPDL	`https://github.com/brownie/cashlib`
CACE	`http://www.cace-project.eu`
TASTY	`http://code.google.com/p/tastyproject`
Might Be Evil	`http://mightbeevil.com`
VIFF	`http://viff.dk`

6.2.2 Standardization

Let us briefly look at cryptographic standards and approaches towards standardizing more recent cryptographic achievements. Furthermore, we take a brief look at standardization attempts in the cloud computing field.

Cryptography

The IEEE P1363 standards contains specifications for public key cryptography (including elliptic curves), and with its more recent additions also lattice-based cryptography (IEEE P1363.1), password-based public key cryptography (IEEE P1363.2), as well as a standard for pairing-based cryptographic techniques (IEEE P1363.3).

Many cryptographic primitives covered by the aforementioned standards are also standardized by other bodies such as the International Organization for Standardization (ISO) and the joint ISO/IEC (International Electrotechnical Commission). Furthermore, there are also country specific standardization bodies such as the U.S. NIST which, besides providing standards also recommends appropriate key sizes for cryptosystems. The most well-known seems to be the NIST curves in the context of elliptic curve cryptography.

In the context of key size recommendations, we point the attention of the reader to `http://www.keylength.com/` for a project providing key size recommendations compiled from different sources.

Finally, we want to mention that for various privacy preserving techniques, such as anonymous signatures (including group signatures) and anonymous entity authentication, ISO/IEC has already standardization attempts at the level of a draft international standard (DIS) as ISO/IEC DIS 20008 and ISO/IEC DIS 20009 respectively. Nevertheless, it must be mentioned that most of the cryptographic concepts discussed in this book lack existing standardization efforts and it will still take some time to have standards available.

Cloud Computing

Today, there is a large number of standardization efforts led by cloud computing vendors and standardization bodies. Due to this large number, it makes it equally difficult for cloud computing vendors as well as users to determine which efforts in standardization will emerge to be predominant. Additionally, there are multiple standardization efforts in some fields of cloud computing, whereas they are missing in other fields. We refer the reader to [23] for an interesting discussion on cloud standardization problems.

Nevertheless, standardization is an important subject for clouds, as it helps to avoid vendor lock-in, to improve the interoperability of different cloud computing vendors and allows benchmarking, and the absence of standards makes it difficult for customers to compare and evaluate cloud offerings.

We will exemplarily briefly present two standardization efforts in the context of infrastructure as a service (IaaS) offers, namely migration of virtual machine (VM) images across platforms and unified interfaces for accessing data stored in the cloud. DMTF with its Open Virtualization Format intends to standardize how VMs are moved from one hosted platform to another and SNIA with its Cloud Data Management Interface standardizes the way clients interface with cloud storage resources. An up-to-date overview on cloud computing standardization efforts in various fields can be found at `http://cloud-standards.org`.

Security issues associated with cloud computing are addressed by the Cloud Security Alliance (`https://cloudsecurityalliance.org`), a nonprofit organization with a mission to promote the use of best practices for providing security assurance within cloud computing. In the context of security, we currently also see a shift towards providing hardware security modules in the cloud. For example, CloudHSM by Amazon (`http://aws.amazon.com/en/cloudhsm`) allows secure management of cryptographic keys in the cloud without relying on trust in the respective cloud provider.

6.3   SELECTED CLOUDS

In this section, we briefly mention cloud offers from major vendors in the infrastructure as a service (IaaS), the platform as a service (PaaS) as well as the software as a service (SaaS) setting. Then, since IaaS offers and in particular cloud storage services provide relatively low security guarantees, we provide an overview of current academic approaches to enhance existing cloud storage services in a way to provide higher security guarantees.

6.3.1   Commercial Clouds

The basic idea behind cloud computing is that operators of large computing farms rent IT-related capabilities as a service to users, by allowing them to access technology-enabled services, without any need for knowledge of, expertise with, or control over how the technology infrastructure that supports those services work. Today, this approach is often termed as "everything as a service" (XaaS) and we will briefly review the most important concepts for commercial clouds below.

Infrastructure as a Service: IaaS refers to a provision model in which a cloud provider delivers infrastructure components such as CPU, memory, and storage, typically realized via a platform virtualization environment (for running client-specified virtual machines), as a service. Thus, clients can obtain and boot new virtual server instances on demand, which allows them to quickly scale capacity, both up and down, as the computing requirements change. Amazon's Elastic Compute Cloud (EC2) or Amazon's Simple Storage Service (S3) are prominent examples for IaaS offers.

Platform as a Service: PaaS refers to a provision model in which a cloud provider offers a platform for building and running Web-based applications. The PaaS model provides all of the facilities required to support the complete life cycle of building and delivering Web applications and services entirely available from the Internet, all with no software downloads or installation for developers and end users. An example for a PaaS is the Google App Engine, which is a platform for developing and hosting Web applications in Google-managed data centers, or Microsoft's Azure platform.

Software as a Service: SaaS refers to a provision model in which a cloud provider offers his or her clients ready to use applications through a subscription or a pay-as-you-go model. A prominent example for Saas is Google Apps, which provides several Web applications functionality similar to traditional office suites (email, calendar, instant messaging, word processing, spreadsheets, etc.)

We note that we have only given random examples of the respective services, since cloud services are an extremely dynamic market and typically all of the large players provide their own cloud storage offers.

6.3.2 Secure Cloud Storage Architectures

Missing or inadequate security and privacy related features in currently deployed cloud storage systems requires customers to fully trust in the integrity of the cloud provider as well as the provider's security practices. However, besides securing the cloud from within the cloud infrastructure, an alternative possibility is to (transparently) add relevant security and privacy features from the outside without affecting the cloud provider's interfaces and inner workings. Within the last few years several approaches to eliminate security deficiencies within state-of-the-art cloud storage systems have been proposed [24–34], thereby focusing on various security and privacy related issues as presented subsequently. More details on the results presented here can be found in [35].

6.3.2.1   Properties

We identify the following properties supported by existing architectures. By *confidentiality*, we mean data privacy with regard to (colluding) cloud providers. By *integrity*, we mean measures to verify block or file integrity and do not consider using error-correcting codes or erasure codes as a means to provide integrity. Although they tolerate corruptions to some degree, which then can be corrected, it is not the goal to detect whether modifications have happened. Information dispersal and consequently using the cloud of clouds paradigm (see Section 5.4) is understood as a means to provide *availability*. By *authenticity*, we mean additional means to check whether a file was written/modified by an authorized entity. *Retrievability* is understood in the sense of PoRs (see Section 5.1.1) or PDPs (see Section 5.1.2); that is, whether it is possible to challenge cloud providers to prove possession of a file without the necessity to be in possession of a local copy of the file for proof verification. *Freshness* and *consistency* are interesting in the context of a multiwriter setting; that is, whether it is possible to verify if the cloud provider(s) deliver the actual version of a file and if the approach has some means to guarantee write-consistency in the presence of multiple parallel writers to the same file, respectively. The meaning of *access control* is obvious and *auditability* means whether it is possible to prove cloud violations (e.g., a dropped write operation) to a third party. *Cloud logic* means whether the storage cloud is required to execute code. If this is required, it is necessary to augment current cloud storage services, such as Amazon S3, by additional functionality. *Implementation* means whether a (prototypical) implementation is available and which language was used.

Note that not all properties can be treated as being independent from others. For instance, if only a single writer is considered in the design of an approach, properties like freshness and consistency are not meaningful. The same argument holds for access control (i.e., if a system is for instance designed as a backup solution to work with a single client).

6.3.2.2 Approaches

We provide an overview of recent approaches to secure (distributed) cloud storage built on top of existing cloud storage services and enhancing them with additional features. Since they are designed with different goals and applications in mind (e.g., enterprise versus private customers), they provide quite different features. Table 6.2 presents the overview and indicates whether the aforementioned properties are supported by the different approaches.

DepSKY [30] is a distributed cloud storage system that is capable of integrating different cloud storage services and abstracting away details of the cloud storage providers by offering an object store interface to its clients. For all stored data objects, integrity is verifiable by means of digital signatures contained in the metadata of every object. *HAIL* [25] is a concept for distributed cloud storage providing high availability by unifying the use of file redundancy within a cloud provider and across independent cloud providers. *IRIS* [29] represents an authenticated file system that lets enterprises store data in the cloud and be resilient against potentially untrustworthy cloud providers. It enables an enterprise tenant or an external auditor to verify the integrity and freshness of any data retrieved from the file system and supports typical file system operations. *Tahoe-LAFS* [24] is an open source distributed cloud storage system and focuses on high availability – even if some of the cloud providers fail or are taken over by an attacker, the entire filesystem continues to function correctly, including preservation of privacy and security. *Cleversafe* [32] is an architecture for a distributed cloud storage system and uses a variant of Rivest's all-or-nothing transform [36]. For example, consider a symmetric encryption of a file into a sequence of n ciphertext blocks. Furthermore, put the encryption key through an n-out-of-n secret-sharing, and attach one share per ciphertext block. Then, the chunk can only be deciphered, if *all* of it is available, so as to recover the full key. Cleversafe provides both, an object- and a block-interface (to support standards like NFS, CIFS, iSCSI, etc.), for storing objects. *CloudProof* [26] is a cloud storage approach focusing on auditability (i.e., audit the cloud that integrity, write serializability and freshness are preserved by all operations, and to detect and proof violations to third parties). *RACS* [28] represents an redundant array of cloud storage (i.e., a cloud storage proxy disperses data across multiple cloud providers by means of optimal erasure codes). *NubiSave* [33] is a distributed cloud storage approach and builds upon a modular open source implementation called NubiSave, which provides a layered architecture (integration layer, preprocessing layer, transport layer) for a gateway to realize distributed cloud storage with a focus on easy integration of additional features (e.g., different information dispersal algorithms). *CS2* [31] represents a semantic cloud storage system, which integrates searchable encryption in combination with so-called search authenticators: Besides confidential search operations on encrypted data, a client should also be able to check whether the set of files returned for a search query is correct. Furthermore, their cloud storage system provides what they call global integrity (i.e., the integrity of stored data can be checked regardless of whether the entire data needs to be retrieved by a client). *RDSKVS* [34] represents an abstraction of a key-value store (KVS) as realized by many commercial cloud storage services in form of a read/write register that allows multiple clients to access data in the cloud in a multiple reader and multiple writer (MRMW) setting. They support standard operations of KVSs (i.e., store, retrieve, list, and remove).

Table 6.2
State-of-the-Art (Distributed) Cloud Storage System Properties

Property	DepSKY	HAIL	IRIS	Tahoe-LAFS	Cleversafe	CloudProof	RACS	NubiSave	CS2	RDSKVS
Confidentiality	✓	×	×	✓	✓	✓	×	✓	✓	×
Integrity	✓	✓	✓	✓	×	✓	×	✓	✓	×
Availability	✓	✓	✓	✓	✓	×	✓	✓	×	✓
Authenticity	×	×	✓	✓	×	✓	×	×	×	×
Retrievability	×	✓	✓	×	×	×	×	×	✓	×
Freshness	✓	×	✓	✓	×	✓	×	×	×	✓
Consistency	✓	×	✓	×	✓	✓	×	×	×	✓
Access control	×	×	×	✓	✓	✓	×	×	×	×
Auditing	×	×	✓	×	×	✓	×	×	×	×
Cloud logic	×	✓	×	×	×	✓	×	×	✓	×
Implementation	Java	C++	C#	Python	Java	C#	Python	Python	C++	Java

6.4   OUTLOOK

Many of the presented techniques are rather young and most of them are subject of intensive ongoing research. With the number of security systems being developed in research highly exceeding the number of those that get implemented and tested under real-life conditions, it is always somewhat difficult to reliably assess which security system will do well and which will not. Also, many primitives do work well in theory or come with good asymptotic complexity assurances, while performing dramatically less well in practice. Fully homomorphic encryption is just one example of a primitive that enjoys wonderful properties on the paper, but is still not sufficiently developed to really become a practical, handy, and efficient tool. It is therefore advisable not to automatically go for the latest inventions in research, but to stick with well-understood and well-tested primitives that have been subject of investigation for a couple of years. In this way, one can use the entire cryptographic research community's efforts as a certificate for the quality or badness of a security system, when choosing one for implementation. Let us illustrate this with two examples.

As a remedy to the aforementioned issues of secure multiparty computation to be used as an alternative or even substitute to fully homomorphic encryption, recent proposals [4] were made that use trusted hardware (either a partially trusted central server, or personal smartcards) to simplify SMC and to make it more efficient. Whether this is practical or not will be up to the specific application at hand, although we emphasize that [4] is more of a practical architecture proposal than a theoretical paper. Its actual usability is yet to be found out.

As a neat feature of SMC, it can to some extent be endowed with error-detection facilities [6, 37], thus yielding to *verifiability* of the result's correctness. A recent approach to the problem of letting the receiver check the validity of the result has been given by [38], who essentially use a combination of Yao's garbled circuits (Section 4.2.4) with FHE (Section 4.2.3). The practicability of this proposal is yet subject of ongoing investigation.

The general demand of verifiability can, however, go much beyond checking functional correctness of a cloud service, which can in a simple setting as well be tested using well-known methods from software testing (see [39]). Beyond pure functional correctness, we can ask for *strong service identity* [39], which means that all instances of a service that a cloud (respectively any of its nodes) hosts must be kept identical to the initial service specification for the entire lifecycle of the system. Compared to the frameworks of PDP and PoR (see Section 5.1.1 and Section 5.1.2), this would be the cloud provider's proof of running the *correct* algorithm, software, platform, or system. Depending on whether we deal with IaaS, PaaS, or SaaS, the particular realization may come in different disguises. Mostly, it is a matter of supervising or hypervising virtual machine implementations (see [39] for a detailed account).

Cloud computing is currently seeing much interest and therefore is highly changing and systems and standards appear somewhat volatile at the moment. Nevertheless, cryptography knows a considerable lot of primitives with interesting new challenges and applications in the cloud domain. Unfortunately, however, despite what is technically possible, one must not ignore what is legally permissible and what appears trustworthy to customers. Complicated and opaque security mechanisms may raise concerns and thus may yield to the paradoxical effect of destroying trust rather than creating it. On the bright side, the benefits and services that a cloud can offer may again outweigh a user's concerns. It will surely remain fascinating to see what future cloud cryptography and security will bring.

References

[1] M. Van Dijk and A. Juels, "On the Impossibility of Cryptography Alone for Privacy-Preserving Cloud Computing," in *USENIX HotSec*, pp. 1–8, USENIX Association, 2010.

[2] B. Barak, O. Goldreich, R. Impagliazzo, S. Rudich, A. Sahai, S. P. Vadhan, and K. Yang, "On the (Im)possibility of Obfuscating Programs," in *CRYPTO*, vol. 5677 of *LNCS*, pp. 1–18, Springer, 2001.

[3] A. Bogdanov and C. H. Lee, "Limits of Provable Security for Homomorphic Encryption," Tech. Rep. TR12-156, ECCC, 2012.

[4] J. Loftus and N. P. Smart, "Secure Outsourced Computation," in *AFRICACRYPT*, vol. 6737 of *LNCS*, pp. 1–20, Springer, 2011.

[5] M. Ben-Or, S. Goldwasser, and A. Wigderson, "Completeness Theorems for Non-Cryptographic Fault-Tolerant Distributed Computation," in *STOC*, pp. 1–10, ACM, 1988.

[6] T. Rabin and M. Ben-Or, "Verifiable Secret Sharing and Multiparty Protocols With Honest Majority," in *STOC*, pp. 73–85, ACM, 1989.

[7] M. Hirt and U. Maurer, "Player Simulation and General Adversary Structures in Perfect Multiparty Computation," *Journal of Cryptology*, vol. 13, pp. 31–60, 2000. 10.1007/s001459910003.

[8] D. Chaum, C. Crépeau, and I. Damgard, "Multiparty Unconditionally Secure Protocols," in *STOC*, pp. 11–19, ACM, 1988.

[9] Y. Wang and Y. Desmedt, "Perfectly Secure Message Transmission Revisited," *IEEE Transactions on Information Theory*, vol. 54, no. 6, pp. 2582–2595, 2008.

[10] M. Fitzi, M. K. Franklin, J. Garay, and S. H. Vardhan, "Towards Optimal and Efficient Perfectly Secure Message Transmission," in *TCC*, vol. 4392 of *LNCS*, pp. 311–322, Springer, 2007.

[11] M. Gomulkiewicz, M. Klonowski, and M. Kutylowski, "Provable Unlinkability against Traffic Analysis Already after $O(\log(n))$ Steps!," in *ISC*, vol. 3225 of *LNCS*, pp. 354–366, Springer, 2004.

[12] A. Meyerson and R. Williams, "On the Complexity of Optimal K-Anonymity," in *PODS*, pp. 223–228, ACM, 2004.

[13] K. LeFevre, D. J. DeWitt, and R. Ramakrishnan, "Incognito: Efficient Full-Domain K-Anonymity," in *SIGMOD*, pp. 49–60, ACM, 2005.

[14] A. Kerckhoffs, "La Cryptographie Militaire," *Journal des sciences militaires*, vol. IX, pp. 5–38, Jan. 1883.

[15] A. M. Eljetlawi and N. Ithnin, "Graphical Password: Comprehensive Study of the Usability Features of the Recognition Base Graphical Password Methods," *ICCIT*, vol. 2, pp. 1137–1143, 2008.

[16] I. Jermyn, A. Mayer, F. Monrose, M. K. Reiter, and A. D. Rubin, "The Design and Analysis of Graphical Passwords," in *USENIX Security Symposium*, pp. 1–1, USENIX Association, 1999.

[17] X. Suo, Y. Zhu, and G. S. Owen, "Graphical Passwords: A Survey," in *Computer Security Applications*, p. 10, 2005.

[18] Q. Yan, J. Han, Y. Li, J. Zhou, and R. H. Deng, "Designing Leakage-Resilient Password Entry on Touchscreen Mobile Devices," in *SIGSAC*, ASIA CCS, (New York, NY, USA), pp. 37–48, ACM, 2013.

[19] Y. Zhang, A. Juels, M. K. Reiter, and T. Ristenpart, "Cross-Vm Side Channels and Their Use to Extract Private Keys," in *CCS*, pp. 305–316, ACM, 2012.

[20] T. Ristenpart, E. Tromer, H. Shacham, and S. Savage, "Hey, You, Get Off of My Cloud: Exploring Information Leakage in Third-Party Compute Clouds," in *CCS*, pp. 199–212, ACM, 2009.

[21] W. Henecka, S. Kögl, A.-R. Sadeghi, T. Schneider, and I. Wehrenberg, "TASTY: Tool for Automating Secure Two-Party Computations," in *CCS*, pp. 451–462, ACM, 2010.

[22] Might Be Evil. http://www.mightbeevil.org/.

[23] S. Ortiz Jr., "The Problem with Cloud-Computing Standardization," *IEEE Computer*, vol. 44, no. 7, pp. 13–16, 2011.

[24] Z. Wilcox-O'Hearn and B. Warner, "Tahoe: The Least-Authority Filesystem," in *Storage*, pp. 21–26, ACM, 2008.

[25] K. D. Bowers, A. Juels, and A. Oprea, "HAIL: A High-Availability and Integrity Layer for Cloud Storage," in *CCS*, pp. 187–198, ACM, 2009.

[26] R. A. Popa, J. Lorch, D. Molnar, H. J. Wang, and L. Zhuang, "Enabling Security in Cloud Storage SLAs with CloudProof," in *USENIX Annual Technical Conference*, 2011.

[27] A. Shraer, C. Cachin, A. Cidon, I. Keidar, Y. Michalevsky, and D. Shaket, "Venus: Verification For Untrusted Cloud Storage," in *CCSW*, pp. 19–30, ACM, 2010.

[28] H. Abu-Libdeh, L. Princehouse, and H. Weatherspoon, "RACS: A Case for Cloud Storage Diversity," in *SoCC*, pp. 229–240, 2010.

[29] E. Stefanov, M. van Dijk, A. Oprea, and A. Juels, "Iris: A Scalable Cloud File System with Efficient Integrity Checks," in *ACSAC*, pp. 229–238, ACM, 2012.

[30] A. N. Bessani, M. P. Correia, B. Quaresma, F. André, and P. Sousa, "DepSky: Dependable and Secure Storage in a Cloud-of-Clouds," in *EuroSys*, pp. 31–46, 2011.

[31] S. Kamara, C. Papamanthou, and T. Roeder, "CS2: A Searchable Cryptographic Cloud Storage System," Tech. Rep. MSR-TR-2011-58, Microsoft Research, 2011.

[32] J. K. Resch and J. S. Plank, "AONT-RS: Blending Security and Performance in Dispersed Storage Systems," in *USENIX FAST*, pp. 191–202, USENIX Association, 2011.

[33] J. Spillner, G. Bombach, S. Matthischke, J. Muller, R. Tzschichholz, and A. Schill, "Information Dispersion over Redundant Arrays of Optimal Cloud Storage for Desktop Users," in *UCC*, pp. 1–8, IEEE, 2011.

[34] C. Basescu, C. Cachin, I. Eyal, R. Haas, A. Sorniotti, M. Vukolic, and I. Zachevsky, "Robust Data Sharing with Key-Value Stores," in *DSN*, pp. 1–12, IEEE, 2012.

[35] D. Slamanig and C. Hanser, "On Cloud Storage and the Cloud of Clouds Approach," in *ICITST*, pp. 649 – 655, IEEE, 2012.

[36] R. L. Rivest, "All-or-Nothing Encryption and the Package Transform," in *FSE*, vol. 1267 of *LNCS*, pp. 210–218, Springer, 1997.

[37] T. P. Pedersen, "Non-Interactive and Information-Theoretic Secure Verifiable Secret Sharing," in *CRYPTO*, vol. 576 of *LNCS*, pp. 129–140, Springer, 1992.

[38] R. Gennaro, C. Gentry, and B. Parno, "Non-Interactive Verifiable Computing: Outsourcing Computation to Untrusted Workers," in *CRYPTO*, vol. 6223 of *LNCS*, pp. 465–482, Springer, 2010.

[39] S. Bouchenak, G. Chockler, H. Chockler, G. Gheorghe, N. Santos, and A. Shraer, "Verifying Cloud Services: Present and Future," *Operating Systems Review*, 2013.

List of Symbols

$\mathbb{R}$	set of the real numbers
$\mathbb{Z}$	set of integers
$\mathbb{N}$	set of natural numbers, including zero
F_{p^n}	finite field of order p^n
Σ^*	set of all strings over (the alphabet) Σ
$\mathbb{Z}_n$	residue class modulo n
$\mathbb{Z}_n^*, \mathsf{F}_{p^n}^*$	group of units (invertible elements) in the respective finite field
$\mathsf{G}, (\mathsf{G}, +), (\mathsf{G}, \cdot)$	a (general) group (additive or multiplicative notation)
$\mathsf{R}, (\mathsf{R}, +, \cdot)$	a (general) ring
$\langle g \rangle$	(sub-) group generated by the element g
$E(\mathsf{F}_q)$	elliptic curve group over the field F_q
$\mathsf{S}[p]$	substructure (subgroup, etc.) of order p in S.
QR_n	set of quadratic residue modulo n (i.e., numbers having a "square-root" modulo n)
2^X	power set of X
$\in_R$	random selection from a set
$\|x\|$	absolute value (if x is a number), or length of x (if x is a string)
$a \operatorname{DIV} b$	integer division
$a \operatorname{MOD} b$	remainder of a divided by b
$\oplus$	bitwise exclusive-OR
$a\|b$	a divides b
$a\|\|b$	string concatenation of a and b
$a \ll b$	a is much less than b
$\gcd(x, y)$	greatest common divisor of x and y
$\operatorname{lcm}(x, y)$	least common multiple of x and y

$EEA(x, y)$	extended Euclidian algorithm, returning a triple (g, a, b) such that $gcd(x, y) = g = ax + by$
$poly(n)$	a general (not further specified) polynomial in n
$negl(\kappa)$	a general (not further specified) negligible function in κ
κ	security parameter (usually an integer or string)
$\lfloor x \rfloor, \lceil x \rceil$	floor and ceiling functions
Adv	adversary's advantage
$\texttt{Encrypt}(m; pk)$	shorthand notation for m's encryption under pk, via $\texttt{Encrypt}(m; pk)$
$\mathcal{O}$	Landau asymptotic order or point at infinity
$\Pr[X]$	probability of the event X
$\leq_p, \leq_T$	polynomial or Turing reduction
$ord(x)$	order of the element x
$L(a, b), J(a, b)$	Legendre and Jacobi symbol; commonly written as $\left(\frac{a}{b}\right)$ in textbooks
$\langle \mathbf{x}, \mathbf{y} \rangle$	inner product $\langle \mathbf{x}, \mathbf{x} \rangle = \sum_{i=1}^{n} x_i y_i$, for vectors $\mathbf{x} = (x_1, \ldots, x_n), \mathbf{y} = (y_1, \ldots, y_n)$.
$\simeq$	isomorphy relation
$h(X), h(X|Y)$	entropy and conditional entropy, of the random variable X, conditional on Y, respectively
$H(x)$	hash value of the (string) x

Abbreviations

ABE	attribute-based encryption
AES	advanced encryption standard
BCD	Bose-Chaudhuri-Hocquenghem
BDHP	bilinear Diffie-Hellman problem
BGN	Boneh-Goh-Nissim
CDS	Cramer-Damgård-Schoenmakers
CIA(+)	confidentiality, integrity, availability (and authenticity)
CL	Camenish-Lysyanskaya
DH	Diffie-Hellman
DL	discrete logarithm
(C/D)DHP	(computational/decisional) Diffie-Hellman problem
(C/D)DLP	(computational/decisional) Discrete Logarithm problem
ECC	error-correcting code, or also elliptic-curve cryptography
ECDLP	elliptic curve discrete logarithm problem
FDH	full-domain hash
FHE	fully homomorphic encryption
FS	Fiat-Shamir
GC	garbled circuit
GM	group manager
IaaS	infrastructure as a service
IBE	identity-based encryption
IDA	information-dispersal algorithm
IND-CCA1	indistinguishability under chosen ciphertext attacks
IND-CCA2	indistinguishability under adaptive chosen ciphertext attacks
IND-CPA	indistinguishability under chosen plaintext attacks

IP	internet protocol
LWE	learning with errors (assumption)
(H)MAC	(hash) message authentication code
MC	multicoupon
ORAM	oblivious random access memory
OT	oblivious transfer
PaaS	platform as a service
(A)PAKE	(anonymous) password-based authenticated key exchange
PBE	predicate-based encryption
PDP	provable data possession
PEKS	public key encryption with keyword search
PET	privacy-enhancing technology
PERKS	PEKS with registered keywords
PKE	public key encryption
PKI	public key infrastructure
(S)PIR	(symmetric) private information retrieval
PoR	proof of retrievability
PoW	proof of ownership
PRP	pseudorandom permutation
QID	quasi-identifier
ROM	random oracle model
RSA	Rivest-Shamir-Adleman
SaaS	software as a service
SDK	system development kit
SHA	secure hash-algorithm
SHE	somewhat homomorphic encryption
SMC	secure multiparty computation
SP	service provider or storage provider
SQL	structured query language
TCP	transmission control protocol
TTP	trusted third party
VM	virtual machine
XaaS	everything as a service
XML	extensible markup language
WLOG	without loss of generality
(HV)ZKP	(honest-verifier) zero-knowledge proof

About the Authors

Stefan Rass graduated with a double masters degree in mathematics and computer science from the Alpen-Adria University (AAU) in Klagenfurt in 2005. He received a Ph.D. in mathematics. Since 2009, he has been a postdoctoral researcher at the AAU and he became an assistant professor in 2011. Between 2005 and today, he contributed to EU projects (e.g., related to quantum cryptography) and various industrial research projects, some of which are partially based on his research results. His scientific interests include general system security, in particular the design of security infrastructures and enterprise risk management, as well as applications of quantum cryptography and information-theoretic security. His research is focused on applied security and a mix of theoretical and practical contributions. Dr. Rass has authored numerous papers related to information theoretic security and classical (complexity-theory-based) cryptography. Besides research, he serves as a reviewer for scientific conferences and journals, as well as consultant for the industry and federal agencies like the Austrian Regulatory Authority for Broadcasting and Telecommunications, in projects concerned with the design or evaluation of security products. He is a member of IEEE and the German Informatics Society (GI), teaching courses on theoretical computer science, complexity theory, system security, and cryptography.

Daniel Slamanig received his Ph.D. in computer science from the Alpen-Adria University in Klagenfurt in 2011, where he was working in the area of public key cryptography focusing on privacy-preserving cryptography. From 2011 to 2012, he worked as a postdoctoral researcher at the Carinthia University of Applied Sciences (CUAS) where he led a project on privacy-preserving cloud computing and taught introductory and advanced courses and seminars on cryptography, IT-security, and computer science. Since 2012 he has been a postdoctoral researcher at the Institute of Applied Information Processing and Communication (IAIK) at Graz University of Technology (TUG). He is involved as a researcher in various (EU funded) projects in the field of secure cloud storage and privacy preserving identity management. His main research interests include cryptography, privacy, and information security. Currently, he is particularly interested in privacy-enhancing cryptographic primitives and cryptographic protocols in cloud computing and storage as well as the design of digital signature variants. Dr. Slamanig has published numerous papers in international conferences and journals, acts as a reviewer for various journals and conferences, and is a member of the International Association for Cryptologic Research (IACR) and the Austrian Computer Society (OCG).

Index